Longman School
Shakespeare

NEW EDITION
for GCSE

Romeo and Juliet

Editor: John O'Connor
Textual Consultant: Dr Stewart Eames

Volume Editor: John O'Connor

GCSE Assessment Practice:
Chris Sutcliffe (AQA)
Pam Taylor (Edexcel)
Margaret Graham (WJEC)
John Reynolds (OCR)

Longman
Part of Pearson

Longman is an imprint of Pearson Education Limited, a company incorporated in England and Wales, having its registered office at Edinburgh Gate, Harlow, Essex, CM20 2JE. Registered company number: 872828

www.pearsonschoolsandfecolleges.co.uk

Longman is a registered trademark of Pearson Education Limited

First published 2004
This new edition published 2010

12 11
10 9 8 7 6 5 4

British Library Cataloguing in Publication Data
A catalogue record for this book is available from the British Library

ISBN 9781408236895

Typeset by Juice Creative Ltd, Hertfordshire
Cover photo © Getty Images: Darren Robb
Printed and bound in Malaysia, KHL – CTP

We are grateful to the following for permission to reproduce copyright photographs:

Getty Images: *page 237*: Andrea Pistolesi/The Image Bank

Every effort has been made to contact copyright holders of material reproduced in this book. Any omissions will be rectified in subsequent printings if notice is given to the publishers.

ACT 1: SCENE BY SCENE

The Chorus sets the scene in Verona and outlines the story of the two lovers.

1 Benvolio tries to stop a fight between Capulet and Montague servants, but is attacked by Tybalt. The Prince threatens the death penalty if the families disturb the streets in this way ever again. Romeo has been unhappy, and his parents, Lord and Lady Montague, discuss this with Benvolio. Romeo reveals to Benvolio that he is in love, but that the girl is rejecting him.

2 Capulet agrees to allow Paris to woo his daughter, Juliet. Learning that Rosaline, the girl Romeo loves, is to be a guest at the Capulet ball, Benvolio suggests that they gate-crash it.

3 Lady Capulet tells Juliet of Paris's request to marry her and Juliet agrees to consider Paris as a possible husband.

4 Romeo is worried about going to the Capulet ball because of a troubling dream. Mercutio says that the dream was only caused by Queen Mab, who comes to people in their sleep and gives them strange fantasies.

5 Tybalt is angry that Romeo has gate-crashed the ball and threatens revenge. Romeo meets Juliet and they fall in love, but both are later dismayed to learn that they are from rival families.

ACT 2: SCENE BY SCENE

The Chorus talks about the difficulties that Romeo and Juliet will have to overcome.

1 Leaving the party, Romeo hides from his friends and refuses to come when Mercutio calls him.

2 Hiding inside the Capulet's garden, Romeo sees Juliet at a window and hears her declare her love for him. They express their love for one another and Juliet asks Romeo to send a message the next day telling her when and where they can be married.

3 Romeo visits Friar Lawrence. When Romeo tells him about Juliet, he agrees to marry them because it might help to heal the bitterness between the feuding families.

4 Benvolio tells Mercutio that Romeo has been sent a challenge to a duel by Tybalt, a dangerous fighter. Juliet's Nurse arrives and Romeo asks her to tell Juliet to meet him that afternoon, when the Friar will marry them.

5 When the Nurse finally returns to an impatient Juliet, she passes on Romeo's instructions.

6 Friar Lawrence warns Romeo about the danger of his sudden love for Juliet, but agrees to marry the lovers in secret.

ACT 3: SCENE BY SCENE

1 Tybalt comes looking for Romeo, determined to get revenge. When they meet, Romeo refuses to fight him. Angry with Romeo for putting up with Tybalt's insults, Mercutio challenges Tybalt himself and is fatally wounded. To get revenge for the dead Mercutio, Romeo kills Tybalt and then flees. The Prince banishes him from Verona.

2 When the Nurse reports that Romeo has killed Tybalt, Juliet grieves for him, but is also distraught at Romeo's banishment. She asks the Nurse to bring Romeo to her.

3 The Friar unsuccessfully tries to comfort Romeo, who is devastated at being banished. The Nurse arrives to tell him that Juliet wants to see him before he leaves.

4 Capulet tells Paris that Juliet is mourning for Tybalt, but decides that she will marry Paris in three days' time.

5 At dawn the next day, Juliet makes Romeo leave before he is captured. When told that she is to marry Paris, Juliet refuses and her father angrily threatens to throw her out unless she agrees. The Nurse advises her to go through with the marriage to Paris, but Juliet plans to seek help from the Friar.

ACT 4: SCENE BY SCENE

1 Juliet sees Paris at the Friar's cell. Realising how desperate Juliet is, the Friar suggests Juliet take a potion to make her seem dead. The Friar will write to Romeo and arrange for him to collect Juliet when she wakes in the Capulet tomb.

2 On the Friar's advice, Juliet apologises to her father and pretends to agree to marry Paris the following day.

3 Despite imagining the horrors of what might go wrong, Juliet drinks the potion.

4 Hearing Paris arriving for the wedding, Capulet orders that Juliet should be woken up.

5 The Nurse finds Juliet apparently dead. The Friar tries to comfort the mourners as plans are made for her funeral.

ACT 5: SCENE BY SCENE

1 In Mantua, Balthasar tells Romeo that Juliet is dead. Deciding to join Juliet in the tomb that night, Romeo buys poison and leaves for Verona.

2 Friar Lawrence learns that the letter he had sent to Romeo has not been delivered. He rushes off to the tomb.

3 At the Capulet tomb, Romeo is challenged by Paris. They fight, and Paris is killed. Romeo looks at Juliet for the last time, kisses her and drinks the poison. Friar Lawrence enters to find Romeo dead. When Juliet wakes, the Friar tries to explain what has happened, but flees when he hears people approaching. Juliet kisses Romeo and stabs herself. The Friar, under arrest, explains to the Prince what has happened. In their grief, Capulet and Montague make peace.

THE HOUSE OF CAPULET

CAPULET
Juliet's father
He promises Paris that
Juliet can marry him.

LADY CAPULET
Juliet's mother
She supports her
husband when Juliet
refuses to marry Paris.

COUSIN CAPULET
Capulet's older cousin
A guest at the feast.

JULIET
*Capulet's 14-year-old
daughter*
She falls in love with
Romeo and marries him
in secret.

TYBALT
Juliet's cousin
He kills Mercutio and is
then himself killed by
Romeo.

NURSE
*Juliet's nurse since she
was a baby*
She helps Juliet to marry
Romeo in secret.

PETER
The Nurse's servant
He goes with the Nurse
when she meets Romeo.

SAMPSON AND GREGORY
Servants
They fight with the
Montagues in the brawl.

SERVANT
He cannot read and asks
Romeo to tell him who
is on the guest list for
the feast.

THE PRINCE'S FAMILY

ESCALUS
Prince of Verona
He banishes Romeo
for killing Tybalt.

MERCUTIO
A relative of the Prince
He is Romeo's friend and
is killed by Tybalt.

COUNT PARIS
A relative of the Prince
Capulet arranges for him
to marry Juliet.

THE HOUSE OF MONTAGUE

MONTAGUE
Romeo's father

LADY MONTAGUE
Romeo's mother
She dies of grief when
Romeo is banished.

ROMEO
Montague's son
He falls in love with Juliet
and secretly marries her,
but is banished when he
kills Tybalt.

BENVOLIO
Romeo's cousin and friend
He has to report to the
Prince how Romeo came
to kill Tybalt.

BALTHASAR
Romeo's servant
He takes news to Romeo
when he is banished to
Mantua.

ABRAHAM
Servant
He is involved in the
brawl with the Capulets.

OTHERS IN VERONA

FRIAR LAWRENCE
A priest and Romeo's friend
He secretly marries Romeo
and Juliet, and tries to help
Juliet avoid marrying Paris.

FRIAR JOHN
Another priest
He is prevented from
delivering Friar Lawrence's
letter to Romeo in Mantua.

MUSICIANS
They are hired to play
at the wedding of Juliet
and Paris.

WATCHMEN
Paris's page fetches them
when Romeo and Paris
fight at the Capulet tomb.

IN MANTUA

AN APOTHECARY
A poor pharmacist
He sells poison to Romeo.

CHARACTER LIST

THE CHORUS

THE HOUSE OF CAPULET

    CAPULET

    LADY CAPULET

    JULIET *their daughter*

    TYBALT *Juliet's cousin*

    Juliet's **NURSE**

    Capulet's **SERVANT**

    PETER *the Nurse's servant*

    an old **COUSIN**

    SAMPSON *a servant*

    GREGORY *a servant*

    Tybalt's **PAGE**

    other **SERVANTS** *and* **FOLLOWERS**

THE HOUSE OF MONTAGUE

    MONTAGUE

    LADY MONTAGUE

    ROMEO *their son*

    BENVOLIO *Romeo's friend*

    BALTHASAR *Romeo's servant*

    ABRAHAM *a servant*

    other **SERVANTS**

THE PRINCE'S FAMILY

PRINCE ESCALUS *of Verona*

MERCUTIO *a relative of the Prince*

COUNT PARIS *another relative*

Paris's PAGE

Mercutio's PAGE

ATTENDANTS *and* GUARDS

ALSO FROM VERONA

FRIAR LAWRENCE *a Franciscan friar*

FRIAR JOHN *his friend*

an OFFICER

Men of the WATCH

MUSICIANS

GUESTS *at the Capulet feast*

CITIZENS

IN MANTUA

an APOTHECARY

Scenes are set in Verona, except for Act 5 Scene 1, which takes place in Mantua.

The Chorus introduces the story, set in Verona. A long-standing feud between the Montague and Capulet families will be ended only by the deaths of the lovers, Romeo and Juliet.

1 **households**: families
both … dignity: as noble as each other
3 **ancient grudge**: long-term hatred
mutiny: outburst of violence
4 **civil blood**: i.e. citizens' injuries and deaths
5 **From … foes**: born from these two enemies, lethal to one another
6 **star-crossed**: ill-fated
7 **misadventured**: pitiful and tragic
overthrows: downfalls
8 **strife**: feud
9 **passage**: course
death-marked: doomed to death
11 **but … end**: except for the deaths of their children
12 **traffic**: business
14 **What … mend**: i.e. the actors' hard work will try to make up for any weaknesses in their performance of the play

THINK ABOUT for GCSE

Structure and form

- The Prologue is written in the form of a sonnet (a fourteen-line poem often divided into sections/quatrains). How are the first three sections (lines 1 to 4, 5 to 8, and 9 to 12) used to introduce the performance?

Enter CHORUS.

CHORUS   Two households, both alike in dignity,
In fair Verona where we lay our scene,
From ancient grudge break to new mutiny,
Where civil blood makes civil hands unclean.
From forth the fatal loins of these two foes   5
A pair of star-crossed lovers take their life;
Whose misadventured piteous overthrows
Doth with their death bury their parents' strife.
The fearful passage of their death-marked love,
And the continuance of their parents' rage,   10
Which, but their children's end, nought could remove,
Is now the two hours' traffic of our stage –
    The which, if you with patient ears attend,
    What here shall miss, our toil shall strive to mend.

Exit.

In this scene ...

- A street fight breaks out between the Capulets and the Montagues.
- The Prince stops the riot and threatens the death penalty for anyone caught fighting in Verona's streets again.
- Romeo's parents ask Benvolio why Romeo has been behaving strangely.
- Romeo tells Benvolio that he is in love with a girl who refuses to be won over.

Two Capulet servants, Sampson and Gregory, brag about their part in the feud with the Montagues.

THINK ABOUT
for GCSE

Themes and issues

- What are Sampson and Gregory boasting about (lines 1 to 27)? What does this reveal about the way they view their sense of family **honour**?

Performance and staging

- Lines 1 to 4 contain wordplay: to 'carry coals' is to be humiliated, 'colliers' (coal-miners) were considered dirty and dishonest, 'choler' (pronounced 'collar') means anger, and a 'collar' was also a hangman's noose. Why might some directors cut these jokes in a performance? Why might others decide to keep them?

s.d. **bucklers**: small shields

1   **carry coals**: i.e. do work that is below us

2   **colliers**: coal-miners

3   **choler**: anger
    draw: i.e. draw our swords

4   **draw ... collar**: i.e. avoid hanging

5   **moved**: made angry

8   **stand**: i.e. fight

11   **take the wall**: walk where the road is cleanest, i.e. show my superiority

12–13   **goes to the wall**: is defeated by the strong

14–15   **weaker vessels**: 'the weaker sex'

19   **'Tis all one**: It makes no difference

23   **maidenheads**: virginities

25   **They must ... it**: The ones who sense it are the ones who feel it (i.e. the maids)

A street in Verona.

Enter SAMPSON *and* GREGORY *(servants of the house of Capulet), armed with swords and bucklers.*

SAMPSON	Gregory, on my word, we'll not carry coals.
GREGORY	No, for then we should be colliers.
SAMPSON	I mean, an we be in choler, we'll draw.
GREGORY	Ay, while you live, draw your neck out of collar.
SAMPSON	I strike quickly, being moved.
GREGORY	But thou art not quickly moved to strike.
SAMPSON	A dog of the house of Montague moves me.
GREGORY	To move is to stir, and to be valiant is to stand: therefore, if thou art moved thou runn'st away.
SAMPSON	A dog of that house shall move me to stand. I will take the wall of any man or maid of Montague's.
GREGORY	That shows thee a weak slave, for the weakest goes to the wall.
SAMPSON	'Tis true, and therefore women, being the weaker vessels, are ever thrust to the wall: therefore I will push Montague's men from the wall, and thrust his maids to the wall.
GREGORY	The quarrel is between our masters, and us their men.
SAMPSON	'Tis all one. I will show myself a tyrant. When I have fought with the men, I will be civil with the maids: I will cut off their heads.
GREGORY	The heads of the maids?
SAMPSON	Ay, the heads of the maids, or their maidenheads – take it in what sense thou wilt.
GREGORY	They must take it in sense that feel it.

5

10

15

20

25

Two Montague servants approach. The Capulets try to start a fight.

29 **poor-John**: cheap dried fish
tool: weapon

31 **naked weapon**: unsheathed sword

33 **Fear me not**: Have no fears about me

34 **marry**: indeed ('by the Virgin Mary')

35 **take ... sides**: have the law on our side

36 **list**: like

37 **bite my thumb**: make an insulting gesture

THINK ABOUT *for* GCSE

Language

• The dialogue in lines 1 to 31 is full of sexual innuendoes (double-meanings). They include: 'stir' (have sex), 'stand' (have an erection), 'thrust', 'pretty piece of flesh' and 'tool'. What does this language tell you about Sampson and Gregory?

48 **I am for you**: i.e. I am ready to fight you

SAMPSON	Me they shall feel while I am able to stand – and 'tis known I am a pretty piece of flesh.
GREGORY	'Tis well thou art not fish: if thou hadst, thou hadst been poor-John. Draw thy tool – here comes two of the house of Montagues.

30

Enter ABRAHAM *and* BALTHASAR *(servants of the house of Montague).*

SAMPSON	My naked weapon is out. Quarrel! I will back thee.
GREGORY	How? Turn thy back and run?
SAMPSON	Fear me not.
GREGORY	No, marry. I fear *thee*!
SAMPSON	Let us take the law of our sides: let them begin.

35

GREGORY	I will frown as I pass by, and let them take it as they list.
SAMPSON	Nay, as they dare. I will bite my thumb at them, which is disgrace to them if they bear it.
ABRAHAM	Do you bite your thumb at us, sir?
SAMPSON	I do bite my thumb, sir.

40

ABRAHAM	Do you bite your thumb at *us*, sir?
SAMPSON	(*Aside to* GREGORY) Is the law of our side if I say 'Ay'?
GREGORY	(*Aside to* SAMPSON) No.
SAMPSON	No, sir, I do not bite my thumb at you, sir, but I bite my thumb, sir.

45

GREGORY	Do you quarrel, sir?
ABRAHAM	Quarrel, sir? No, sir.
SAMPSON	But if you do, sir, I am for you. I serve as good a man as you.
ABRAHAM	No better.

50

SAMPSON	Well, sir –

Sampson and Gregory grow bolder when Tybalt, a Capulet, arrives, and the fight begins. Benvolio, a Montague, tries to stop them, but it quickly turns into a public brawl.

56 **swashing**: slashing

59 **Put up**: Sheathe your swords

60 **heartless hinds**: 1 servants lacking courage; 2 female deer without male protection

63 **manage**: use
   part: separate

THINK ABOUT for GCSE

Characterisation

• What impression do you get of Tybalt from his first appearance?

• What are your first impressions of Capulet?

Performance and staging

• If you were the director, how would you want the Montague servants and Benvolio to react when Tybalt arrives (line 59)?

67 **bills**: long-handled axes
   partisans: spears

69 **long sword**: heavy, old-fashioned weapon

72 **spite**: defiance

Enter BENVOLIO.

GREGORY	(*Aside to* SAMPSON) Say 'better'! – Here comes one of my master's kinsmen.
SAMPSON	(*To* ABRAHAM) Yes – better, sir.
ABRAHAM	You lie!

55

SAMPSON	Draw, if you be men! Gregory, remember thy swashing blow!

They fight.

BENVOLIO *draws his sword and tries to separate them.*

BENVOLIO	Part, fools! Put up your swords! You know not what you do.

Enter TYBALT.

TYBALT	What, art thou drawn among these heartless hinds? Turn thee, Benvolio! Look upon thy death.

60

BENVOLIO	I do but keep the peace! Put up thy sword Or manage it to part these men with me.
TYBALT	What, drawn, and talk of peace? I hate the word As I hate hell, all Montagues, and thee. Have at thee, coward!

65

They fight.

Enter a city OFFICER, *with three or four armed citizens, who rush in to try to stop the fighting.*

OFFICER	Clubs, bills and partisans! Strike! Beat them down! Down with the Capulets! Down with the Montagues!

Enter old CAPULET, *in his dressing-gown, followed by* LADY CAPULET, *his wife.*

CAPULET	What noise is this? Give me my long sword, ho!
LADY CAPULET	A crutch, a crutch! Why call you for a sword?

70

CAPULET	My sword I say! Old Montague is come, And flourishes his blade in spite of me!

The Prince of Verona speaks angrily to Montague and Capulet. He threatens the death penalty for anyone caught fighting on the streets again. Montague asks Benvolio how the fighting began.

76 **Profaners**: mis-users
neighbour-stainèd steel: swords, stained with your neighbours' blood

78 **quench**: put out
pernicious: destructive

81 **mistempered**: 1 angry; 2 made for use in a bad cause

82 **movèd**: angry

83 **civil brawls**: public riots
airy word: trivial comment

87 **cast**: throw down
grave ... ornaments: staffs etc., fitting for their age and status

89 **Cankered**: i.e. rusty
cankered hate: cancerous hatred

91 **Your lives ... peace**: i.e. you will be executed, for having broken the peace

95 **our farther pleasure**: what else I decide to do

98 **set ... abroach**: opened up this old quarrel

100 **adversary**: enemy

101 **ere**: before

103 **prepared**: already drawn

THINK ABOUT for GCSE

Structure and form

• What threat does the Prince make to Montague and Capulet? Why might this be important later in the play?

Themes and issues

• What do you think of the Prince's statements? Do you think his **authority** is firm enough, for example?

Enter old MONTAGUE *and* LADY MONTAGUE, *his wife.*

MONTAGUE   Thou villain, Capulet! (*To his wife*) Hold me not – let
             me go!

LADY MONTAGUE Thou shalt not stir one foot to seek a foe.

Enter PRINCE ESCALUS *(ruler of Verona), with guards and
attendants.*

PRINCE   Rebellious subjects, enemies to peace,   75
             Profaners of this neighbour-stainèd steel –
             Will they not hear? What ho! You men, you beasts,
             That quench the fire of your pernicious rage
             With purple fountains issuing from your veins!
             On pain of torture, from those bloody hands   80
             Throw your mistempered weapons to the ground,
             And hear the sentence of your movèd Prince.
             Three civil brawls bred of an airy word
             By thee, old Capulet, and Montague,
             Have thrice disturbed the quiet of our streets,   85
             And made Verona's ancient citizens
             Cast by their grave beseeming ornaments
             To wield old partisans in hands as old,
             Cankered with peace, to part your cankered hate.
             If ever you disturb our streets again,   90
             Your lives shall pay the forfeit of the peace!
             For this time, all the rest depart away.
             You, Capulet, shall go along with me,
             And Montague, come you this afternoon,
             To know our farther pleasure in this case,   95
             To old Freetown, our common judgement-place.
             Once more, on pain of death, all men depart!

All exit, except MONTAGUE, LADY MONTAGUE, *and* BENVOLIO.

MONTAGUE   Who set this ancient quarrel new abroach?
             Speak, nephew. Were you by when it began?

BENVOLIO   Here were the servants of your adversary   100
             And yours, close fighting ere I did approach.
             I drew to part them. In the instant came
             The fiery Tybalt, with his sword prepared,
             Which, as he breathed defiance to my ears,

Benvolio, Montague and Lady Montague discuss Romeo's recent behaviour. He has been keeping to himself and seems depressed.

106 **nothing hurt withal**: not at all hurt by his strokes
108 **on ... part**: some on one side, some on the other
109 **either part**: both sides

111 **Right**: Very
fray: brawl

114 **abroad**: outside

116 **rooteth**: grows

118 **ware**: 1 aware; 2 wary
119 **stole ... covert**: crept into the shadows
120 **measuring his affections**: judging his feelings
121 **most sought ... found**: wanted most of all to be alone
122 **Being ... self**: my own company being too much for me
123 **my humour**: what I wanted
124 **shunned**: kept away from
126 **augmenting**: adding to

130 **Aurora**: goddess of the dawn
131 **heavy**: sad
132 **pens**: shuts

135 **portentous**: ominous
humour: moody behaviour
136 **counsel**: advice

138 **of**: from

139 **importuned**: tried to question

141 **his own ... counsellor**: discussing his feelings only with himself

THINK ABOUT for GCSE

Characterisation

• What are the first things we learn about Romeo (lines 112 to 136)? Why are Benvolio and Montague so concerned about him?

20

He swung about his head and cut the winds,   105
Who, nothing hurt withal, hissed him in scorn.
While we were interchanging thrusts and blows,
Came more and more, and fought on part and part,
Till the Prince came, who parted either part.

Lady Montague O where is Romeo? Saw you him today?   110
Right glad I am he was not at this fray.

Benvolio Madam, an hour before the worshipped sun
Peered forth the golden window of the east,
A troubled mind drove me to walk abroad –
Where, underneath the grove of sycamore   115
That westward rooteth from this city side,
So early walking did I see your son.
Towards him I made, but he was ware of me,
And stole into the covert of the wood.
I, measuring his affections by my own,   120
Which then most sought where most might not be found,
Being one too many by my weary self,
Pursued my humour not pursuing his,
And gladly shunned who gladly fled from me.

Montague Many a morning hath he there been seen,   125
With tears augmenting the fresh morning's dew,
Adding to clouds more clouds with his deep sighs.
But all so soon as the all-cheering sun
Should in the farthest east begin to draw
The shady curtains from Aurora's bed,   130
Away from light steals home my heavy son,
And private in his chamber pens himself,
Shuts up his windows, locks fair daylight out,
And makes himself an artificial night.
Black and portentous must this humour prove,   135
Unless good counsel may the cause remove.

Benvolio My noble uncle, do you know the cause?

Montague I neither know it, nor can learn of him.

Benvolio Have you importuned him by any means?

Montague Both by myself and many other friends: 140
But he, his own affections' counsellor,

Benvolio promises to try to discover the reason behind Romeo's unhappiness, and Montague and Lady Montague leave. Romeo admits to Benvolio that he is in love.

142 **true**: trustworthy
143 **close**: secretive
144 **sounding**: being worked out
145 **envious**: intending harm

150 **So please you**: If you please
151 **his grievance**: what's the matter with him
152 **I would ... stay**: I hope that, by staying here, you will be fortunate enough
153 **shrift**: confession (given to a priest)

THINK ABOUT for GCSE

Language

• Shakespeare often uses imagery from the world of nature. What does the 'bud' image (lines 145 to 147) in Montague's speech tell us about Romeo's behaviour?

162 **Out ... love**: I love her, but she doesn't love me
163 **so gentle ... view**: which looks so pleasant
164 **tyrannous ... proof**: difficult when we experience it
165 **muffled**: Cupid was blindfolded.
166 **pathways ... will**: ways to get what he wants

22

Is to himself – I will not say how true –
But to himself so secret and so close,
So far from sounding and discovery
As is the bud bit with an envious worm   145
Ere he can spread his sweet leaves to the air,
Or dedicate his beauty to the sun.
Could we but learn from whence his sorrows grow,
We would as willingly give cure as know.

Enter ROMEO.

BENVOLIO   See where he comes. So please you, step aside.   150
             I'll know his grievance or be much denied.

MONTAGUE   I would thou wert so happy by thy stay
             To hear true shrift. Come, madam, let's away.

                    Exit MONTAGUE, *with* LADY MONTAGUE.

BENVOLIO   Good morrow, cousin.

ROMEO   Is the day so young?

BENVOLIO   But new struck nine.

ROMEO   Ay me, sad hours seem long.   155
             Was that my father that went hence so fast?

BENVOLIO   It was. What sadness lengthens Romeo's hours?

ROMEO   Not having that which, having, makes them short.

BENVOLIO   In love?

ROMEO   Out –   160

BENVOLIO   Of love?

ROMEO   Out of her favour where I am in love.

BENVOLIO   Alas, that Love, so gentle in his view,
             Should be so tyrannous and rough in proof!

ROMEO   Alas, that Love, whose view is muffled still,   165
             Should without eyes see pathways to his will!
             Where shall we dine? O me! What fray was here?
             Yet tell me not, for I have heard it all.
             Here's much to do with hate, but more with love.

Benvolio asks who the girl is, but Romeo does not tell him.

171 **of nothing ... create**: created out of nothing in the first place
172 **serious vanity**: weighty emptiness
173 **well-seeming**: attractive
175 **Still-waking**: always awake
176 **that ... this**: but am not loved in return

177 **coz**: cousin

178 **oppression**: unhappiness
179 **transgression**: offence / overstepping the limit
181 **propagate**: increase
   pressed: oppressed

185 **purged**: cleansed
186 **vexed**: troubled
187 **discreet**: cautious / sensitive
188 **gall**: bitter-tasting poison

189 **Soft**: Not so fast

THINK ABOUT for GCSE

Language

• Romeo's speech (from line 169) is based on opposites and contains many oxymorons (expressions which seem to contradict themselves), such as 'loving hate'. These are often found in Elizabethan love-poetry. What others are there? What do they suggest about Romeo's state of mind?

193 **in sadness**: seriously

195 **sadly**: can also mean 'seriously'

199 **aimed so near**: guessed as much

	Why then, O brawling love, O loving hate,	170
	O anything of nothing first create!
	O heavy lightness, serious vanity,
	Misshapen chaos of well-seeming forms!
	Feather of lead, bright smoke, cold fire, sick health,
	Still-waking sleep, that is not what it is!	175
	This love feel I, that feel no love in this.
	Dost thou not laugh?

BENVOLIO   No, coz, I rather weep.

ROMEO   Good heart, at what?

BENVOLIO   At *thy* good heart's oppression.

ROMEO   Why, such is love's transgression.
          Griefs of mine own lie heavy in my breast,   180
          Which thou wilt propagate to have it pressed
          With more of thine. This love that thou hast shown
          Doth add more grief to too much of mine own.
          Love is a smoke made with the fume of sighs:
          Being purged, a fire sparkling in lovers' eyes;   185
          Being vexed, a sea nourished with loving tears.
          What is it else? A madness most discreet,
          A choking gall, and a preserving sweet.
          Farewell, my coz.

BENVOLIO   Soft, I will go along –
          And if you leave me so, you do me wrong.   190

ROMEO   Tut, I have lost myself. I am not here.
          This is not Romeo: he's some other where.

BENVOLIO Tell me in sadness, who is that you love?

ROMEO   What, shall I groan and tell thee?

BENVOLIO   Groan? Why no –
          But sadly tell me who.   195

ROMEO   Bid a sick man in sadness make his will –
          A word ill urged to one that is so ill.
          In sadness, cousin, I do love a woman.

BENVOLIO I aimed so near when I supposed you loved.

Romeo says that the girl cannot be won over. He rejects Benvolio's suggestion that he should forget her and look at other girls.

200 **mark-man**: marksman / skilful archer

201 **right fair mark**: good target

203 **Dian's wit**: i.e. the good sense to avoid love (Diana was the Roman goddess of hunting and virginity)

204 **proof**: armour
chastity: sexual purity

205 **uncharmed**: i.e. unaffected by love's spell

206 **will ... terms**: i.e. rejects love-talk

207 **bide ... eyes**: accept loving glances

208 **ope ... gold**: accept money

210 **her store**: i.e. her treasury of beauty

211 **still**: always

212 **in that sparing**: by saving herself

214 **Cuts ... posterity**: i.e. her beauty will not be handed on to her children

216 **merit bliss**: i.e. go to heaven for her sexual purity

217 **forsworn to**: sworn that she will not

THINK ABOUT *for* GCSE

Themes and issues

• **Love**: The wordplay between Romeo and Benvolio (lines 199 to 203), starting with the expression 'I aimed so near', is based on archery. How does it build up from there? Who is Cupid and how does he fit in?

Language

• What does Romeo's language in lines 202 to 210 suggest about his attitude to the girl?

223 **call ... more**: think about her excellent beauty even more

228 **passing fair**: exceedingly attractive

230 **passed**: surpassed / exceeded

232 **pay that doctrine**: teach you that lesson
else ... debt: i.e. I won't have done what I owe you as a friend

ROMEO	A right good mark-man! And she's fair I love.	**200**
BENVOLIO	A right fair mark, fair coz, is soonest hit.	

ROMEO Well, in that hit you miss. She'll not be hit
With Cupid's arrow. She hath Dian's wit,
And in strong proof of chastity well-armed,
From Love's weak childish bow she lives uncharmed. **205**
She will not stay the siege of loving terms,
Nor bide th' encounter of assailing eyes,
Nor ope her lap to saint-seducing gold.
O, she is rich in beauty – only poor
That when she dies, with beauty dies her store. **210**

BENVOLIO Then she hath sworn that she will still live chaste?

ROMEO She hath, and in that sparing makes huge waste,
For beauty, starved with her severity,
Cuts beauty off from all posterity.
She is too fair, too wise, wisely too fair, **215**
To merit bliss by making me despair.
She hath forsworn to love, and in that vow
Do I live dead, that live to tell it now.

BENVOLIO Be ruled by me: forget to think of her.

ROMEO O, teach me how I should forget to think! **220**

BENVOLIO By giving liberty unto thine eyes:
Examine other beauties.

ROMEO   'Tis the way
To call hers – exquisite – in question more.
These happy masks that kiss fair ladies' brows,
Being black, puts us in mind they hide the fair. **225**
He that is strucken blind cannot forget
The precious treasure of his eyesight lost.
Show me a mistress that is passing fair:
What doth her beauty serve, but as a note
Where I may read who passed that passing fair? **230**
Farewell. Thou canst not teach me to forget.

BENVOLIO I'll pay that doctrine, or else die in debt.

Exeunt.

In this scene ...

- Count Paris asks Capulet for his permission to woo Juliet.
- Benvolio persuades Romeo to go to the Capulet feast, where he can see girls who are more beautiful than the one he loves.

Count Paris wants to marry Juliet and asks her father for his consent. Capulet at first says that Juliet is too young to marry. But he agrees to let Paris woo her and he invites him to a feast at his house that evening.

THINK ABOUT for GCSE

Characterisation

- What impression have you formed of Capulet from this opening conversation? What is his attitude to Juliet getting married?

Relationships

- How old is Juliet? Which of Capulet's comments tells us that she is an only child? What might these facts suggest about Capulet's attitude to his daughter?

1   **bound**: ordered to keep the peace
2   **In ... alike**: or will face the same punishment

4   **reckoning**: reputation
5   **at odds**: as enemies
6   **suit**: request

7   **But saying o'er**: Simply repeating
8   **stranger**: newcomer

11   **Ere**: before

13   **marred**: spoiled

15   **hopeful ... earth**: 1 hope which forms the centre of my world; 2 lady who will inherit my wealth
18   **she agreed**: if she consents
19   **according**: agreeing

22   **store**: number

26   **comfort**: happiness
27   **well-apparelled**: i.e. clothed in flowers and leaves
30   **Inherit**: i.e. enjoy / experience
32   **mine**: i.e. my daughter
33   **stand in number**: be counted as one of the group
     in reckoning none: not high on your list

Another street.

Enter CAPULET, *Count* PARIS, *and Capulet's* SERVANT.

CAPULET But Montague is bound as well as I,
In penalty alike, and 'tis not hard, I think,
For men so old as we to keep the peace.

PARIS Of honourable reckoning are you both,
And pity 'tis you lived at odds so long. 5
But now, my lord, what say you to my suit?

CAPULET But saying o'er what I have said before:
My child is yet a stranger in the world;
She hath not seen the change of fourteen years.
Let two more summers wither in their pride 10
Ere we may think her ripe to be a bride.

PARIS Younger than she are happy mothers made.

CAPULET And too soon marred are those so early made.
Earth hath swallowed all my hopes but she.
She is the hopeful lady of my earth. 15
But woo her, gentle Paris, get her heart –
My will to her consent is but a part.
And she agreed, within her scope of choice
Lies my consent and fair according voice.
This night I hold an old accustomed feast, 20
Whereto I have invited many a guest,
Such as I love – and you among the store,
One more most welcome, makes my number more.
At my poor house look to behold this night
Earth-treading stars that make dark heaven light. 25
Such comfort as do lusty young men feel
When well-apparelled April on the heel
Of limping winter treads – even such delight
Among fresh female buds shall you this night
Inherit at my house. Hear all, all see, 30
And like her most whose merit most shall be –
Which on more view of many, mine, being one,
May stand in number, though in reckoning none.

Capulet gives his servant a list of the guests to be invited to the feast. The servant cannot read and so asks Romeo and Benvolio for help.

34 **sirrah**: you there

37 **stay**: wait

39 **meddle**: busy himself
   yard: measuring rod
40 **last**: wooden foot shape used by shoemakers

47 **another's anguish**: the suffering of a second pain
48 **holp**: helped
   backward: in reverse
49 **another's languish**: a further suffering
51 **rank**: foul
52 **plantain leaf**: leaf used to help cuts heal

53 **broken shin**: cut on the leg

55 **bound**: tied up

57 **Good e'en**: i.e. Good afternoon

58 **gi'**: give you

60 **without book**: 1 by heart; 2 from experience

THINK ABOUT for GCSE

Performance and staging

• In productions, this servant is usually Peter (the Nurse's man in Act 2 Scene 4) and would have been played by the comic actor in Shakespeare's company. If you were the director, what would you want the actor playing him to do in order to make this scene funny?

Relationships

• What does Benvolio think about Romeo's behaviour?

Come, go with me.
(*To the* SERVANT, *giving him a guest-list*)
         Go, sirrah, trudge about
Through fair Verona. Find those persons out   35
Whose names are written there, and to them say
My house and welcome on their pleasure stay.

Exit CAPULET, *with* PARIS.

SERVANT   Find them out whose names are written here? It is
written that the shoemaker should meddle with his yard
and the tailor with his last, the fisher with his pencil   40
and the painter with his nets. But I am sent to find those
persons whose names are here writ, and can never find
what names the writing person hath here writ. I must to
the learnèd. (*He sees* BENVOLIO *and* ROMEO *coming*) In
good time!   45

Enter BENVOLIO *and* ROMEO.

BENVOLIO   Tut, man, one fire burns out another's burning!
One pain is lessened by another's anguish:
Turn giddy, and be holp by backward turning.
One desperate grief cures with another's languish:
Take thou some new infection to thy eye,   50
And the rank poison of the old will die.

ROMEO   Your plantain leaf is excellent for that.

BENVOLIO   For what, I pray thee?

ROMEO   For your broken shin.

BENVOLIO   Why, Romeo, art thou mad?

ROMEO   Not mad, but bound more than a madman is –   55
Shut up in prison, kept without my food,
Whipped and tormented, and – Good e'en, good fellow.

SERVANT   God gi' good e'en. I pray, sir, can you read?

ROMEO   Ay – mine own fortune in my misery.

SERVANT   Perhaps you have learned it without book. But I pray,   60
can you read anything you see?

ROMEO   Ay, if I know the letters and the language.

Romeo reads out the guest-list, which includes the girl he loves – Rosaline. Benvolio suggests that they should go to the feast, where Romeo can see other girls who are more beautiful.

63 Rest you merry: i.e. Goodbye and good luck

66 County: Count

83 crush: drink

86 Sups: has supper

88 unattainted: unbiased

92 Maintains such falsehood: accepts lies like that

93 these: i.e. my eyes

THINK ABOUT
for GCSE

Relationships

- Look at lines 46 to 51, and 85 to 90. What advice does Benvolio give Romeo?

SERVANT	Ye say honestly. (*Walking away*) Rest you merry.
ROMEO	Stay, fellow! I can read. (***He takes the guest-list and reads it***)

'Signior Martino and his wife and daughters;   65
County Anselme and his beauteous sisters;
The lady widow of Vitruvio;
Signior Placentio and his lovely nieces;
Mercutio and his brother Valentine;
Mine uncle Capulet, his wife and daughters;   70
My fair niece Rosaline and Livia;
Signior Valentio and his cousin Tybalt;
Lucio and the lively Helena.'
A fair assembly! Whither should they come?

SERVANT	Up –	75
ROMEO	Whither? To supper?	
SERVANT	To our house.	
ROMEO	Whose house?	
SERVANT	My master's.	
ROMEO	Indeed, I should have asked thee that before.	80

SERVANT   Now I'll tell you without asking. My master is the
great rich Capulet – and if you be not of the house of
Montagues, I pray come and crush a cup of wine. Rest
you merry.

Exit.

BENVOLIO   At this same ancient feast of Capulet's   85
Sups the fair Rosaline whom thou so loves,
With all the admirèd beauties of Verona.
Go thither, and with unattainted eye
Compare her face with some that I shall show,
And I will make thee think thy swan a crow.   90

ROMEO   When the devout religion of mine eye
Maintains such falsehood, then turn tears to fire;
And these who, often drowned, could never die,

Romeo agrees to go to the
Capulet feast, but refuses to
accept that he will find any
girl there more beautiful than
Rosaline.

94 **Transparent**: 1 bright / clear; 2
   obvious
   heretics: disbelievers (in a religion),
   who might be executed by burning

97 **none ... by**: when there were no other
   beauties present

98 **poised**: only balanced

99 **that ... scales**: i.e. those eyes

102 **scant**: hardly

104 **splendour ... own**: i.e. Rosaline's
    beauty

THINK ABOUT for GCSE

Structure and Form

• In what ways has Act 1
  Scene 2 helped to set up the
  fateful encounter with Juliet
  at the Capulet ball?

Language

• What do you notice about
  the language Romeo uses
  in describing his love in
  lines 91 to 94? Think about
  the meanings of 'devout'
  and 'heretics', for example.
  What point is he making?

Transparent heretics, be burnt for liars.
One fairer than my love? The all-seeing sun   95
Ne'er saw her match since first the world begun!

BENVOLIO   Tut, you saw her fair, none else being by –
Herself poised with herself in either eye.
But in that crystal scales let there be weighed
Your lady's love against some other maid   100
That I will show you shining at this feast,
And she shall scant show well that now seems best.

ROMEO   I'll go along – no such sight to be shown,
But to rejoice in splendour of mine own.

Exeunt.

In this scene ...

- Lady Capulet tells Juliet that Count Paris wants to marry her.
- Juliet agrees to consider Paris as a husband.

Lady Capulet and the Nurse discuss Juliet's age. The Nurse recalls an event from Juliet's childhood.

2 maidenhead: virginity

3 God forbid: Perhaps the Nurse has realised that 'lady-bird' was sometimes slang for prostitute.

8 the matter: what I want to talk about
give leave: leave us alone

10 thou's: you shall
counsel: private discussion

11 pretty age: i.e. the right age for marriage

THINK ABOUT for GCSE

Relationships

- Why does Lady Capulet call the Nurse back in line 9, do you think? What does it reveal about their relationship?

Context

- What does the dialogue between Lady Capulet and the Nurse reveal about the status of the Nurse in the Capulet household?

14 teen: grief

15 but: only

16 Lammas-tide: a harvest feast on August 1st

17 odd: a few

19 Susan: the Nurse's own daughter (who died young)

24 was weaned: stopped being breast-fed

26 laid ... dug: Women would put the bitter-tasting substance on the nipple to put the child off sucking.

28 bear a brain: have a great memory

Inside the house of the Capulets.

Enter LADY CAPULET *and the* NURSE.

LADY CAPULET	Nurse, where's my daughter? Call her forth to me.
NURSE	Now, by my maidenhead at twelve year old, I bade her come. What, lamb! What, lady-bird! God forbid! Where's this girl? What, Juliet!

Enter JULIET.

JULIET	How now? Who calls?	5
NURSE	Your mother.	
JULIET	Madam, I am here. What is your will?	
LADY CAPULET	This is the matter. Nurse, give leave a while – We must talk in secret. – Nurse, come back again. I have remembered me, thou's hear our counsel. Thou know'st my daughter's of a pretty age.	10
NURSE	Faith, I can tell her age unto an hour.	
LADY CAPULET	She's not fourteen.	
NURSE	I'll lay fourteen of my teeth – and yet, to my teen be it spoken, I have but four – she's not fourteen. How long is it now to Lammas-tide?	15
LADY CAPULET	A fortnight and odd days.	
NURSE	Even or odd, of all days in the year come Lammas-Eve at night shall she be fourteen. Susan and she – God rest all Christian souls – were of an age. Well, Susan is with God: she was too good for me. But, as I said, on Lammas-Eve at night shall she be fourteen – that shall she, marry, I remember it well. 'Tis since the earthquake now eleven years, and she was weaned – I never shall forget it – of all the days of the year, upon that day. For I had then laid wormwood to my dug, sitting in the sun under the dove-house wall. My lord and you were then at Mantua – nay, I do bear a brain! But, as I said, when	20 25

The Nurse finishes her story and Lady Capulet asks Juliet how she feels about marriage.

29 **dug**: breast
30 **tetchy**: irritable
31 **Shake ... dove-house**: the dove-house shook
32 **I trow**: believe me
    bid me trudge: tell me to go away
33 **stand high-lone**: stand up by herself
33–4 **by the rood**: by the holy cross (an oath)
35 **broke her brow**: cut her forehead
36 **'a**: he
38 **fall backward**: a sexual double-meaning
38–9 **hast more wit**: know a bit more
39 **by my holidame**: by my holiness (an oath)
41 **come about**: come true eventually
    warrant: promise you
    and I should: even if I were to
43 **stinted**: stopped
47 **it**: its
48 **stone**: testicle

50 **comest to age**: are old enough

54 **And I might**: If only I could
55 **once**: one day

56 **Marry**: by (the Virgin) Mary

58 **How ... married**: What do you think of the idea of getting married

61 **thy teat**: the nipple you sucked (i.e. the Nurse's)

THINK ABOUT for GCSE

Characterisation

• What are your first impressions of the Nurse?

Performance and staging

• If you were the director, how would you ask the actor playing Lady Capulet to react while the Nurse is telling – and repeating – her story (lines 18 to 55)?

it did taste the wormwood on the nipple of my dug and
felt it bitter, pretty fool, to see it tetchy, and fall out with   30
the dug! 'Shake', quoth the dove-house. 'Twas no need,
I trow, to bid me trudge. And since that time it is eleven
years for then she could stand high-lone. Nay, by the
rood, she could have run and waddled all about – for
even the day before, she broke her brow, and then my   35
husband – God be with his soul, 'a was a merry man –
took up the child. 'Yea,' quoth he, 'dost thou fall upon
thy face? Thou wilt fall backward when thou hast more
wit, wilt thou not, Jule?' And, by my holidame, the pretty
wretch left crying, and said 'Ay'. To see now how a jest   40
shall come about! I warrant, and I should live a thousand
years, I never should forget it. 'Wilt thou not, Jule?' quoth
he – and, pretty fool, it stinted, and said 'Ay'!

LADY CAPULET   Enough of this. I pray thee hold thy peace.

NURSE   Yes, madam. Yet I cannot choose but laugh, to think it   45
              should leave crying, and say 'Ay'. And yet I warrant it
              had upon it brow a bump as big as a young cockerel's
              stone – a perilous knock! – and it cried bitterly. 'Yea,'
              quoth my husband, 'fall'st upon thy face? Thou wilt fall
              backward when thou comest to age, wilt thou not, Jule?'   50
              It stinted, and said 'Ay'!

JULIET   And stint thou too, I pray thee, Nurse, say I.

NURSE   Peace, I have done. God mark thee to his grace, thou
              wast the prettiest babe that e'er I nursed. And I might
              live to see thee married once, I have my wish.   55

LADY CAPULET   Marry, that 'marry' is the very theme
              I came to talk of. Tell me, daughter Juliet,
              How stands your dispositions to be married?

JULIET   It is an honour that I dream not of.

NURSE   An honour! Were not I thine only nurse, I would say   60
              thou hadst sucked wisdom from thy teat.

Juliet is told that Paris wants to marry her. She cautiously agrees to consider him as a husband.

63 **ladies of esteem**: honourable society women

65 **much ... years**: at roughly the same age

69 **a man of wax**: i.e. the ideal model of a man

76 **every married lineament**: all his features, combined in harmony

77 **one ... content**: each one goes well with another

78 **what obscured**: whatever you cannot see clearly

79 **margent**: margin (which often contained notes and comments)

80 **unbound**: 1 without a cover; 2 unmarried

81 **cover**: i.e. a wife

82 **lives in the sea**: i.e. knows where it is supposed to live

82–3 **'tis much ... hide**: the cover of a book should reflect the beautiful contents (i.e. Juliet would show off Paris's worth)

84–5 **That book ... story**: i.e. people admire a book both for its fine story and its rich binding

86–7 **share ... less**: i.e. be admired as much as Paris is when you are married to him

88 **grow**: 1 gain in status; 2 become pregnant

90 **I'll look ... move**: I expect I shall like him, if I am attracted by his looks

91–2 **no more ... fly**: I will go no further in love except with your permission

95 **in extremity**: in a mess

96 **wait**: serve at table
   straight: immediately

THINK ABOUT for GCSE

Themes and issues

• What do Lady Capulet's speeches, in lines 62 to 67, and 72 to 87, reveal about her attitude to **love** and marriage?

LADY CAPULET Well, think of marriage now. Younger than you,
Here in Verona, ladies of esteem,
Are made already mothers. By my count,
I was your mother much upon these years   65
That you are now a maid. Thus then in brief:
The valiant Paris seeks you for his love.

NURSE A man, young lady! Lady, such a man as all the world
... Why, he's a man of wax!

LADY CAPULET Verona's summer hath not such a flower.   70

NURSE Nay, he's a flower – in faith, a very flower!

LADY CAPULET What say you? Can you love the gentleman?
This night you shall behold him at our feast.
Read o'er the volume of young Paris' face,
And find delight writ there with beauty's pen.   75
Examine every married lineament,
And see how one another lends content –
And what obscured in this fair volume lies,
Find written in the margent of his eyes.
This precious book of love, this unbound lover,   80
To beautify him, only lacks a cover.
The fish lives in the sea – and 'tis much pride
For fair without the fair within to hide.
That book in many's eyes doth share the glory
That in gold clasps locks in the golden story.   85
So shall you share all that he doth possess
By having him, making yourself no less.

NURSE No less? Nay, bigger! Women grow by men.

LADY CAPULET Speak briefly: can you like of Paris' love?

JULIET I'll look to like, if looking liking move.   90
But no more deep will I endart mine eye
Than your consent gives strength to make it fly.

Enter the SERVANT.

SERVANT Madam, the guests are come, supper served up, you
called, my young lady asked for, the Nurse cursed in
the pantry, and everything in extremity. I must hence to   95
wait. I beseech you, follow straight.

They go off to the feast where Paris is waiting to meet Juliet.

97 **the County stays**: Count Paris is waiting
98 **to**: to add to

Relationships

• What kind of relationship to Juliet does the Nurse have? How can you tell?

• What does this scene reveal about the relationship between Lady Capulet and Juliet? Think about how close they are, for example.

LADY CAPULET   We follow thee. Juliet, the County stays.

NURSE   Go, girl. Seek happy nights to happy days.

Exeunt.

In this scene ...

- Romeo has had a dream which has made him uneasy about attending the Capulet feast.
- Mercutio tells him about Queen Mab and declares that dreams are only trivial fantasies.
- They enter the Capulet house, despite Romeo's concerns.

Romeo, Benvolio and their friend Mercutio arrive outside the Capulets' house. Mercutio tries to shake Romeo out of his love-sickness.

THINK ABOUT for GCSE

Themes and issues

- What effects has **love** had on Romeo, according to his statements here?

Context

- Romeo and his friends are planning to enter the Capulet ball as maskers. According to their opening conversation (lines 1 to 32), what did maskers typically do to entertain people?

1 **speech ... excuse**: Maskers would introduce themselves with an introductory speech.
3 **The date ... prolixity**: i.e. These days such long-winded speeches are unfashionable
4 **hoodwinked**: blindfolded
5 **Tartar's ... lath**: typical Cupid's bow, made of cheap wood (i.e. a prop)
6 **crow-keeper**: scarecrow
7 **without-book**: learned by heart
8 **After the prompter**: with the prompter's help
10 **measure ... measure**: 'serve them' a dance
11 **ambling**: dancing
12 **heavy**: low-spirited

16 **stakes**: fixes

18 **above ... bound**: higher than an ordinary leap in dancing
19 **sore ... shaft**: seriously wounded by Cupid's arrow
21 **bound a pitch**: i.e. leap up high

23 **sink in it**: enjoy love-making
24 **oppression**: weight
tender thing: delicate female
26 **rude**: rough

[handwritten top:] R + friends are about to gatecrash Capulet's party

ACT 1 SCENE 4

[handwritten:] It was the custom of such uninvited guests to have a speech prepared + to perform a dance for the guests. — Benvolio

Outside the house of the Capulets.

[handwritten:] Montague, Romeo's car2   relative of the prince

Enter ROMEO, BENVOLIO, and MERCUTIO, with five or six other gentlemen wearing masks. Servants light their way with flaming torches, and one carries a drum.

[handwritten left:] masquerade ball (fancy dress)

[handwritten right:] lads' night out — trying to help Romeo take his mind off Rosaline

[handwritten:] announce the party has begun

ROMEO	What, shall this speech be spoke for our excuse?
	Or shall we on without apology?
BENVOLIO	The date is out of such prolixity.
	We'll have no Cupid hoodwinked with a scarf,
	Bearing a Tartar's painted bow of lath, 5
	Scaring the ladies like a crow-keeper –
	Nor no without-book prologue, faintly spoke
	After the prompter, for our entrance,
	But let them measure us by what they will,
	We'll measure them a measure and be gone. 10
ROMEO	Give me a torch: I am not for this ambling.
	Being but heavy, I will bear the light.
MERCUTIO	Nay, gentle Romeo, we must have you dance.
ROMEO	Not I, believe me. You have dancing shoes
	With nimble soles: I have a soul of lead 15
	So stakes me to the ground I cannot move.
MERCUTIO	You are a lover: borrow Cupid's wings,
	And soar with them above a common bound.
ROMEO	I am too sore empiercèd with his shaft
	To soar with his light feathers – and so bound, 20
	I cannot bound a pitch above dull woe.
	Under love's heavy burden do I sink.
MERCUTIO	And to sink in it should you burden love –
	Too great oppression for a tender thing.
ROMEO	Is love a tender thing? It is too rough, 25
	Too rude, too boisterous, and it pricks like thorn.

[handwritten annotations throughout:]
- *what shall we say is our excuse for being here?*
- *Romeo for normal maskers introduce themselves with an intro speech upon arrival*
- *long-winded speeches are out of vogue — Shakespeare private joke*
- *being not going to produce our dance by having someone dress up as Cupid*
- *scarecrow*
- *no learned off speeches*
- *Nor are we going to recite a memorised speech to introduce ourselves*
- *let them judge us however they like*
- *we won't give a speech, we'll give them a dance*
- *serve them a dance*
- *dancing*
- *I feel sad, so let me be the one who carries the torch*
- *grumpy / self-centred / self-pity / self-indulgent*
- *moose / morose   low-spirited*
- *Not me.   You're wearing dancing shoes*
- *C'mon man! You're up 4 a dance*
- *With nimble soles my soul is made of lead — metaphor*
- *what does that mean? I can't move myself*
- *+ its so heavy it keeps me stuck to the ground*
- *boost his morale / pep talk / try to cheer him up — be the man*
- *fly high*
- *Cupid's arrow — pun on soar / sore*
- *I can't leap because I'm miserable*
- *His arrow has pierced me too deeply*
- *So I can't fly with his cheerful feather*
- *leap up high   too*
- *I sink under heavy weight of love*
- *enjoy love — Mercutio*
- *If you sink, you're dragging love down / it's not right to*
- *delicate / female*
- *Is love really tender?*
- *It's not right to drag something down as tender as love*
- *philosophising now*
- *rough / randy*

45

Romeo has worries about attending the feast because he has had a disturbing dream. Mercutio tells him that he must have been visited by Queen Mab.

28 **Prick … pricking**: 1 hurt love in return for hurting you; 2 ease sexual desire by satisfying it

29 **case**: cover (mask)
   visage: face

30 **visor for a visor**: mask for an ugly face

31 **What … deformities**: if nosy people notice my ugliness

32 **beetle … me**: i.e. the mask has overhanging eyebrows and red cheeks

34 **betake … legs**: start dancing

35 **wantons**: irresponsible people

37–8 **proverbed … on**: the old proverb applies to me: 'the onlooker sees the best of the game'

39 **The game … done**: i.e. Let's quit while we are ahead

40 **dun's the mouse**: 'be silent and unseen' (a proverb)

41 **Dun**: a stick-in-the-mud
   draw … mire: pull you out of the mud

42 **save your reverence**: if you'll excuse me for saying so

43 **burn daylight**: waste time

46 **good**: intended

46–7 **our judgement … wits**: there is five times more sense in that than in what our senses usually tell us

49 **no wit**: not wise

THINK ABOUT for GCSE

Language

• Mercutio and Romeo love playing with words. Look at the puns in lines 9 to 10, 12, 15, 18 to 19, 20 to 21, 26 to 28, 30, 39 to 41, and 51. Do you find them irritating or entertaining?

Scene may appear unnecessary
- As audience we know it +
his friends are on way to feast.
we know that Romeo is worried,
melancholy while Mercutio is
more sensible, logical, reasonable.
why include it? esp as it doesn't
add to plot

46   Scene vitally imp. for
theme of fate + R's conviction
that the night's events will lead to his death

Annotations (handwritten):

Mercutio is gently mocking Romeo by turning all of R. Statements above love into blantantly sexual metaphors. love portrayed as a pastime technique — love portrayed as a person / personification

R. refuses to engage in the banter

✳ Prescient sense — that something bad will happen

MERCUTIO   If love be rough with you, be rough with love:
If [your] prick love when it pricks you, you'll beat it down   mask

Prick love for pricking, and you beat love down.

Give me a case to put my visage in:
A mask to [disguise] my face mask

self deprecating saying he is ugly

A visor for a visor! What care I

What curious eye doth quote deformities? — what do ±30 care
Let this mask with its black eyebrows blush for me   people notice my — if wrinkles / see my flaws

Here are the beetle brows shall blush for me.   image does this convey?

He puts on a mask.

BENVOLIO   Come, knock and enter – and no sooner in,
The min we get in let's all start dancing   gives instructions — the min we get in, start dancing

But every man betake him to his legs.   start dancing

ROMEO   A torch for me. Let wantons light of heart   35

If he/ladies want to dance let them, I'll look on.   Tickle the senseless rushes with their heels,   J. morose

For I am proverbed with a grandsire phrase: glum, pessimistic
I'll just hold a torch + watch you sing

I'll be a candle-holder and look on.   let's quit while we're ahead – defeatist
I'll sit this one out

The game was ne'er so fair, and I am done.

MERCUTIO   Tut, dun's the mouse, the constable's own word.   40 morose

If you're being a [dun] in the mud we'll get you out of   – does R. want to be here?
If thou art Dun, we'll draw thee from the mire –

mean out of love you'll excuse me for my rude   Or, save your reverence, love, wherein thou stickest
come we're wasting precious daylight

If you're stuck, we'll help you out   Up to the ears. Come, we burn daylight, ho!
great expression of friendship come on, let's go stop

ROMEO   Nay, that's not so.   You're stuck up to your ears because of love.
No, we're not. it's night

MERCUTIO   I mean, sir, in delay

We waste our lights in vain, like lights by day.   45

Take our good meaning, for our judgement sits

Five times in that, ere once in our five wits.

ROMEO   We mean well in going to this mass ball   And we mean well in going to this mask –

But it's not smart of us to go   But 'tis no wit to go. — It's not wise to go in
Has a foreboding sense

MERCUTIO   Why, may one ask?

ROMEO   I had a dream tonight   I dreamt a dream tonight.

MERCUTIO   And so did I.   50   so did I

ROMEO   well, what your dream?   Well, what was yours?

MERCUTIO   my dream told me that dreamers often lie   That dreamers often lie.   never worry about your dreams – they're often false – stop

ROMEO   often dreams are true – They lie in bed + dream about the who   In bed asleep, while they do dream things true.   faith about dreams

MERCUTIO   O, then I see Queen Mab hath been with you.

BENVOLIO   Queen Mab? What's she?   the fairy who supposedly brings dreams to sleeping humans

47

Mercutio tells them who Queen Mab is and what she does while people are asleep.

55 **midwife**: i.e. she 'delivers' people's dreams
57 **On ... alderman**: on the ring of a senior town councillor
58 **atomies**: tiny creatures
60 **spinners**: spiders
61 **cover**: canopy
62 **traces**: harness

64 **film**: gossamer

66–7 **worm ... maid**: It was believed that worms grew in lazy girls' fingers.
69 **joiner-squirrel**: The squirrel hollows out nuts like a carpenter.
70 **Time ... mind**: for as long as people can remember
71 **state**: splendour
73 **on curtsies**: of bowing (and flattering people)
     straight: immediately

79 **smelling ... suit**: finding a client who will pay to have their case argued at court
80 **tithe-pig**: Pigs were sometimes given as the tenth of a person's income which had to go to the parson.
82 **benefice**: paid church appointment
85 **breaches**: attacks through gaps blown in castle walls
     ambuscadoes: ambushes
86 **healths ... deep**: i.e. heavy drinking
     anon: immediately
90 **plaits**: tangles
91 **bakes ... hairs**: makes unclean people's hair matted
92 **much misfortune bodes**: is very unlucky
93 **hag**: evil fairy

THINK ABOUT for GCSE

Performance and staging

• How could the actor playing Mercutio make the very long Queen Mab speech (lines 55 to 96) come alive for the audience? Think about what actions might accompany it, for example.

Handwritten note at top: Mercutio's famous Queen Mab Speech – imp. for stunning quality of its poetry
M- saying to Romeo he should set aside his L.S. over Rosaline + come to the Capulet feast. R. says he is depressed because of a dream, Merc launches on a lengthy, playful description of Queen Mab – the fairy who supposedly brings dreams to sleeping humans

MERCUTIO

She is the fairies' midwife – and she comes *[she's the fairies' midwife]* 55
In shape no bigger than an agate stone *[And she's no bigger than a stone on a / ring (an alderman's ring)]*
On the forefinger of an alderman,
Drawn with a team of little atomies *[She rides around in a wagon]*
Over men's noses as they lie asleep. *[and she rides over men's noses as they lie sleeping]*
Her waggon-spokes made of long spinners' legs, *[The spokes of the wagon are made of spider legs]* 60
The cover of the wings of grasshoppers. *[the cover (canopy) made of grasshoppers' wings.]*
Her traces of the smallest spider-web, *[The harness is made of the smallest spider webs]*
Her collars of the moonshine's watery beams, *[the collars are made out of moonbeams]*
Her whip of cricket's bone, the lash of film – *[Her whip is a thread attached to a cricket's bone]*
Her waggoner a small grey-coated gnat, *[Her wagon driver is a small gnat in a grey coat]* 65
Not half so big as a round little worm *[He's not half the size of a little round worm]*
Pricked from the lazy finger of a maid. *[that comes from the finger of a lazy girl.]*
Her chariot is an empty hazel-nut,
Made by the joiner-squirrel or old grub, *[They have made wagons for the fairies]*
Time out o' mind the fairies' coachmakers. *[for as long as anyone can remember]* 70
And in this state she gallops night by night
Through lovers' brains, and then they dream of love; *[She rides over courtiers' knees + they dream of curtsies]*
O'er courtiers' knees, that dream on curtsies straight;
O'er lawyers' fingers, who straight dream on fees;
O'er ladies' lips, who straight on kisses dream – *[Mab puts blisters on their lips]* 75
Which oft the angry Mab with blisters plagues, *[Because their breaths smell sweet]*
Because their breaths with sweetmeats tainted are.
Sometime she gallops o'er a courtier's nose *[whatever part of body she rides over in her wagon]*
And then dreams he of smelling out a suit; *[Sometimes she tickles a parson's nose]*
And sometime comes she with a tithe-pig's tail, *[Priest – the dream of larger donation]* 80
Tickling a parson's nose as 'a lies asleep: *[corresponds what people dream]*
Then dreams he of another benefice.
Sometime she driveth o'er a soldier's neck,
And then dreams he of cutting foreign throats, *[ambushes]*
Of breaches, ambuscadoes, Spanish blades, 85
Of healths five fathom deep – and then anon
Drums in his ear, at which he starts and wakes,
And being thus frighted, swears a prayer or two,
And sleeps again. This is that very Mab *[who tangles the hair in horses' manes at night]*
That plaits the manes of horses in the night, *[+ makes the tangles hard to undo the dirty hairs]* 90
And bakes the elf-locks in foul sluttish hairs *[which brings bad luck if they're untangled]*
Which, once untangled, much misfortune bodes.
This is the hag, when maids lie on their backs, *[This is the hag who]*

Left margin handwritten notes:
Main point – that the dreams Queen Mab brings are directly related to the person who dreams them – lovers dream of love, soldiers dream of war, etc.
But in the process of making this v. ordinary point Mercutio falls into a sort of wild bitterness in which he seems to see dreams as destructive + delusional

witty character
can mock Romeo

Bottom handwritten note:
Mab- fairy tale – bringing dreams to sleeping by end of speech, she is 'the hag' who teaches maidens to have sex – descended into a dark pic.

49

Mercutio claims that dreams are nothing more than trivial fantasies. They go in to the feast, despite Romeo's uneasiness that the evening may lead to future tragedy.

94   **learns**: teaches
     bear: 1 bear the weight of a man; 2 bear children
95   **of good carriage**: 1 graceful; 2 good at love-making
97   **nothing**: could mean 'no-thing' (the female sexual organ)

99   **Begot**: born
     vain fantasy: idle dreaming

104   **Turning his side**: reversing his direction
105   **blows ... ourselves**: distracts us from our intentions
107   **my mind misgives**: I have an uneasy feeling
108   **yet ... stars**: fated to happen, but not yet revealed
109   **date**: appointed time
110–11 **expire ... Of**: put an end to
112   **vile forfeit**: awful penalty
      untimely: early
113   **He**: God
      steerage of my course: control over my direction

THINK ABOUT
for GCSE

Characterisation

• In some productions, Mercutio has to be stopped by Romeo (line 96) because he seems to be building up into a mad frenzy. What do you think the Queen Mab speech reveals about him?

Themes and issues

• What seems to be worrying Romeo as they approach the party? Do you think that he is just in low spirits, or does he have some genuine sense of the **fate** in store for him?

Mab teaches them how to hold a lover & bear a child.

That presses them and learns them first to bear,
Making them women of good carriage.   95
This is she –

ROMEO   Peace, peace, Mercutio, peace!
Thou talk'st of nothing. *You're talking nonsense* or *(no-things!*
                                                        (the
                                                        female
MERCUTIO   True, I talk of dreams, *sexual*
which are the products of a brain doing nothing.   *organ)*
Which are the children of an idle brain,
Begot of nothing but vain fantasy,
Dreams are Which is as thin of substance as the air,   100
nothing but And more inconstant than the wind, who woos
silly imaginations Even now the frozen bosom of the north,
as thin as And being angered, puffs away from thence,
air & less stable Turning his side to the dew-dropping south.
predictable
than the wind
BENVOLIO This wind you talk of blows us from ourselves: 105
Dinner is over & we shall get there too late Supper is done, and we shall come too late.
I'm worried we'll get here too late early I fear, too early – for my mind misgives
I have a feeling
ROMEO   Some consequence, yet hanging in the stars, *this party tonight*
Something that will end with my own death Shall bitterly begin his fearful date *will be the start of*
Get pupils With this night's revels, and expire the term   110 *something bad*
to Of a despisèd life closed in my breast,
translate By some vile forfeit of untimely death. *my life is going*
But whoever is in charge of where But He that hath the steerage of my course
✱ *can steer me wherever they want* Direct my sail! On, lusty gentlemen. *– audience knows he*
                                                        will suffer an untimely
BENVOLIO Strike, drum!   115 *death*
Beat the drum (announce their presence)
ROMEO and BENVOLIO put on their masks. All the maskers *prologue*
march round to the beat of the drum, then exeunt.

– here the
audience
feels fate
take a
tighter
grasp on
him

In this scene ...

- Tybalt is bitterly angry that Romeo has gate-crashed the Capulet feast, and says that he will not forget the insult.
- Romeo meets Juliet and they quickly begin to fall in love.
- After the lovers part, each is shocked to find out that they have fallen in love with someone who should be their enemy.

The household servants clear away after the feast and prepare the room for dancing. Capulet warmly welcomes his guests.

1 **take away**: remove the dirty dishes
2 **trencher**: plate

5 **joint-stools**: seats (stools made by joiners)
5–6 **court-cupboard**: sideboard
6 **look to the plate**: deal with the silverware
Good thou: Be a good man
7 **march-pane**: marzipan
8 **Susan ... Nell**: probably the servant's girl-friends

THINK ABOUT for GCSE

Performance and staging

- How would you direct the opening of this scene to make it energetic and full of life?

Characterisation

- What aspect of Capulet's personality that we have not seen before is revealed by his behaviour in lines 15 to 40?

14 **longer ... all**: survivor takes all
s.d. **maskers**: masked guests

16 **walk a bout**: have a dance

18 **deny**: refuse
makes dainty: seems reluctant
19 **Am I come near**: Have I guessed the truth

The great hall in the Capulets' house.

Enter two household SERVANTS, *clearing away after the feast.*

Enter ROMEO, MERCUTIO, BENVOLIO, *and their company, all in masks. They stand to one side as the* SERVANTS *begin to clear the hall for dancing.*

SERVANT 1 Where's Potpan, that he helps not to take away? He shift a trencher? He scrape a trencher?

[handwritten: isn't to helping to clear the table / He should be moving + scraping plates]

SERVANT 2 When good manners shall lie all in one or two men's hands, and they unwashed too, 'tis a foul thing.

[handwritten: when only one or two men have all the good manners / and even then are dirty they are bad]

SERVANT 1 Away with the joint-stools, remove the court-cupboard, look to the plate. Good thou, save me a piece of march-pane – and, as thou loves me, let the porter let in Susan Grindstone and Nell. (**He calls**) Antony and Potpan!

[handwritten: Take away the seats, remove the sideboard, deal with the plates/silverware. Be a good man, save me a piece of marzipan + if you love me let the porter let in / Prob. the servant's gfs]

5

Enter two more SERVANTS.

SERVANT 3 Ay, boy, ready.   10

[handwritten: Yes body, I'm ready]

SERVANT 1 You are looked for and called for, asked for and sought for, in the great chamber.

[handwritten: They're looking for you in the great chamber]

SERVANT 4 We cannot be here and there too. Cheerly, boys! Be brisk a while, and the longer liver take all.

[handwritten: we can't be in 2 places at once, both here + there. – Be quick / For a while + the survivor/winner takes it all.]

Enter CAPULET *and* LADY CAPULET, *Capulets' older* COUSIN, JULIET, *the* NURSE, *and* TYBALT, *with his page-boy. The other guests from the feast, and musicians, follow.*

[handwritten: Juliet's cousin]

The SERVANTS *stand aside.* CAPULET *greets the maskers.*

CAPULET Welcome, gentlemen! Ladies that have their toes Unplagued with corns will walk a bout with you. Ah ha, my mistresses! Which of you all Will now deny to dance? She that makes dainty, She, I'll swear, hath corns. Am I come near ye now? Welcome, gentlemen. I have seen the day   15

20

[handwritten: The ladies who don't have corns on their toes will dance with you / ladies which of you will / refuse to dance now. She that seems reluctant / I'll swear she has corns. Have I guessed the truth? Does that hit close to home?]

[handwritten left margin: Capulet making the rounds through groups of guests, joking with + encouraging them to dance.]

[handwritten: There was a time]

53

Capulet and his cousin talk fondly about their younger days. As the guests dance, Romeo sets eyes on Juliet and is stunned by her beauty.

21   **visor**: mask

25   **A hall**: Make some space
     foot it: get dancing
26   **turn ... up**: pack away the trestle tables
28   **unlooked-for sport**: unexpected entertainment

32   **By 'r lady:** By the Virgin Mary (an oath)

34   **nuptial**: wedding
35   **Pentecost**: Whitsun

39   **a ward**: i.e. he had a guardian as he was not of age

Language

• What words and phrases reveal that Romeo is thinking of Juliet's beauty in terms of brightness in contrast to the surrounding dark? Look at lines 44 to 53.

46   **Ethiop**: in Shakespeare's time, any black African
47   **dear**: precious

That I have worn a visor, and could tell
A whispering tale in a fair lady's ear
Such as would please. – 'Tis gone, 'tis gone, 'tis gone!
You are welcome, gentlemen! Come, musicians, play!

The maskers mingle with the other guests. Music, and a
dance, begins.

A hall, a hall – give room! And foot it, girls!   25
(*To the* SERVANTS) More light, you knaves, and turn the
tables up! –
And quench the fire, the room is grown too hot.
– Ah, sirrah, this unlooked-for sport comes well!
Nay sit, nay sit, good Cousin Capulet –
For you and I are past our dancing days.   30
How long is't now since last yourself and I
Were in a mask?

COUSIN   By 'r lady, thirty years.

CAPULET   What, man? 'Tis not so much, 'tis not so much!
'Tis since the nuptial of Lucentio –
Come Pentecost as quickly as it will –   35
Some five and twenty years, and then we masked.

COUSIN   'Tis more, 'tis more. His son is elder, sir:
His son is thirty.

CAPULET   Will you tell me that?
His son was but a ward two years ago.
(*Watching the dance*) Good youth i' faith. O, youth's
a jolly thing!   40

ROMEO   (*To a* SERVANT) What lady's that which doth enrich the
hand
Of yonder knight?

SERVANT   I know not, sir.

ROMEO   O, she doth teach the torches to burn bright!
It seems she hangs upon the cheek of night   45
As a rich jewel in an Ethiop's ear –
Beauty too rich for use, for earth too dear.
So shows a snowy dove trooping with crows,
As yonder lady o'er her fellows shows.

55

Tybalt recognises Romeo and angrily reports his discovery of the gate-crasher to Capulet. Capulet has heard good things about Romeo and loses his temper with Tybalt for threatening to disturb the party.

50 **The measure done**: Once this dance is over
51 **rude**: rough (compared with Juliet's)
52 **Forswear it**: Swear that it was not so

55 **rapier**: sword

55 **slave**: villain
56 **antic face**: comic, grotesque mask
57 **fleer ... solemnity**: mock our celebrations
58 **stock ... kin**: my family honour
59 **hold**: consider
60 **storm**: behave so angrily

62 **spite**: contempt

THINK ABOUT for GCSE

Language

- What does Romeo's language tell you about the nature of his feelings for Juliet at first sight, for example in line 52?

Performance and staging

- If you were the director, how would you ask Capulet and Tybalt to act during their confrontation (lines 54 to 92)? Think about how each character is feeling as the argument becomes heated, how they should say particular lines, and what actions they might perform.

65 **Content thee**: Calm down
66 **'A bears him**: He behaves
   portly: well-mannered
68 **well-governed**: good-mannered

70 **do him disparagement**: treat him in an ill-mannered way

73 **Show ... presence**: behave pleasantly
74 **ill-beseeming semblance**: very inappropriate way to look

77 **goodman**: i.e. not a gentleman
   Go to: Stop this behaviour

80 **make a mutiny**: cause a disturbance
81 **set cock-a-hoop**: behave wildly

when this dance is over, I'll see where she stands

The measure done, I'll watch her place of stand, 50

And then I'll touch her hand with my rude   *? ugly one*

And, touching hers, make blessed my rude hand.

my eyes are liars,

Did my heart love till now? Forswear it, sight! –

because I never saw true beauty before tonight

For I ne'er saw true beauty till this night.

TYBALT

I can tell by his voice that this man is a Montague

This, by his voice, should be a Montague.

Fetch me my rapier, boy.

Get me my sword, boy.

                                                    Exit PAGE.

what does this villain
dare to come here

                        What! – Dares the slave 55

with his face covered by a mask

Come hither, covered with an antic face,

To sneer at + scorn our celebration?

To fleer and scorn at our solemnity?

Now by my family honour

Now, by the stock and honour of my kin,

I do not consider it a sin to kill him

To strike him dead I hold it not a sin!

CAPULET

what's going on here nephew? why are you acting so angrily?

Why, how now, kinsman! Wherefore storm you so? 60

TYBALT

our enemy

Uncle, this is a Montague, our foe! –

He's a scoundrel came here in contempt

A villain that is hither come in spite,

To scorn at our solemnity this night.

to mock our party tonight

CAPULET

Young Romeo is it?

Is it young Romeo?

TYBALT

                        'Tis he, that villain Romeo.

CAPULET

calm down   *leave him alone*

Content thee, gentle coz, let him alone. 65

He behaves like a well-mannered gentleman

'A bears him like a portly gentleman –

And to tell you him, he has a reputation through verona

And to say truth, Verona brags of him

of being virtuous + well-mannered young man

To be a virtuous and well-governed youth.

I would not, for the wealth of all this town,

treat him in an insulting way

Here in my house do him disparagement. 70

Just ignore him.

Therefore be patient, take no note of him.

That is my will + if you respect my wishes

It is my will, the which if thou respect,

You'll look nice + stop frowning

Show a fair presence and put off these frowns,

because that's not the way you should behave at a feast

An ill-beseeming semblance for a feast.

TYBALT

It's no right way to act when a villain like him shows up

It fits when such a villain is a guest. 75

I won't tolerate it!

I'll not endure him!

CAPULET

You will tolerate it, I say you will.

                        He shall be endured.

I am the boss here   *stop his behaviour. rise up.*

What, goodman boy? I say he shall! Go to!

You'll not tolerate him? God help me!

Am I the master here, or you? Go to!

You'll start a riot among my guests!

You'll not endure him! God shall mend my soul,

You'll make a mutiny among my guests! 80

You will set cock-a-hoop! You'll be the man!

You'll be the rabble-rouser.

Tybalt backs down from confronting Romeo, but plans revenge. Romeo and Juliet meet and exchange loving words.

82 **shame**: insult

83 **saucy**: insolent

84 **trick ... scathe you**: stupid behaviour might do you harm

85 **contrary me**: go against *my* will

86 **Well said**: Bravo
    princox: young upstart

rhyme scheme ⟶
this sonnet is
same as opening
Sonnet (Prologue)
Connects - to the
dark fate that will
meet the lovers
— destructive love

when R + J first speak,
they speak 14 lines before
their 1st kiss. Significance?
14 lines = shared sonnet.
Sonnet = poem (14 lines) - perfect
idealized poetic form often
used to write about love.

89 **perforce**: forced upon me
    wilful choler: the anger I want to show

90 **in ... greeting**: i.e. they are in conflict

92 **gall**: poison

THINK ABOUT for GCSE

Characterisation

• What impression have you formed of Tybalt from this scene and Act 1 Scene 1?

Structure and form

• Lines 93 to 106 are written in the form of a sonnet. (This was a fourteen-line poem, divided into sections, often used by poets writing about love-affairs.) How are the different stages in the dialogue between Romeo and Juliet represented through the three sections (93 to 96, 97 to 100, and 101 to 106)?

93 **profane**: debase / make dirty

94 **holy shrine**: i.e. Juliet's hand

95 **pilgrims**: people who travel to holy places

97 **you do wrong**: i.e. your hand was not rough – so no kiss was called for

98 **mannerly**: proper / fitting

100 **palm to ... kiss**: Pilgrims would touch a holy statue's hand, not kiss it. (Pilgrims also carried palm-leaves.)

105 **Saints ... move**: 1 Statues do not move; 2 Saints do not set things in motion
    grant ... sake: they answer prayers

Language of excitement + Wonder – Shakespeare doesn't disappoint – he has delayed them meeting for 4 scenes – bursting with energy

TYBALT Why, uncle, 'tis a shame.

But uncle, we're being disrespected/insulted (USA = 'dissed')

CAPULET Go to, go to!

Go on, go on!

You are a saucy boy! Is't so indeed?

cheeky/insolent *Is that how it is really? – back*

This trick may chance to scathe you. – I know what.

This stupid behaviour may come back to do you harm – rosite you

You must contrary me! Marry, 'tis time – I'll teach you a lesson 85

You have to contradict me do us

(*To dancers nearby*) Well said, my hearts! – You are

Bravo

 — a princox! Go!

guests

young upstart (jumped up) me

Be quiet, or – (*To the* SERVANTS) More light, more light,

for shame! –

I'll make you quiet! – (*To dancers*) What! – Cheerly

I'll shut you up *keep having fun, my friends*

my hearts!

He leaves TYBALT, *and goes back to his guests as the dancing*
continues.

TYBALT Patience perforce with wilful choler meeting

Combination of patience forced on me with anger/rage

Tone – Severe

Makes my flesh tremble in their different greeting. 90

is making my body tremble – causing conflict

menacing

I will withdraw. But this intrusion shall,

I will leave, I'll leave now, but Romeo's intrusion

forbidding

Now seeming sweet, convert to bitterest gall!

hostile

which seems so sweet to him, will turn bitter/poison to him

aggressive

Menacing – ominous – remember R.'s dream + **Exit.** *later*

ROMEO (*Taking* JULIET'*s hand*) If I profane with my unworthiest *Sense of*

hand *Your hand is like a holy place that my*

Dialogue with rel. This holy shrine, the gentle sin is this: *hand is unworthy to visit. If you're offended by his foreboding*

language of My lips, two blushing pilgrims, ready stand *my two lips are standing here like blushing pilgrims* 95

pilgrimage To smooth that rough touch with a tender kiss. *ready to smooth things with a tender kiss*

JULIET Good pilgrim, you do wrong your hand too much, *you don't give your hand enough credit – your hand was not rash*

Pilgrims Which mannerly devotion shows in this – *By holding my hand you show polite devotion*

worship For saints have hands that pilgrims' hands do touch, *After all, pilgrims touch the hands of statues of Saints*

+ devotion And palm to palm is holy palmers' kiss. *Holding one palm against another is like a kiss* 100

piety

ROMEO Have not saints lips, and holy palmers too? *Don't saints + pilgrims have lips too?*

JULIET Ay, pilgrim, lips that they must use in prayer. *They have lips that they're supposed to pray with*

ROMEO O then, dear saint, let lips do what hands do: *well then saint, let lips do what hands do.*

They pray: grant thou – lest faith turn to despair. *I'm praying for you to kiss me so my faith doesn't turn to despair*

JULIET Saints do not move, though grant for prayers' sake. 105

Saints/statues don't move, even when they grant prayers ie Saints can't set things in motion – give R. licence to make 1st move?

Pilgrim = a person who journeys to a sacred place for religious reasons; one who embarks on a quest for something conceived of as sacred

Romeo and Juliet kiss. The
Nurse interrupts, telling Juliet
that her mother wants her.
Romeo asks the Nurse who
Juliet is and is dismayed to hear
that she is a Capulet. He and his
friends leave.

106 move not: remain still

107 purged: purified

109 trespass ... urged: you encouraged this
sin very sweetly

110 by the book: like an expert

112 What: Who

115 withal: with

117 the chinks: plenty of money

118 O dear account: What a heavy price
to pay
my foe's debt: i.e. in the power of my
enemy
119 The ... best: Let's quit while we're
ahead
122 trifling ... towards: there are light
refreshments on the way

126 fay: faith
it waxes: it's getting

THINK ABOUT for GCSE

Themes and issues

• How seriously should we
take Romeo's new-found
love for Juliet? Does his
language suggest that he is
now genuinely in love, or is
this just another infatuation?

Language

• What does the religious
imagery used by Romeo
and Juliet suggest about the
way they view their love?
How does it affect the way
we see it?

ROMEO   Then move not, while my prayer's effect I take.

Then remains still, don't move while I act out my prayer

He kisses her.

Thus from my lips, by thine, my sin is purged.

purified   now my sin / sin has been

JULIET   Then have my lips the sin that they have took.

Do my lips now have the sin they took from you? taken from my lips by

ROMEO   Sin from my lips? O trespass sweetly urged!
Give me my sin again.

Sin from my lips? You encouraged my sin.   sweetly?   yours

flirtatious / playful   *Give me my sin back*

He kisses her again.

JULIET   — You kiss by the book.   110

(1) marvellous   You kiss like an expert (like you studied it)
(2) kisses by book - kisses as if he learned how to   You've been around

NURSE   (*Approaching them*) Madam, your mother craves a
word with you.

proficient but not original   *insult) or compliment   kiss in manual*

ROMEO   (*As* JULIET *goes*) What is her mother?

who is her mum?

NURSE   Marry, bachelor,
Her mother is the lady of the house,
And a good lady, and a wise and virtuous.
I nursed her daughter that you talked withal.   115
I tell you, he that can lay hold of her
Shall have the chinks.

Young man   Her mother is the lady of the house
let me tell you, the man who marries her will become very wealthy

ROMEO   (*aside*)   Is she a Capulet?
O dear account! My life is my foe's debt.

This is a heavy price to pay! My life is in the hands of my enemy.

BENVOLIO   Away, be gone! The sport is at the best.

Let's go.   let's quit while we're ahead.

ROMEO   Ay, so I fear – the more is my unrest.   120

I'm in more trouble than ever, I fear

CAPULET   Nay, gentleman, prepare not to be gone! –
We have a trifling foolish banquet towards.

we have a little refreshment coming up

The maskers whisper their excuses to him.

Is it e'en so? Why, then I thank you all.
I thank you, honest gentlemen. Good night.
(*To the* SERVANTS) More torches here! Come on, then
let's to bed.   125
Ah, sirrah, by my fay, it waxes late –
I'll to my rest.

by man I swear   It's getting   *(faith)*
I'm away to bed

*Torch-bearers show the maskers out. Guests prepare to
depart. All exit, leaving only* JULIET *and the* NURSE.

When the Nurse tells Juliet who Romeo is, she realises that she has fallen in love with a Montague, the family she is supposed to hate.

128   **yond**: over there

135   **My grave ... bed**: I am likely to die unmarried

138   **sprung from**: born from

139   **Too ... late**: I saw him before I knew who he was; now that I know, it's too late

140   **Prodigious ... me**: This is a very ominous start to our love

143   **Anon**: Coming

THINK ABOUT for GCSE

Characterisation

- What have you learned about Juliet from this scene? Think about the differences between her attitudes to love and Romeo's attitudes, for example.
- Why do you think Juliet enquires after Romeo's identity in a roundabout way (lines 128 to 134)?

here

JULIET   Come hither, Nurse. What is yond gentleman? *that gentleman over here*

NURSE   The son and heir of old Tiberio.

JULIET   What's he that now is going out of door?   **130**

NURSE   Marry, that I think be young Petruchio.

JULIET   What's he that follows there, that would not dance? *who's he are following over here, he are who wouldn't dance*

NURSE   I know not. — *I don't know*

JULIET   *future husband* Go ask his name. (*Exit* NURSE) If he be married, *If he's married I'll die*
v. strong sentiment   My grave is like to be my wedding bed. *rather than marry anyone else*   **135**

NURSE   (*Returning*) His name is Romeo, and a Montague,
The only son of your great enemy.

JULIET   My only love sprung from my only hate! *The only man I love born from the only men I hate!*
antithesis (opposite)   Too early seen unknown, and known too late! *I saw him before I knew who he was; now I knew but it's too late*
Prodigious birth of love it is to me, *This is a bad beginning to our love*   **140** *late*
That I must love a loathèd enemy.

NURSE   What's this? What's this?

JULIET   A rhyme I learnt even now *A rhyme I learned from someone*
Of one I danced withal. *I danced with Love*

JULIET *is called from another room.*

NURSE   Anon, anon! *Right away, right away (coming)*
Come let's away. The strangers all are gone.

                                    Exeunt.

63

The Chorus talks about the change in Romeo's feelings and points out the obstacles in the way of Romeo and Juliet's love.

1   **old desire**: i.e. Romeo's old love for Rosaline
2   **young ... heir**: his new love longs to take its place
3   **fair**: beautiful woman
5   **again**: in return
6   **Alike**: both lovers equally
7   **foe supposed**: i.e. Juliet (a Capulet)
    complain: express his feelings / plead for love
10 **use to**: usually
11 **means**: opportunities

14 **Tempering ... sweet**: easing their difficult situation with the great sweetness of their meetings

THINK ABOUT for GCSE

Structure and form

- In some productions this second Chorus speech is cut. What purposes does it have? Would you cut it, or leave it in?

- A Shakespeare sonnet usually has three four-line sections (called 'quatrains') followed by a couplet. How does the sonnet form here help to express the situation that Romeo and Juliet are in?

Enter CHORUS.

CHORUS   Now old desire doth in his death-bed lie,
         And young affection gapes to be his heir.
         That fair for which love groaned for and would die,
         With tender Juliet matched, is now not fair.
         Now Romeo is beloved, and loves again,   5
         Alike bewitchèd by the charm of looks –
         But to his foe supposed he must complain,
         And she steal love's sweet bait from fearful hooks.
         Being held a foe, he may not have access
         To breathe such vows as lovers use to swear –   10
         And she as much in love, her means much less
         To meet her new-belovèd anywhere.
            But passion lends them power, time means, to meet,
            Tempering extremities with extreme sweet.

                                                        Exit.

In this scene ...

- Leaving the Capulet feast, Romeo hides from Benvolio and Mercutio.
- Mercutio speaks mockingly about Romeo's love for Rosaline and he and Benvolio leave.

Outside the Capulets' garden, Benvolio and Mercutio are looking for Romeo, who is listening, hidden. Mercutio pretends to be a magician trying to make Romeo appear.

THINK ABOUT for GCSE

Themes and issues

- **Love**: Mercutio talks about Cupid in line 13. Why do you think he is referred to so often in this play? Think about who he is, what his arrows represent, and why he is always shown blindfolded.

Performance and staging

- How could the actor playing Mercutio do the 'conjuring' (lines 17 to 21)? What gestures and movements would make the scene comic?

2 **dull earth**: i.e. his physical body
   centre: heart, now in Juliet's possession

4 **stol'n him**: crept off secretly

5 **orchard**: garden

6 **conjure**: call him up, like a spirit

7 **Humours**: odd moods (i.e. 'moody')

8 **likeness**: form

10 **Ay me**: a lover's sigh

11 **gossip**: good old lady-friend

12 **purblind son and heir**: Cupid, her blind son

13 **Abraham**: i.e. rogue
    trim: accurately

14 **King Cophetua**: a king in an old ballad

16 **ape**: In fairgrounds apes were taught to lie 'dead' until 'revived' by a fake cure.

20 **demesnes**: estates (i.e. sexual parts)
    adjacent: nearby

The street, beside the gardens of the Capulet house.

Enter ROMEO, *walking away, then stopping.*

ROMEO	Can I go forward when my heart is here?
	Turn back, dull earth, and find thy centre out.

He scrambles into the garden and conceals himself as
MERCUTIO *and* BENVOLIO *approach, and listens.*

Enter MERCUTIO *and* BENVOLIO.

BENVOLIO	Romeo! My cousin Romeo! Romeo!	
MERCUTIO	He is wise,	
	And on my life hath stol'n him home to bed.	
BENVOLIO	He ran this way and leapt this orchard wall.	5
	Call, good Mercutio.	
MERCUTIO	Nay, I'll conjure too.	
	Romeo! Humours! Madman! Passion! Lover!	
	Appear thou in the likeness of a sigh!	
	Speak but one rhyme and I am satisfied –	
	Cry but 'Ay me' – pronounce but 'love' and 'dove'! –	10
	Speak to my gossip Venus one fair word,	
	One nickname for her purblind son and heir,	
	Young Abraham Cupid – he that shot so trim	
	When King Cophetua loved the beggar maid.	
	He heareth not, he stirreth not, he moveth not! –	15
	The ape is dead, and I must conjure him.	
	(*Imitating a magician trying to raise a spirit*)	
	I conjure thee, by Rosaline's bright eyes,	
	By her high forehead and her scarlet lip,	
	By her fine foot, straight leg and quivering thigh,	
	And the demesnes that there adjacent lie,	20
	That in thy likeness thou appear to us!	
BENVOLIO	And if he hear thee, thou wilt anger him.	

Mercutio makes sexual jokes about Romeo's love for Rosaline. He and Benvolio leave, believing that Romeo is hiding from them.

24 **raise**: can mean 'have an erection'
    spirit: can mean 'semen'
    circle: can mean 'vagina'
25 **stand**: be erect
26 **laid … down**: had sex and satisfied him
27 **were some spite**: would really make him angry
    invocation: conjuring spell
31 **be consorted**: spend time
    humorous: 1 dark and humid; 2 moody
33 **mark**: target
34 **medlar**: kind of apple (thought to look like the female sexual organ)

37 **that**: if only
38 **open-arse**: another name for the medlar
    Poperin pear: kind of pear shaped like a penis (also wordplay on 'pop-her-in')
39 **truckle-bed**: i.e. my poor little bed
40 **field-bed**: i.e. sleeping in the open

42 **means**: intends

THINK ABOUT *for* GCSE

Characterisation

- Mercutio's language is full of sexual innuendoes (double-meanings), for example lines 24 to 29, and 38. What does that suggest about him and his attitude to women and love?

MERCUTIO	This cannot anger him. 'Twould anger him	
	To raise a spirit in his mistress' circle,	
	Of some strange nature, letting it there stand	25
	Till she had laid it, and conjured it down –	
	That were some spite! My invocation	
	Is fair and honest. In his mistress' name	
	I conjure only but to raise up him.	

BENVOLIO Come. He hath hid himself among these trees 30
To be consorted with the humorous night.
Blind is his love, and best befits the dark.

MERCUTIO If love be blind, love cannot hit the mark.
Now will he sit under a medlar tree,
And wish his mistress were that kind of fruit 35
As maids call medlars when they laugh alone.
O Romeo, that she were! O that she were
An open-arse and thou a Poperin pear!
Romeo, good night. I'll to my truckle-bed:
This field-bed is too cold for me to sleep. 40
Come, shall we go?

BENVOLIO   Go, then – for 'tis in vain
To seek him here that means not to be found.

Exit, with MERCUTIO.

In this scene ...

- Inside the Capulets' garden, Romeo sees Juliet at her window.
- Not realising that Romeo is listening, Juliet speaks, and he answers her.
- Despite Juliet's worry that it is all happening so quickly, they declare their love for one another.
- Romeo promises to send Juliet a message the next morning explaining when and where they can be married, and they part.

Inside the Capulets' garden, Romeo sees Juliet at her bedroom window and marvels at her beauty. As he watches her, she speaks.

2 **soft**: wait

6 **her maid**: As a virgin, Juliet is a 'hand-maid' of Diana, goddess of both the moon and chastity.

8 **vestal livery**: clothes worn by Diana's virgins

sick and green: Girls were thought to suffer from 'green-sickness', a thinness of the blood.

9 **fools**: Professional jesters also sometimes wore green as well as their traditional multi-coloured costume.

11 **O that**: I wish

13 **discourses**: speaks clearly

16 **entreat**: ask

17 **spheres**: People believed that planets and stars were fixed in crystal spheres encircling the earth.

18 **there**: i.e. in heaven

21 **airy region**: sky

stream: shine

28 **wingèd messenger**: angel

THINK ABOUT for GCSE

Language

- What do the images Romeo uses suggest about the way he views Juliet? Look at lines 4 to 9, 15 to 22, and 26 to 32.

Themes and issues

- What differences are there between Romeo's view of **love** and Mercutio's? Look, for example, at Act 1 Scene 4, lines 27 to 28, and Act 2 Scene 1.

ACT 2 SCENE 2

The garden, beside the Capulet house.

ROMEO *comes forward (reacting to* MERCUTIO*'s joking).*

ROMEO He jests at scars that never felt a wound.

Enter JULIET, *coming to her window-balcony above.* ROMEO, *below, sees the light at the window, then realises it is* JULIET.

– But soft! What light through yonder window breaks?
It is the east, and Juliet is the sun.
Arise, fair sun, and kill the envious moon,
Who is already sick and pale with grief   5
That thou her maid art far more fair than she.
Be not her maid, since she is envious:
Her vestal livery is but sick and green,
And none but fools do wear it. Cast it off.
– It is my lady! – O, it is my love!   10
O that she knew she were!
She speaks – yet she says nothing. What of that?
Her eye discourses. I will answer it.
– I am too bold. 'Tis not to me she speaks.
Two of the fairest stars in all the heaven,   15
Having some business, do entreat her eyes
To twinkle in their spheres till they return.
What if her eyes were there, they in her head?
The brightness of her cheek would shame those stars
As daylight doth a lamp. Her eyes in heaven   20
Would through the airy region stream so bright
That birds would sing and think it were not night!
See how she leans her cheek upon her hand.
O that I were a glove upon that hand,
That I might touch that cheek!

JULIET   Ay me!

ROMEO   (*Aside*) She speaks.   25
O speak again, bright angel! – For thou art
As glorious to this night, being o'er my head,
As is a wingèd messenger of heaven

71

Not realising that he can hear her, Juliet declares that she loves Romeo despite the fact that he is a Montague. He calls out to her and she recognises his voice.

29 **white upturnèd**: looking up

31 **lazy-pacing**: slow-moving

33 **Wherefore art**: Why are

35 **be but**: only be

39 **though … Montague**: i.e. whatever you call yourself
40 **nor … nor**: neither … nor

46 **owes**: owns / possesses
47 **doff**: cast off
48 **for**: in exchange for

THINK ABOUT for GCSE

Themes and issues

• What do Juliet's statements about names (lines 33 to 49) reveal about her attitude to the Montague–Capulet **conflict** at this moment?

• Is Juliet realistic in believing that names don't matter? Think about where names have been important and powerful earlier in the play: for example in the way the fight starts in Act 1 Scene 1, and for Juliet in Act 1 Scene 5, lines 134 to 141.

52 **bescreened in**: covered by the screen of
53 **counsel**: secret and private thoughts

61 **if … dislike**: if you don't like either of them

Unto the white-upturnèd wondering eyes
Of mortals that fall back to gaze on him   30
When he bestrides the lazy-pacing clouds,
And sails upon the bosom of the air.

JULIET   O Romeo, Romeo! Wherefore art thou Romeo?
Deny thy father and refuse thy name –
Or if thou wilt not, be but sworn my love   35
And I'll no longer be a Capulet.

ROMEO   (*Aside*) Shall I hear more, or shall I speak at this?

JULIET   'Tis but thy name that is my enemy.
Thou art thyself, though not a Montague.
What's 'Montague'? It is nor hand, nor foot,   40
Nor arm, nor face, nor any other part
Belonging to a man. O, be some other name!
What's in a name? That which we call a rose
By any other word would smell as sweet.
So Romeo would, were he not Romeo called,   45
Retain that dear perfection which he owes
Without that title. Romeo, doff thy name –
And for that name, which is no part of thee,
Take all myself.

ROMEO   I take thee at thy word.
Call me but love, and I'll be new-baptized.   50
Henceforth, I never will be Romeo.

JULIET   What man art thou, that thus bescreened in night
So stumblest on my counsel?

ROMEO   By a name
I know not how to tell thee who I am.
My name, dear saint, is hateful to myself   55
Because it is an enemy to thee.
Had I it written, I would tear the word.

JULIET   My ears have yet not drunk a hundred words
Of thy tongue's uttering, yet I know the sound.
Art thou not Romeo, and a Montague?   60

ROMEO   Neither, fair maid, if either thee dislike.

Juliet fears for Romeo's safety if he is caught in the garden. She says that she is uneasy because she has let him know that she loves him, but she is anxious to know whether he loves her in return.

66 **o'erperch**: fly over
67 **limits**: barriers

73 **proof … enmity**: armoured against their hatred

76 **but**: unless

78 **proroguèd**: postponed / put off
wanting of: lacking

81 **lent me counsel**: gave me advice
82 **pilot**: sailor / navigator
wert thou: even if you were
83 **vast**: deserted
84 **adventure … merchandise**: run the risk to gain goods like that
86 **Else**: otherwise

88 **Fain … form**: I would gladly follow the traditional rules of courtship
89 **compliment**: polite social conventions

92 **perjuries**: lies / breaking of oaths
93 **Jove**: Jupiter, King of the gods

96 **say thee nay**: contradict you
97 **So … woo**: so you have to go on courting me

THINK ABOUT for GCSE

Context

• Juliet is worried that Romeo has heard her say that she loves him (lines 85 to 89). Why might it have been unwise for a girl in her situation to let a man know that she loved him?

• What does Juliet's speech (lines 85 to 106) reveal about her character, background and upbringing?

JULIET	How cam'st thou hither, tell me, and wherefore?
	The orchard walls are high and hard to climb –
	And the place death, considering who thou art,
	If any of my kinsmen find thee here.	65

ROMEO	With love's light wings did I o'erperch these walls,
	For stony limits cannot hold love out –
	And what love can do, that dares love attempt.
	Therefore thy kinsmen are no stop to me.

| JULIET | If they do see thee, they will murder thee. | 70 |

ROMEO	Alack, there lies more peril in thine eye
	Than twenty of their swords. Look thou but sweet
	And I am proof against their enmity.

| JULIET | I would not for the world they saw thee here. |

ROMEO	I have night's cloak to hide me from their eyes.	75
	And but thou love me, *let* them find me here.
	My life were better ended by their hate
	Than death proroguèd, wanting of thy love.

| JULIET | By whose direction found'st thou out this place? |

ROMEO	By love, that first did prompt me to inquire.	80
	He lent me counsel, and I lent him eyes.
	I am no pilot, yet wert thou as far
	As that vast shore washed with the farthest sea,
	I should adventure for such merchandise.

JULIET	Thou knowest the mask of night is on my face,	85
	Else would a maiden blush bepaint my cheek
	For that which thou hast heard me speak tonight.
	Fain would I dwell on form – fain, fain deny
	What I have spoke. – But farewell compliment!
	Dost thou love me? I know thou wilt say 'Ay' –	90
	And I will take thy word. Yet if thou swear'st
	Thou mayst prove false. At lovers' perjuries
	They say Jove laughs. O gentle Romeo,
	If thou dost love, pronounce it faithfully.
	Or if thou think I am too quickly won,	95
	I'll frown, and be perverse, and say thee nay,
	So thou wilt woo – but else, not for the world.

Romeo tries to declare his love for Juliet, but she is uneasy about the suddenness of their love.

98 **fond**: foolish

99 **'haviour light**: behaviour too forward

101 **cunning ... strange**: cleverness in playing hard-to-get

103 **ere ... ware**: before I realised

105 **not ... love**: do not judge my surrender to be a sign of immodest love

106 **discoverèd**: revealed

109 **inconstant**: changeable

110 **circled orb**: the imagined sphere in which the moon moves

114 **idolatry**: idol-worship

THINK ABOUT *for* **GCSE**

Language

- In this play, many different views of love are expressed, often through imagery. What do the images in the following lines suggest that love is: lines 109 to 111, 118 to 120, 121 to 122, and 133 to 134?

- How accurately does each of these images represent (a) Romeo's love for Juliet; and (b) her love for him?

117 **contract**: i.e. their exchange of lovers' promises

118 **rash**: hasty
unadvised: ill-considered

129 **would it were**: wish I still had it

130 **Would'st ... it**: Do you want to take it back

In truth, fair Montague, I am too fond,
And therefore thou mayst think my 'haviour light.
But trust me, gentleman, I'll prove more true   100
Than those that have more cunning to be strange.
I should have been more strange, I must confess,
But that thou overheard'st, ere I was ware,
My true-love passion. Therefore pardon me,
And not impute this yielding to light love,   105
Which the dark night hath so discoverèd.

ROMEO   Lady, by yonder blessèd moon I vow,
That tips with silver all these fruit-tree tops –

JULIET   O swear not by the moon, th' inconstant moon,
That monthly changes in her circled orb,   110
Lest that thy love prove likewise variable.

ROMEO   What shall I swear by?

JULIET   Do not swear at all. –
Or if thou wilt, swear by thy gracious self,
Which is the god of my idolatry,
And I'll believe thee.

ROMEO   If my heart's dear love –   115

JULIET   Well, do not swear. Although I joy in thee,
I have no joy of this contract tonight.
It is too rash, too unadvised, too sudden –
Too like the lightning, which doth cease to be
Ere one can say 'It lightens'. Sweet, good night.   120
This bud of love, by summer's ripening breath,
May prove a beauteous flower when next we meet.
Good night, good night! As sweet repose and rest
Come to thy heart as that within my breast.

ROMEO   O wilt thou leave me so unsatisfied?   125

JULIET   What satisfaction canst thou have tonight?

ROMEO   Th' exchange of thy love's faithful vow for mine.

JULIET   I gave thee mine before thou didst request it –
And yet I would it were to give again.

ROMEO   Would'st thou withdraw it? For what purpose, love?   130

Juliet hears the Nurse calling her. Before she goes, she asks Romeo to send her a message the following day telling her when and where they can be married.

THINK ABOUT for**GCSE**

Context

• When Juliet returns to the window, she immediately talks of marriage (lines 142 to 148). Why might Juliet feel that she should marry Romeo as quickly as possible? Think about a young woman's reputation at that time, and her father's plans for her.

Language

• What does Romeo mean by his statement about love and lovers (lines 156 to 157)? How effective is his comparison?

131 **frank**: generous

133 **bounty**: generosity and what I want to give you

137 **Anon**: I'm coming

141 **flattering-sweet**: delightful
      substantial: real

143 **bent**: intention

145 **procure**: arrange
146 **rite**: marriage ceremony

151 **beseech**: beg
      By and by: Straight away

152 **cease thy suit**: give up your courtship of me

155 **want**: lack

JULIET	But to be frank and give it thee again:
	And yet I wish but for the thing I have.
	My bounty is as boundless as the sea,
	My love as deep. The more I give to thee,
	The more I have, for both are infinite. 135

The NURSE is heard calling from inside the house.

	I hear some noise within. Dear love, adieu!
	– Anon, good Nurse! – Sweet Montague, be true.
	Stay but a little: I will come again.

She goes from the window.

ROMEO	O blessèd, blessèd night! I am afeard,
	Being in night, all this is but a dream, 140
	Too flattering-sweet to be substantial.

JULIET returns above.

JULIET	Three words, dear Romeo, and good night indeed.
	If that thy bent of love be honourable,
	Thy purpose marriage, send me word tomorrow
	By one that I'll procure to come to thee, 145
	Where and what time thou wilt perform the rite –
	And all my fortunes at thy foot I'll lay,
	And follow thee, my lord, throughout the world.

NURSE	(*From inside the house*) Madam!

JULIET	I come! Anon! – But if thou mean'st not well, 150
	I do beseech thee –

NURSE	(*Calling again*) Madam!

JULIET	By and by! I come!
	– To cease thy suit, and leave me to my grief.
	Tomorrow will I send.

ROMEO	So thrive my soul, –

JULIET	A thousand times good night!

She goes again.

ROMEO	A thousand times the worse, to want thy light! 155
	Love goes toward love as schoolboys from their books,
	But love from love, toward school with heavy looks.

Juliet returns and says she will send someone by nine in the morning for Romeo's message. The lovers are reluctant to part.

158 **Hist**: the sound a falconer makes to call a hawk
159 **tassel-gentle**: male falcon
160 **Bondage is hoarse**: i.e. being 'imprisoned' in the house, she has to whisper
161 **Echo**: a nymph in classical myth who pined away for love

166 **attending**: listening

166 **nyas**: a young hawk taken from its nest for training

172 **to**: in order to
    still: always

THINK ABOUT for GCSE

Performance and staging

• How might this scene have been staged in Shakespeare's playhouse?

Language

• How does the language of falconry and bird-keeping help Romeo and Juliet to express their feelings here?

177 **wanton's bird**: spoilt child's pet bird

179 **gyves**: fetters / handcuffs

182 **would**: wish

He moves slowly away – as JULIET *returns once more to her window.*

JULIET	Hist, Romeo, hist! O for a falconer's voice,
	To lure this tassel-gentle back again.
	Bondage is hoarse, and may not speak aloud – **160**
	Else would I tear the cave where Echo lies,
	And make her airy tongue more hoarse than mine
	With repetition of my Romeo's name.
ROMEO	It is my soul that calls upon my name.
	How silver-sweet sound lovers' tongues by night, **165**
	Like softest music to attending ears!
JULIET	Romeo!
ROMEO	My nyas?
JULIET	What o'clock tomorrow
	Shall I send to thee?
ROMEO	By the hour of nine.
JULIET	I will not fail. 'Tis twenty years till then.
	I have forgot why I did call thee back. **170**
ROMEO	Let me stand here till thou remember it.
JULIET	I shall forget, to have thee still stand there,
	Remembering how I love thy company.
ROMEO	And I'll still stay, to have thee still forget,
	Forgetting any other home but this. **175**
JULIET	'Tis almost morning. I would have thee gone –
	And yet no farther than a wanton's bird,
	Who lets it hop a little from her hand,
	Like a poor prisoner in his twisted gyves,
	And with a silk thread plucks it back again, **180**
	So loving-jealous of his liberty.
ROMEO	I would I were thy bird.

Juliet goes in and Romeo leaves, planning to seek advice and help from Friar Lawrence.

183 much cherishing: too much affection

188 Hence will I: I will go from here
ghostly … cell: Friar Lawrence's hidden-away room
189 crave: ask for
hap: good fortune

THINK ABOUT for GCSE

Language

- The phrase 'sweet sorrow' (line 184) is an oxymoron (an expression that seems to contradict itself while still making sense). In what ways does it represent Juliet's mixed feelings as she says goodbye? Look at lines 176 to 181, and 182 to 184, for example.

Characterisation

- In many productions Juliet seems much more practical than Romeo. What is there in this scene to support that interpretation?

JULIET	Sweet, so would I –
	Yet I should kill thee with much cherishing.
	Good night, good night. Parting is such sweet sorrow,
	That I shall say 'good night' till it be morrow.

185

She goes in.

ROMEO	Sleep dwell upon thine eyes, peace in thy breast.
	Would I were sleep and peace, so sweet to rest!
	Hence will I to my ghostly sire's close cell,
	His help to crave, and my dear hap to tell.

Exit.

scene ...

- Romeo visits Friar Lawrence and tells him that he and Juliet have fallen in love.
- The Friar finally agrees to marry the couple, believing that their marriage will bring their two families together.

When Romeo arrives at Friar Lawrence's cell, the Friar is collecting plants and herbs which have medicinal properties.

3 **fleckled**: dappled with spots of light

4 **From ... wheels**: out of the way of the sun-god's chariot

5 **ere**: before

7 **osier cage**: willow basket

8 **baleful**: harmful

9–10 **that's ... womb**: is both the mother of all natural things and their grave

11 **divers kind**: various species

14 **None ... some**: there are no plants which do not have some good qualities

15 **mickle**: great
powerful grace: i.e. healing power

17 **For ... vile**: For there is nothing, however lowly

19–20 **Nor aught ... abuse**: nor is there anything, however good, which will not turn away from its natural goodness if it is misused

22 **by action dignified**: can become good if it is used in the right way

23 **infant rind**: tender young skin

25 **that part**: the scent
each part: each part of the body

26 **stays ... heart**: stops the heart and the senses too

27 **still**: always

28 **grace**: the ability to receive God's goodness
rude will: giving in to physical desires

30 **canker**: caterpillar

THINK ABOUT for GCSE

Language

- The Friar's speech (lines 1 to 30) contains many antitheses (opposites). What subjects do these relate to?

- Why do you think the language of this play is so full of opposites and contradictions?

Near Friar Lawrence's cell.

Enter FRIAR LAWRENCE, *alone, with a basket.*

The smiling morning is replacing the frowning night

FR. LAWRENCE   The grey-eyed morn smiles on the frowning night,
Check'ring the eastern clouds with streaks of light;
darkness is stumbling out of the sun's path
And fleckled darkness like a drunkard reels
getting dark
like a drunk man
From forth day's path and Titan's fiery wheels.
before the sun comes up and burns away the dew
Now, ere the sun advance his burning eye   5
I have to fill the basket of mine
The day to cheer and night's dank dew to dry,
I must upfill this osier cage of ours
with harmful weeds + medicinal flowers.
With baleful weeds and precious-juiced flowers.
The earth is nature's mother + also   nature's tomb
The earth that's nature's mother is her tomb:
What is her burying grave, that is her womb.   10
From the earth's womb, many different sort of children came
And from her womb children of divers kind
We sucking on her natural bosom find:
Many for many virtues excellent,
There are no plants which do not have some good qualities
None but for some, and yet all different.
great   healing power
O, mickle is the powerful grace that lies   15
In plants, herbs, stones, and their true qualities.
There is nothing however lowly that does not
For nought so vile that on the earth doth live
provide the earth with some special quality
But to the earth some special good doth give –
Nor is there anything however good, which will not turn
Nor aught so good but, strained from that fair use,
away from its
Revolts from true birth, stumbling on abuse.   20
virtue turns to vice if it is misused.
Virtue itself turns vice, being misapplied,
natural goodness
vice sometimes become virtue through
And vice sometime by action dignified.
if it is
the right actions
misused

Enter ROMEO *behind (unseen by the* FRIAR).

tender young skin
Within the infant rind of this weak flower
there is both poison + remedy medicine.
Poison hath residence and medicine power.
smell it it cheers – makes you feel good
For this, being smelt, with that part cheers each part;   25
But if you taste it you die
Being tasted, stays all senses with the heart.
opposed kings
good + evil
Two such opposèd kings encamp them still
exist in everything
In man as well as herbs – grace and rude will.
– grace v physical desire
And where the worser is predominant,
where evil is dominant
good v evil
death soon kills the body like cancer
Full soon the canker death eats up that plant.   30

ROMEO   Good morrow, father.

The Friar assumes that, because Romeo is up so early, he must have been with Rosaline. Romeo tells the Friar that he has fallen in love with Juliet, and asks the Friar to marry them.

31 **Benedicite**: God bless you

33 **argues ... head**: suggests that your mind is troubled

35 **Care ... eye**: Old men are kept awake by worries

37 **unbruisèd**: not yet injured by life
   unstuffed: carefree

40 **uproused ... distemp'rature**: forced to get up early because you are troubled

46 **that name's woe**: the unhappiness that name caused me

THINK ABOUT for GCSE

Language

- Look at Romeo's explanation about what has happened (lines 49 to 54). Why does Romeo use language about enemies and wounds to describe what he has been doing? What does he know about the character and interests of the person he is talking to?

Relationships

- What does the Friar's reaction to Romeo's language (lines 55 to 56) suggest about him and his relationship with Romeo?

51–2 **Both ... lies**: Your help and holy medicine can be the remedy for both of us

54 **intercession ... foe**: request for help will benefit my enemy too

55 **homely in thy drift**: straightforward in the way you explain it

56 **Riddling ... shrift**: i.e. If you don't explain clearly, you won't receive proper forgiveness for your sins

63 **pass**: walk along together

67 **forsaken**: given up

FR. LAWRENCE   Benedicite!

God bless you

What early tongue so sweet saluteth me? — *who greets me so early in the morning*

Young son, it argues a distempered head

something wrong if you're getting out of bed this early

So soon to bid good morrow to thy bed.

Care keeps his watch in every old man's eye,   35

old men has worries

And where care lodges, sleep will never lie –

worried men never get any sleep

But where unbruisèd youth with unstuffed brain

But young men shouldn't have a care in the world

Doth couch his limbs, there golden sleep doth reign.

They should get to bed early and get plenty of sleep.

Therefore thy earliness doth me assure

he fact that you're awake

Thou art uproused with some distemp'rature.   40

his early tells me you're troubled

Or if not so, then here I hit it right –

You have not been to bed tonight.

Our Romeo hath not been in bed tonight.

old men — worried never sleep

young men — haven't any worries

ROMEO   That last is true: the sweeter rest was mine.

I enjoyed a sweeter rest than sleep

FR. LAWRENCE God pardon sin! Wast thou with Rosaline?

ROMEO   With Rosaline, my ghostly father? No.   45

I have forgot that name, and that name's woe.

I have forgotten not girl) & all the sadness she brought me

FR. LAWRENCE That's my good son. But where hast thou been then?

ROMEO   I'll tell thee ere thou ask it me again.

I have been feasting with mine enemy,

Where on a sudden one hath wounded me   50

suddenly someone wounded me with love +

That's by me wounded. Both our remedies

was wounded with love by me.

Within thy help and holy physic lies.

You have the sacred power to cure both of us.

I bear no hatred, blessèd man; for lo,

My intercession likewise steads my foe.

my request will benefit my enemy

FR. LAWRENCE Be plain, good son, and homely in thy drift;   55

speak plainly, make your meaning clear, my son.

Riddling confession finds but riddling shrift.

A jumbled confession can only receive a jumbled absolution

ROMEO   Then plainly know, my heart's dear love is set

On the fair daughter of rich Capulet.

I love Capulet's daughter

As mine on hers, so hers is set on mine,

I love her and she loves me

And all combined – save what thou must combine   60

By holy marriage. When and where and how

I will tell you more later

We met, we wooed, and made exchange of vow,

who, where, we met, how we fell in love

I'll tell thee as we pass. But this I pray,

I'm begging you

That thou consent to marry us today.

please agree to marry us today

FR. LAWRENCE Holy Saint Francis, what a change is here!   65

Is Rosaline that thou didst love so dear

So soon forsaken? Young men's love then lies

given up

Surprised Romeo has given Rosaline up

The Friar complains that Romeo is changeable in love, but agrees to help him.

69 **brine**: tears
70 **sallow**: pale

72 **season**: 1 give a flavour to; 2 preserve

79 **Pronounce this sentence**: Repeat this moral saying
80 **fall**: be excused for committing sins
81 **chid'st**: told me off
82 **doting**: being infatuated

86 **Doth ... allow**: i.e. Juliet returns Romeo's favour and love

88 **read by rote**: recited what it had learned by heart, i.e. Romeo had only imitated true love
90 **In one respect**: For one reason
92 **rancour**: bitter hatred

93 **stand**: insist

THINK ABOUT *for* GCSE

Themes and issues

• Friar Lawrence says that he has told Romeo off 'for doting, not for **loving**' (line 82). What is the difference, and why is it important here?

Relationships

• Why do you think the Friar agrees so readily to help Romeo? Look at lines 89 to 92. Do you think he is making the right decision?

Young men love with their eyes, not with their hearts

Not truly in their hearts, but in their eyes.
Jesu Maria, what a deal of brine
Hath washed thy sallow cheeks for Rosaline! **70**
How much salt water thrown away in waste
To season love, that of it doth not taste!
The sun not yet thy sighs from heaven clears,
Thy old groans ring yet in mine ancient ears –
Lo, here upon thy cheek the stain doth sit **75**
Of an old tear that is not washed off yet.
If e'er thou wast thyself, and these woes thine,
Thou and these woes were all for Rosaline.
And art thou changed? Pronounce this sentence then:
Women may fall, when there's no strength in men. **80**

Salty tears you shed for Rosaline – you cried so much over her
How many salty tear-drops you wasted
Salting a love you never tasted!
The sun hasn't yet melted away the fog you made
with all your sighs; the groans you used to make are still ringing in my old ears.
There's still a stain on your cheek from an old tear that hasn't been washed off yet
If you were ever yourself, and this sadness was yours, you + your sadness were all for Rosaline.
And now you've changed?
You can't expect women to be faithful when men are so unreliable

ROMEO   Thou chid'st me oft for loving Rosaline.
You have scolded me often for loving Rosaline

FR. LAWRENCE   For doting, not for loving, pupil mine.
For being infatuated, – obsessing about her, not for loving her, my student / pupil.

ROMEO   And bad'st me bury love.
And you told me to bury love

FR. LAWRENCE   Not in a grave
disapproving   To lay one in, another out to have.
I didn't tell you to get rid of one love and replace her with another

ROMEO   I pray thee chide me not. Her I love now **85**
Doth grace for grace and love for love allow.
The other did not so.
Don't scold me. The girl I love now returns my love. The other girl did not love me.

FR. LAWRENCE   O, she knew well
Thy love did read by rote that could not spell.
But come, young waverer, come go with me.
In one respect I'll thy assistant be – **90**
For this alliance may so happy prove
To turn your households' rancour to pure love.
O she knew v. well you were acting like you were in love without really knowing what love means
inconsistent man.
I'll help you with your secret wedding for one reason
This marriage may turn the hatred between your families into pure love.

ROMEO   O let us hence. I stand on sudden haste!
Let's get out of here. I'm in a rush.

FR. LAWRENCE   Wisely and slow. They stumble that run fast.
Go wisely + slowly. Those who rush stumble + fall.

Exeunt.

In this scene ...

- Mercutio and Benvolio discuss Tybalt, who has sent Romeo a challenge to a duel.
- Romeo appears and enjoys some witty wordplay with Mercutio.
- The Nurse arrives, looking for Romeo. He gives her instructions about when and where Juliet is to meet him so that they can be married.

Mercutio and Benvolio wonder what has happened to Romeo. Benvolio says that Romeo has been sent a challenge by Tybalt, a skilled and deadly sword-fighter.

THINK ABOUT for GCSE

Performance and staging

- In a performance, this exchange can be played as Mercutio either admiring or mocking Tybalt's skill as a fencer. If you were the director, which interpretation would you choose?

Context

- What 'cause' (line 25) could Tybalt claim to justify challenging Romeo to a duel?

1 **should**: can
2 **tonight**: last night

9 **answer it**: accept the challenge
11–12 **how ... dared**: that, having been challenged, he is willing to fight
14 **white ... eye**: i.e. Rosaline has fair skin and dark eyes
15 **pin ... cleft**: i.e. centre of his heart, pierced
15–16 **blind bow-boy**: Cupid
16 **butt-shaft**: blunt practice arrow
18 **Why ... Tybalt**: What's so special about Tybalt
19 **Prince of Cats**: Tybalt was the cat's name in many old stories.
20 **captain of compliments**: master of polite ceremony
pricksong: from sheet music, strictly following the notes
21 **proportion**: rhythm
22 **minim rests**: briefest pauses
23 **butcher ... button**: he is so accurate, he can slice an opponent's silk button
24 **of ... house**: from the finest school
25 **cause**: a reason for fighting, such as an insult to a man's honour
25–6 **passado ... hai**: fashionable terms for particular thrusts in fencing

ACT 2 SCENE 4

A street in Verona.

Enter MERCUTIO *and* BENVOLIO.

MERCUTIO	Where the devil should this Romeo be? Came he not home tonight?
BENVOLIO	Not to his father's. I spoke with his man.
MERCUTIO	Why, that same pale hard-hearted wench, that Rosaline, torments him so, that he will sure run mad.
BENVOLIO	Tybalt, the kinsman to old Capulet, hath sent a letter to his father's house.
MERCUTIO	A challenge, on my life.
BENVOLIO	Romeo will answer it.
MERCUTIO	Any man that can write may answer a letter.
BENVOLIO	Nay, he will answer the letter's master, how he dares, being dared.
MERCUTIO	Alas, poor Romeo, he is already dead – stabbed with a white wench's black eye, run through the ear with a love song, the very pin of his heart cleft with the blind bow-boy's butt-shaft. And is he a man to encounter Tybalt?
BENVOLIO	Why, what is Tybalt?
MERCUTIO	More than Prince of Cats. O, he's the courageous captain of compliments! He fights as you sing pricksong – keeps time, distance, and proportion. He rests me his minim rests – one, two, and the third in your bosom. The very butcher of a silk button – a duellist, a duellist! – a gentleman of the very first house of the first and second cause. Ah, the immortal passado! – the punto reverso! – the 'hai'!
BENVOLIO	The what?

5

10

15

20

25

Handwritten annotations: "Didn't he come home last night?" · "father's house" · "a servant" · "hussy She is going to torment him until he goes insane" · "v protective of Romeo" · "Old Capulet's nephew, Romeo's father's house" · "I bet it's a challenge (challenge to a duel)" · "answer / accept the challenge" · "Romeo is willing to fight" · "He's been stabbed by a white girl's black eye. He's been cut through the ear with a love song. The frame of his heart has been split by blind Cupid's arrow." · "Is he man enough to face off with Tybalt" · "what's so special about Tybalt?" · "He fights like you sing" · "Pauses – one, two + the 3rd is your heart." · "a master of duels" · "he knows all the moves" · "Slowly killing the notes (all 2 mind Romeo by soon) / kissing"

91

When Romeo arrives, Mercutio
teases him, believing that
he still longs for Rosaline.
He complains that Romeo
disappeared after the Capulet
feast.

THINK ABOUT *for* **GCSE**

Characterisation

• Nearly all Mercutio's
examples of lovers (lines 41
to 43) came to tragic ends or
caused tragedy. Why does
he select them, rather than
others, do you think? What
does it suggest about him
and his attitude to love?

28 **The pox of**: A curse on
antic … fantasticoes: weird posers
29 **new tuners of accent**: trendy speakers
30 **tall**: brave
31 **grandsire**: grandfather
32 **strange flies**: foreign parasites
32–3 **fashion-mongers**: followers of fashion
33 **pardon-me's**: people with affected
manners
33 **stand**: 1 insist on; 2 stand up
34 **form**: 1 way of doing something; 2 seat
34–5 **old bench**: i.e. old ways
37 **roe**: 1 deer (i.e. his girlfriend);
2 fish eggs (i.e. he looks thin)
38 **numbers**: poetry
39 **Petrarch**: a poet who wrote love
sonnets to Laura
to his lady: compared to Rosaline
41–2 **Dido … Thisbe**: all heroines from
famous love stories
41 **dowdy**: plain-looking woman
42 **hildings … harlots**: sluts … prostitutes
42–3 **a grey … purpose**: quite attractive, but
hardly worth mentioning
44 **French slop**: style of baggy trousers
44–5 **gave … counterfeit**: deceived us
48 **slip**: counterfeit coins were called
'slips'
conceive: work it out
50 **strain courtesy**: forget good manners
51 **constrains**: forces
52 **bow … hams**: 1 bow; 2 have sex;
3 have a sexually transmitted disease
54 **most … it**: got the true meaning

56 **pink**: 1 perfection; 2 a small flower;
3 the hole-pattern in material

59 **pump well-flowered**: shoe
well-decorated

hates newfangled expressions

MERCUTIO *I hate these weird posers*
The pox of such antic, lisping, affecting fantasticoes!
I hate these trendy speakers
These new tuners of accent! – 'By Jesu, a very good
blade!' 'A very tall man!' 'A very good whore!' – Why,   30
is not this a lamentable thing, grandsire, that we should
be thus afflicted with these strange flies, these fashion-
mongers, these 'pardon-me's'! – who stand so much
on the new form that they cannot sit at ease on the old
bench? O, their bones, their bones! – *hates all hates* 35
affected manners, trendy speakers, irritates him

Enter ROMEO.

BENVOLIO Here comes Romeo, here comes Romeo!
without his gf he looks thin – like a dried herring without its eggs

MERCUTIO Without his roe, like a dried herring. O flesh, flesh, how
art thou fishified! Now is he for the numbers that
Mercutio teases R. by referring to the poet Petrarch + 6 mythical + historical women who inspired love poetry
Petrarch flowed in! Laura to his lady was a kitchen *Compared to Romeo's girl, Laura was a kitchen slave. Surely she has a better love to make rhymes for her*
wench – marry, she had a better love to be-rhyme her   40
Dido was plain looking, Cleopatra was gypsy
– Dido a dowdy, Cleopatra a gipsy, Helen and Hero *sluts + prost, quite attractive but hardly worth mentioning*
hildings and harlots, Thisbe a grey eye or so, but not
to the purpose. Signior Romeo, bonjour! There's a
French salutation to your French slop. You gave us the
counterfeit fairly last night. – *You deceived us*   45

ROMEO Good morrow to you both. What counterfeit did I give
you?
You gave us the slip. Can't you work it out

MERCUTIO The slip, sir, the slip! Can you not conceive?

ROMEO Pardon, good Mercutio. My business was great, and in *I was in such a hurry that I forgot about good manners*
such a case as mine a man may strain courtesy.   50

MERCUTIO That's as much as to say, such a case as yours constrains
a man to bow in the hams. – *Mercutio implies Romeo's business was sexual*

ROMEO Meaning to curtsy?

MERCUTIO Thou hast most kindly hit it. – *double-meaning*

ROMEO A most courteous exposition. *explanation*   55

MERCUTIO Nay, I am the very pink of courtesy. *perfection*

ROMEO Pink for flower? – *the pink flower – suggest female genitalia*

MERCUTIO Right.

ROMEO Why, then is my pump well-flowered.
well then my pump/shoe is well decorated with flowers – Romeo playing along with the sexual joke
pump = shoe + penis

In a light-hearted mood Romeo and Mercutio enjoy some clever wordplay, each one trying to outdo the other.

61 **single sole**: 1 thin sole of a shoe; 2 alone or single; 3 immortal soul

62–3 **solely singular**: 1 unique; 2 quite alone (and worn out)

66 **Switch ... match**: Make your horse go faster with whip and spurs, or I'll declare myself the winner

68 **wild-goose**: foolish and futile

69 **Was ... you**: Did I get even with you

72 **there ... goose**: 1 playing the fool; 2 looking for a prostitute

73 **bite ... ear**: a sign of affection (possibly ironic)

75 **sweeting ... sauce**: apple sauce (eaten with goose)

77–8 **here's ... broad**: i.e. you can make your tiny wit go a long way

80 **goose**: obvious fool

83 **by art**: i.e. by using your skill (with words)

84 **natural**: born idiot

85 **bauble**: 1 jester's stick; 2 penis

87 **tale**: 'tail' means penis (wordplay) **against the hair**: 1 against my wish; 2 pubic hair; 3 'hare' was a slang term for prostitute

88 **large**: 1 crude; 2 erect

90 **come**: to have an orgasm

91 **occupy**: i.e. have sex

THINK ABOUT for GCSE

Performance and staging

- Lines 36 to 91 are full of wordplay that modern audiences are not likely to understand and productions often cut this section. What do you think is gained if it is cut, and what would be lost?

Relationships

- What does this dialogue suggest about the relationship between the three men?

Romeo implies that Mercutio is only good for jokes

MERCUTIO *Alright my witty friend, this joke has worn on your*
Sure wit! Follow me this jest now till thou hast 60
pump. It's nice shin as all worn out. The
worn out thy pump – that when the single sole of it is
joke is all you have left
worn, the jest may remain, after the wearing, solely
singular.

a bad joke, It's all silliness.

ROMEO O single-soled jest, solely singular for the singleness!

MERCUTIO *Come break this up Benvolio. I'm losing his duel*
Come between us, good Benvolio! My wit faints. *of wits.* 65

ROMEO *keep going, keep going, or I'll declare*
Switch and spurs, switch and spurs! – or I'll cry a match! *myself the*

MERCUTIO *if our jokes are silly + pointless, I am* *winner*
Nay, if our wits run the wild-goose chase, I am done –
finished for you have more foolishness in one of your jokes
Sexual double meaning for thou hast more of the wild-goose in one of thy wits
than I have in 5 of mine. Was I ever close to
than, I am sure, I have in my whole five. Was I with you
you in playing the fool? looking for a prostitute
there for the goose? 70

ROMEO Thou wast never with me for anything when thou wast
not there for the goose.

MERCUTIO I will bite thee by the ear for that jest. — *word play*
horse play

ROMEO *don't bite me*
Nay, good goose, bite not.

MERCUTIO *Your joke is a very bitter apple, It is a sharp sauce (apple)*
Thy wit is a very bitter sweeting. It is a most sharp sauce. 75 *sauce + goose!*

ROMEO And is it not well served in to a sweet goose?

MERCUTIO O! – here's a wit of cheveril, that stretches from an inch
narrow to an ell broad! — *You can make your joke go*
a long way

ROMEO I stretch it out for that word 'broad' – which, added to
the 'goose', proves thee far and wide a broad goose. 80

MERCUTIO *why isn't all this joking better than groaning about*
Why, is not this better now than groaning for love? Now *love?*
Now you are
art thou sociable; now art thou Romeo! Now art thou *are naturally.*
what you've learned to be and what you
what thou art, by art as well as by nature. For this *up*
This love of yours was like an idiot who runs
drivelling love is like a great natural that runs lolling up
to down looking for a hole to hide his toy in.
and down to hide his bauble in a hole. 85

BENVOLIO Stop there, stop there. — *double pun*
double-meaning

MERCUTIO *You want me to stop my tale before I'm done for penis*
Thou desirest me to stop in my tale against the hair.
tale — tail (penis)
BENVOLIO *otherwise your tale would have gotten too large*
Thou wouldst else have made thy tale large.

MERCUTIO *Oh you're wrong, I would have made it short, I*
O, thou art deceived! I would have made it short, for I
had come to the deeper part of my tale, + +
was come to the whole depth of my tale, and meant 90
more sexual jokes
indeed to occupy the argument no longer.
planned to say nothing more on the topic.

95

The Nurse arrives with her servant, Peter, wanting to speak to Romeo.

92   **goodly gear**: i.e. a sight for sore eyes
A sail: the cry of sailors when a ship was sighted

93   **shirt ... smock**: man and a woman

99   **God ... e'en**: Good afternoon

100   **good e'en**: already past noon

101   **bawdy**: sexually vulgar
dial: clock

102   **prick**: 1 mark on a clock; 2 penis

103   **Out upon you**: Get away with you

105   **mar**: ruin

106–7   **quoth 'a**: did he say / indeed

111   **for fault of**: in the absence of

113   **Very well took**: well understood

115   **confidence**: private discussion; or perhaps she means 'conference' (talk)

116   **endite**: mockingly imitating the Nurse's mistake (line 115) he deliberately uses 'endite' for 'invite'

117   **bawd**: someone who arranges customers for prostitutes
So ho: a hunter's cry

118   **found**: got the scent of

119   **hare**: a slang term for prostitute
lenten pie: pie served without meat (in Lent)

120   **hoar**: 1 stale; 2 pronounced the same as 'whore'
spent: eaten up

THINK ABOUT for GCSE

Performance and staging

- What does Romeo's cry of 'A sail' (line 92) suggest about the Nurse's costume and movement?

- What would the Nurse look like if you were directing the play? Think about how old she would be and how she would be dressed, for example.

Enter the NURSE, *with* PETER, *a servant.*

ROMEO	Here's goodly gear! A sail, a sail!
MERCUTIO	Two, two! A shirt and a smock.
NURSE	Peter!
PETER	Anon.
NURSE	My fan, Peter.
MERCUTIO	Good Peter, to hide her face – for her fan's the fairer face.
NURSE	God ye good morrow, gentlemen.
MERCUTIO	God ye good e'en, fair gentlewoman.
NURSE	Is it good e'en?
MERCUTIO	'Tis no less, I tell ye. For the bawdy hand of the dial is now upon the prick of noon.
NURSE	Out upon you! What a man are you?
ROMEO	One, gentlewoman, that God hath made – for himself to mar.
NURSE	By my troth, it is well said. 'For himself to mar', quoth 'a! Gentlemen, can any of you tell me where I may find the young Romeo?
ROMEO	I can tell you, but young Romeo will be older when you have found him than he was when you sought him. I am the youngest of that name, for fault of a worse.
NURSE	You say well.
MERCUTIO	Yea, is the worst well? Very well took, i' faith: wisely, wisely.
NURSE	If you be he, sir, I desire some confidence with you.
BENVOLIO	She will endite him to some supper.
MERCUTIO	A bawd, a bawd, a bawd! So ho!
ROMEO	What hast thou found?
MERCUTIO	No hare, sir – unless a hare, sir, in a lenten pie, that is something stale and hoar ere it be spent.

95

100

105

110

115

120

97

Mercutio mocks the Nurse with sexual jokes before leaving with Benvolio. The Nurse complains to Romeo about Mercutio's treatment of her.

123   meat: slang for 'prostitute'

125   too ... score: not worth paying for
126   hoars: 1 gets stale; 2 spends time with whores
spent: finished up

131   saucy merchant: rude / insolent character
132   ropery: vulgar jokes

134   stand to: 1 live up to; 2 be sexually aroused

136   take him down: humiliate him (but with an unintended sexual meaning)
137   an ... lustier: even if he were livelier
Jacks: rogues
138   Scurvy: Rotten
139   flirt-gills: immoral women
skains-mates: brawling friends
140   suffer: permit
141   use ... pleasure: 1 make rude fun of me; 2 have casual sex with me
143   weapon: 1 sword; 2 penis
146   vexed: irritated

150–1   lead ... paradise: take advantage of her innocence
151   gross: bad / wicked

THINK ABOUT for GCSE

Language

• Do you find Mercutio's language when talking to the Nurse (lines 117 to 130) funny, or offensively sexist and insulting to her age?

Characterisation

• What is your opinion of Romeo's treatment of the Nurse here?

He walks around the NURSE, *singing.*

An old hare hoar, *old rabbit meat is good to eat*
And an old hare hoar, *If you can't get anything else.*
Is very good meat in Lent: *But if it is so old,*
But a hare that is hoar *that it goes bad before you eat it,*
Is too much for a score, *Then it's a waste of money*   125
When it hoars ere it be spent.

Romeo, will you come to your father's? We'll to dinner
thither. *we'll go here*

ROMEO   I will follow you.   *mocking the*
                                                                     nurse.

MERCUTIO   Farewell, ancient lady. Farewell, lady – (*singing again*)
               lady, lady.   130

                                              Exit, with BENVOLIO.

NURSE   I pray you, sir, what saucy merchant was this that was so *rude character*
               full of his ropery? *vulgar jokes*

ROMEO   A gentleman, Nurse, that loves to hear himself talk, and
               will speak more in a minute than he will stand to in a
               month.   135

NURSE   And 'a stand to anything against me, I'll take him down, *If he says anything against me, I'll humiliate him, even*
               an 'a were lustier than he is – and twenty such Jacks! *if he were stronger. He is*
               And if I cannot, I'll find those that shall. Scurvy knave! I *dirty rat.*
               am none of his flirt-gills, I am none of his skains-mates! *immoral women* *highly sexed friends*
               (*To* PETER) And thou must stand by, too, and suffer every 140
               knave to use me at his pleasure! *1) make fun of*
                                                 2) have casual sex with

PETER   I saw no man use you at his pleasure. If I had, my
Sword/penis weapon should quickly have been out. I warrant you, I *I'll draw my*
               dare draw as soon as another man if I see occasion in a *sword as quick as any other man if I see a fight*
               good quarrel, and the law on my side.   145 *starting + the law is on my side*

NURSE   Now, afore God, I am so vexed that every part about me *irritated/annoyed*
shaking   quivers! – Scurvy knave! – (*To* ROMEO) Pray you, sir, a
with rage/   word. And, as I told you, my young lady bid me inquire
annoyance   you out. What she bid me say I will keep to myself. But
               first let me tell ye, if ye should lead her into a fool's 150
               paradise, as they say, it were a very gross kind of
               behaviour, as they say. For the gentlewoman is young –
               It would be v. wicked of you if you were
               to take advantage of her.

99

Romeo instructs the Nurse to tell Juliet to meet him at the Friar's cell that afternoon, where they will be married. Meanwhile his servant will supply a rope-ladder so that Romeo can climb up to Juliet's room that night.

THINK ABOUT for GCSE

Relationships

• The Nurse has come to bring a message from Juliet, but what comment does she add of her own (lines 147 to 155)? What point is she making to Romeo and why does she make it? What does this add to your impression of the Nurse's relationship with Juliet?

Context

• Juliet seems to be heavily supervised at home. What was one reason why a young girl like her might be allowed to leave the house unaccompanied (lines 163 to 166)? How will this prove useful in advancing her plans?

153 **deal double with**: double-cross

155 **weak dealing**: mean behaviour

156 **commend**: remember
protest: swear / declare (can mean 'declare my love')

160 **mark me**: take notice of what I say

164 **shrift**: confession

166 **shrived**: confessed
thy pains: your trouble

170 **stay**: wait

172 **tackled stair**: rope-ladder
173 **high topgallant**: highest point on a ship
174 **convoy**: means of access
175 **quit thy pains**: reward you for your trouble

179 **secret**: trustworthy
180 **Two ... away**: Two people – minus one – can keep a secret (i.e. keep it to yourself)
181 **warrant**: assure

What does this suggest about the rel. btwn nurse + Juliet? Protective of her.

It would be wicked + evil to take advantage of her, to lead her on

and therefore, if you should deal double with her, truly
it were an ill thing to be offered to any gentlewoman,
and very weak dealing.   155

ROMEO   Nurse, commend me to thy lady and mistress. I protest
         unto thee – *Remember*

NURSE   Good heart! And i' faith I will tell her as much. Lord,
         Lord, she will be a joyful woman!

ROMEO   What wilt thou tell her, Nurse? Thou dost not mark me. 160
         Pay attention to me

NURSE   I will tell her, sir, that you do protest – which, as I take
         it, is a gentleman-like offer.   *Propose – declare her love*

ROMEO   Bid her devise   *Tell her to devise a plan to get out of her*
         Some means to come to shrift this afternoon. *house + come to confession at the abbey this afternoon.*
         And there she shall, at Friar Lawrence's cell, *At Friar Lawrence's cell she can make confess.on*   165
         Be shrived and married. (*Offering money*) Here is for
         thy pains. *+ be married.* *your efforts.*

NURSE   No, truly, sir: not a penny.

ROMEO   Go to, I say you shall.

NURSE   (*Taking the money*) This afternoon, sir? Well, she
         shall be there.

ROMEO   And stay, good Nurse, behind the abbey wall.   170
         wait good nurse. within an hour, one of my men will
         Within this hour my man shall be with thee,
         come to you behind the abbey wall + give
         And bring thee cords made like a tackled stair,
         You a rope ladder. I'll use the rope
         Which to the high topgallant of my joy *ladder climb over the walls at night.*
         Must be my convoy in the secret night. *Then I'll meet Juliet joyfully + in secret.*
         Farewell. Be trusty, and I'll quit thy pains.   175
         Be honest + helpful + I'll repay you for your efforts
         Farewell. Commend me to thy mistress.

NURSE   Now God in heaven bless thee! Hark you, sir.

ROMEO   What say'st thou, my dear Nurse?

NURSE   Is your man secret? Did you ne'er hear say,
         Can your man keep a secret? Haven't you ever heard the saying "Two can conspire to but one away"?
         'Two may keep counsel, putting one away'?   180

ROMEO   I warrant thee, my man's as true as steel.
         assure

Before leaving, the Nurse tells Romeo that Count Paris wants to marry Juliet.

183 **prating**: chattering

184–5 **would ... aboard**: would very much like to marry her

185 **as lief**: as soon

187 **properer**: more handsome

188 **clout**: sheet

189 **versal**: universal / entire

rosemary: the herb of remembrance (used at Elizabethan weddings and funerals)

192 **the dog's name**: 'R' was called the dog's letter, possibly because it sounds like a dog growling.

194 **sententious**: she probably means 'sentences' (moral sayings)

199 **Before**: Walk in front of me

apace: get a move on

THINK ABOUT *for* GCSE

Structure and form

• What has to happen between this point (noon) and midnight to further Romeo and Juliet's happiness? Think about the roles of (a) the Friar; (b) the Nurse; and (c) Romeo's man.

• What does the Nurse say to remind the audience that there is at least one potential obstacle to Romeo and Juliet's future happiness?

Why do you think the nurse tells Romeo that Count Paris wants to marry Juliet?
1 – make him jealous
– make sure he will marry Juliet – why? nurse knows that she really loves him

NURSE   Well, sir. My mistress is the sweetest lady. Lord,
Lord! – when 'twas a little prating thing – O, there is a
nobleman in town, one Paris, that would fain lay knife
aboard – but she, good soul, had as lief see a toad, a   185
very toad, as see him. I anger her, sometimes, and tell
her that Paris is the properer man – but I'll warrant you,
when I say so, she looks as pale as any clout in the
versal world. Doth not 'rosemary' and 'Romeo' begin
with a letter?   190

very much liked
would rather look at a toad than at him
more handsome than you are
Rosemary (herb) – was a token of remembrance between loss's + for the dead.

ROMEO   Ay, Nurse, what of that? Both with an R.

NURSE   Ah, mocker! That's the dog's name. R is for the – No, I
know it begins with some other letter. And she hath the
prettiest sententious of it, of you and rosemary, that it
would do you good to hear it.   195

sentences

ROMEO   Commend me to thy lady.

Give my compliments to your lady.

NURSE   Ay, a thousand times. Peter!

PETER   Anon.

NURSE   (*Handing him her fan*) Before, and apace.

Go ahead.   Go quickly.

Exeunt.

In this scene ...

- When the Nurse returns to Juliet, she keeps putting off giving Romeo's message, complaining of tiredness.
- She finally tells Juliet when and where she is to meet Romeo and be married.

Juliet waits at home, impatient for the return of the Nurse. She finally arrives, moaning about her exhausting errand.

THINK ABOUT *for* **GCSE**

Language

- Juliet's language reflects her mood. What words or phrases in lines 1 to 17 give an idea of movement? What do you notice about the length of line 15, for example?

- How does Juliet convey the contrast between youth and age? Look at the tennis-ball image (lines 12 to 15) and the rhythm of lines 17 to 18. It helps to speak these lines in order to hear their effect.

Characterisation

- What does Juliet's opening speech in this scene reveal about her feelings?

3   **Perchance**: perhaps
4   **heralds**: messengers

6   **louring**: gloomy / threatening
7   **nimble-pinioned**: swift-winged
     draw Love: pull Venus's chariot

12   **affections**: feelings

14   **bandy**: strike (with a racket)

16   **feign ... were**: act as if they were
17   **Unwieldy**: clumsy

25   **give me leave**: leave me alone
26   **What ... have I**: What a tiring journey I've had

The Capulet garden.

Enter JULIET.

JULIET
I sent the Nurse at 9 o'clock.
The clock struck nine when I did send the Nurse –
In half an hour she promised to return.
Perhaps Perchance she cannot meet him – that's not so.
O, she is lame! Love's heralds should be thoughts, *love's messengers should be thoughts,*
Which ten times faster glides than the sun's beams   5 *which fly ten times faster than sunbeams*
Driving back shadows over louring hills. *they should be strong enough to push shadows / dark hills.*
Therefore do nimble-pinioned doves draw Love, *That's the why doves carry Venus so fast and that's why*
Cupid has wings that let him fly as fast as the wind And therefore hath the wind-swift Cupid wings.
Now it's noon Now is the sun upon the highmost hill
Of this day's journey, and from nine to twelve *She has been away* 10
Is three long hours – yet she is not come. *3 hours + hasn't returned*
Had she affections and warm youthful blood, *feelings*
She would be as swift in motion as a ball;
My words would bandy her to my sweet love, *my words would bounce her back to me.*
And his to me. *may act as if they were already dead* 15
But old folks – many feign as they were dead: *old people*
Unwieldy, slow, heavy, and pale as lead. *almost, slow, but colourless, like lead.*

Enter PETER, *followed by the* NURSE.

Here she is! Sweet
O God, she comes! – O honey Nurse, what news?
Did you meet him?
Hast thou met with him? Send thy man away.

NURSE
Wait for me at the gate
Peter, stay at the gate.   20

Exit PETER.

JULIET
Why do you look so sad?
Now good sweet Nurse – O Lord, why look'st thou sad?
Even if the news is sad tell me with a smile on your
Though news be sad, yet tell them merrily. *face.*
If the news is good, you're ruining the sweet news
If good, thou sham'st the music of sweet news
by playing it to me with a sour face like that.
By playing it to me with so sour a face.

NURSE
I'm tired. Leave me alone.
I am aweary: give me leave a while.   25
Ohmm, my bones ache so much! What a tiring journey I'm
Fie, how my bones ache! What a jaunce have I! *had.*

JULIET
I wish I had your bones and I had your news.
I would thou hadst my bones, and I thy news.
Nay, come, I pray thee, speak: good, good Nurse, speak.
Come on now, I beg you. Speak.

105

Juliet becomes increasingly impatient as the Nurse delays telling her what Romeo said.

29 stay: wait

34 excuse: make excuses for not telling

36 stay the circumstance: wait for the details

38 simple: foolish

42 be not ... on: are not worth talking about

44 Go thy ... God: Off you go, girl: be good

THINK ABOUT for GCSE

Relationships

- Look at the Nurse's comments on Romeo in lines 38 to 44. Why do you think she expresses her opinions on him in this roundabout way? What does this reveal about their relationship?

Performance and staging

- If you were the director, how would you want Juliet to react and what would you want her to do while the Nurse gets around to giving her the news? Look at line 50, for example.

50 a' t'other: on the other
51 Beshrew: Curse
52 jauncing: trudging
53 I' faith: I promise you

55 honest: honourable

58 within: indoors

62 hot: impatient (perhaps also 'eager for Romeo')
Marry ... trow: i.e. What a way to behave
63 poultice: cure (dressing used to ease aches)

NURSE	Jesu, what haste! Can you not stay a while?
	Do you not see that I am out of breath?	30
JULIET	How art thou out of breath, when thou hast breath
	To say to me that thou art out of breath?
	The excuse that thou dost make in this delay
	Is longer than the tale thou dost excuse.
	Is thy news good or bad? Answer to that.	35
	Say either, and I'll stay the circumstance.
	Let me be satisfied: is't good or bad?
NURSE	Well, you have made a simple choice – you know not
	how to choose a man. Romeo? No, not he. Though
	his face be better than any man's, yet his leg excels all	40
	men's – and for a hand and a foot and a body, though
	they be not to be talked on, yet they are past compare.
	He is not the flower of courtesy, but, I'll warrant him,
	as gentle as a lamb. Go thy ways, wench: serve God.
	What, have you dined at home?	45
JULIET	No, no! But all this did I know before!
	What says he of our marriage? What of that?
NURSE	Lord, how my head aches! What a head have I!
	It beats as it would fall in twenty pieces.
	My back a' t'other side – ah, my back, my back!	50
	Beshrew your heart for sending me about
	To catch my death with jauncing up and down!
JULIET	I' faith, I am sorry that thou art not well.
	Sweet, sweet, sweet Nurse, tell me – what says my love?
NURSE	Your love says, like an honest gentleman, and a	55
	courteous, and a kind, and a handsome, and, I warrant,
	a virtuous – Where is your mother?
JULIET	Where is my mother? Why, she is within.
	Where should she be? How oddly thou repliest!
	– 'Your love says, like an honest gentleman,	60
	"Where is your mother?"'
NURSE	O God's lady dear!
	Are you so hot? Marry, come up, I trow!
	Is this the poultice for my aching bones?
	Henceforth do your messages yourself.

107

The Nurse finally tells Juliet that she must meet Romeo at the Friar's cell and be married that afternoon. Meanwhile the Nurse will fetch the rope-ladder.

65   **coil**: fuss

66   **shrift**: confession

68   **hie you hence**: hurry off

70   **wanton**: playful / uncontrolled
71   **They'll … straight**: your cheeks blush very readily

75   **drudge**: poor servant
     toil: labour / work hard
76   **bear the burden**: i.e. carry Romeo's weight

THINK ABOUT for GCSE

Structure and form

- In her final speech the Nurse restates her plan. How effective is this as an ending to the scene?

Relationships

- From what you know so far, how would you describe (a) the Nurse's feelings for Juliet; (b) her attitude towards Juliet's mother; and (c) her role and position in the Capulet household?

You're making such a fuss!

JULIET   Here's such a coil! Come, what says Romeo?   65

NURSE   Have you got leave to go to shrift today?

Do you have permission to go out + take confession today?

JULIET   I have.

NURSE   Then hie you hence to Friar Lawrence' cell.
Then hurry up and rush over to Friar Lawrence's cell
There stays a husband to make you a wife.
There's a husband there who's waiting to make you his wife
Now comes the wanton blood up in your cheeks: 70
Now I see the blood rushing to your cheeks:
They'll be in scarlet straight at any news.
You'll blush bright red as soon as you hear any news.
Hie you to church! I must another way,
Go to the church — I must go by a different path to get
To fetch a ladder – by the which your love
a rope ladder — your love will use it
Must climb a bird's nest soon when it is dark.
to climb up to your window while it's dark.
I am the drudge, and toil in your delight,   75
I do the drudge work for your pleasure
But you shall bear the burden soon at night.
But soon you'll be doing a wife's work all night long.
Go! I'll to dinner. Hie you to the cell.
I'll go to lunch. You go to Friar L's cell.

JULIET   Hie to high fortune! Honest Nurse, farewell.
wish me luck. Thank you, dear Nurse.

Exeunt.

109

In this scene ...

• The Friar advises Romeo about the nature of love.

• Juliet arrives and she and Romeo go off to be married.

The Friar warns Romeo about the short lifespan of sudden and violent love, and then Juliet arrives.

THINK ABOUT for GCSE

Structure and form

• Why are lines 1 to 2, and 7 to 8 examples of dramatic irony (a situation in which the audience knows something which the character does not)? Think about the Prologue to Act 1. How might these lines make the audience feel?

Language

• What three images does the Friar use to persuade Romeo to 'love moderately' (lines 9 to 15)? How effective do you find them?

2 **That ... not**: so that the future does not punish us with unhappiness

3 **But come ... can**: I don't care what sorrow comes

4 **countervail**: equal

6 **Do ... close**: Simply join

8 **but**: simply / only

10 **powder**: gunpowder

12 **Is loathsome ... deliciousness**: can become sickly and disgusting

13 **confounds**: destroys

15 **Too swift ... slow**: i.e. more haste, less speed

16–17 **so light ... flint**: i.e. her feet are barely touching the ground

18 **bestride the gossamers**: ride on spiders' threads

19 **idles**: floats around
    wanton: playful

20 **vanity**: the delights of this world (compared with his religion)

21 **ghostly**: spiritual

23 **As ... him**: I must give him a kiss in return

24–5 **if the ... mine**: if you are feeling as much happiness as I am

25 **that**: if

26 **blazon**: richly describe

ACT 2 SCENE 6

Friar Lawrence's cell.

***Enter* FRIAR LAWRENCE, *with* ROMEO.**

FR. LAWRENCE	So smile the heavens upon this holy act
	That after-hours with sorrow chide us not!
ROMEO	Amen, amen! But come what sorrow can,
	It cannot countervail the exchange of joy
	That one short minute gives me in her sight. 5
	Do thou but close our hands with holy words,
	Then love-devouring death do what he dare,
	It is enough I may but call her mine.
FR. LAWRENCE	These violent delights have violent ends,
	And in their triumph die – like fire and powder, 10
	Which, as they kiss, consume. The sweetest honey
	Is loathsome in his own deliciousness,
	And in the taste confounds the appetite.
	Therefore, love moderately. Long love doth so:
	Too swift arrives as tardy as too slow. 15

JULIET enters, hurriedly, and embraces ROMEO.

	Here comes the lady. O, so light a foot
	Will ne'er wear out the everlasting flint.
	A lover may bestride the gossamers
	That idles in the wanton summer air,
	And yet not fall, so light is vanity. 20
JULIET	Good even to my ghostly confessor.
FR. LAWRENCE	Romeo shall thank thee, daughter, for us both.

ROMEO kisses her.

JULIET	As much to him – else is his thanks too much.

She returns his kiss.

ROMEO	Ah, Juliet, if the measure of thy joy
	Be heaped like mine, and that thy skill be more 25
	To blazon it, then sweeten with thy breath

Handwritten annotations:

May the heavens be happy with this holy …

So nothing unfortunate happens later to make us regret it.

whatever misfortunes occur, they can't

ruin the joy I feel with one look at her.

All you have to do

Join our hands with holy words,

then love-devouring death can do whatever it pleases

for me if I can call her mine.

These sudden joys have sudden endings.

They burn up in victory like fire + gunpowder

when they meet, as in a kiss, they explode. Too much honey

can make you sick to your stomach,

And in its taste destroys the appetite

love each other in moderation — that is the key to long-lasting love.

Too fast is as bad as too slow.

Oh, a footstep as light as hers will

never endure the really rough road of life.

Lovers are so light they can walk on a spiderweb

floating on a summer breeze, and yet not fall.

That's how flimsy + unreal pleasure is.

spiritual

kiss is a thank

I'll give him equal thanks, so we're even.

Ah, Juliet, if you're as happy as I am,

And you're better with words, tell me about the happiness you

imagine we'll have in our marriage.

eo and Juliet declare
eir love for one another and
the Friar leads them off to be
married.

28 **Unfold**: i.e. describe
29 **in either**: from the other person
   dear encounter: precious meeting
30 **Conceit**: Understanding
   matter: content
31 **substance**: true meaning
   ornament: flowery language
32 **They are … worth**: If you can say how
   much money you've got, you're not
   really rich
34 **sum up sum**: calculate the total
36 **by your leaves**: with your permission

THINK ABOUT *for* **GCSE**

Language

• How would you describe
  the language Juliet uses to
  describe her love in lines 30
  to 34? What does it reveal
  about her?

This neighbour air – and let rich music's tongue *— tell me*
Unfold the imagined happiness that both *how happy*
Receive in either, by this dear encounter. *you'll think we'll be when married*

JULIET   *I can imagine more than I can say — I have more on my mind than words* Conceit more rich in matter than in words   30
Brags of his substance, not of ornament.
If you can say how much money you've got, you're not really rich. They are but beggars that can count their worth –
My love has made me so rich that I can't count even half of my wealth But my true love is grown to such excess
I cannot sum up sum of half my wealth.

FR. LAWRENCE   *we will do the job quickly* Come, come with me, and we will make short work –   35
Because I'm not leaving you two For, by your leaves, you shall not stay alone
Till Holy Church incorporate two in one.
Alone until you're united in marriage

                                                    Exeunt.

In this scene ...

- Mercutio and Benvolio meet Tybalt, who is looking for Romeo.
- Tybalt insults Romeo. When he does not respond, Mercutio angrily challenges Tybalt himself.
- Mercutio and Tybalt fight. Mercutio is fatally wounded.
- Feeling ashamed that Mercutio has died on his behalf, Romeo fights with Tybalt and kills him.
- As punishment, the Prince exiles Romeo from Verona.

Benvolio is anxious about walking the streets when the Capulets are likely to be around. Mercutio teases Benvolio, accusing him of being a quarreller himself.

THINK ABOUT for GCSE

Structure and form

- How does Shakespeare create tension in the opening of this scene?

Characterisation

- Benvolio's name means something like 'well-wishing'. What does he say here which suggests that he is a peace-maker? Where else in the play has he shown that quality?

1 **retire**: get off the streets
2 **Capels are abroad**: Capulets are out and about
3 **scape**: avoid

6 **claps ... sword**: bangs his sword down

8 **operation ... cup**: time his second glass of wine has taken effect
8–9 **draws ... drawer**: draws his sword on the barman
11 **Jack**: fellow
12–13 **as soon ... moved**: as quickly moved to anger and as angry at being provoked

15 **two such**: two people like you

20 **hazel**: 1 a nut; 2 an eye colour

22 **meat**: food / nourishment
23 **addle**: rotten (as a bad egg)

27 **doublet**: jacket
before Easter: traditionally the time for bringing out new fashions
28 **riband**: laces
29 **tutor ... quarrelling**: teach *me* not to quarrel

ACT 3 SCENE 1

A square in Verona.

Enter MERCUTIO *and* BENVOLIO, *with other Montague servants and Mercutio's page.*

BENVOLIO   I pray thee, good Mercutio, let's retire.
The day is hot, the Capels are abroad,
And if we meet we shall not scape a brawl –
For now, these hot days, is the mad blood stirring.

MERCUTIO   Thou art like one of these fellows that, when he enters   5
the confines of a tavern, claps me his sword upon the
table and says 'God send me no need of thee!' – and,
by the operation of the second cup draws him on the
drawer, when indeed there *is* no need.

BENVOLIO   Am *I* like such a fellow?   10

MERCUTIO   Come, come. Thou art as hot a Jack in thy mood as any
in Italy, and as soon moved to be moody – and as soon
moody to be moved.

BENVOLIO   And what to?

MERCUTIO   Nay, and there were two such, we should have none   15
shortly, for one would kill the other. Thou? Why, thou
wilt quarrel with a man that hath a hair more or a hair
less in his beard than thou hast! Thou wilt quarrel with
a man for cracking nuts, having no other reason but
because thou hast hazel eyes. What eye but such an eye   20
would spy out such a quarrel? Thy head is as full of
quarrels as an egg is full of meat, and yet thy head hath
been beaten as addle as an egg for quarrelling. Thou
hast quarrelled with a man for coughing in the street
because he hath wakened thy dog that hath lain asleep   25
in the sun! Didst thou not fall out with a tailor for
wearing his new doublet before Easter? With another for
tying his new shoes with old riband? And yet thou wilt
tutor *me* from quarrelling!

Tybalt appears with some other Capulets. Mercutio provokes Tybalt, but Tybalt is looking for Romeo. When Romeo arrives, Tybalt calls him a villain.

Themes and issues

- **Conflict**: What different motivations do the three characters have here? Think about why Tybalt approaches Mercutio and what he wants, whether Mercutio is trying to provoke a fight and why he might want to, and what Benvolio is trying to do.

Context

- Tybalt calls Romeo 'villain' (line 58) – an insult to both his character and birth; and 'boy' (line 63) – a slur on his manhood. How might a young gentleman be expected to react in this situation?

30 **And**: If
31 **fee-simple**: absolute ownership (his life would be cheap, because it would be very short)
32 **simple**: stupid
33 **By my head**: a common oath
34 **By my heel**: a scornful oath invented by Mercutio

39 **apt enough to**: ready for
an: if
40 **occasion**: reason

42 **consortest with**: are often in the company of
43 **Consort**: group of musicians
minstrels: paid musicians, i.e. no better than servants
45 **fiddlestick**: i.e. his sword
46 **Zounds**: By God's wounds (an oath)
47 **haunt**: place / thoroughfare
49 **reason ... grievances**: discuss your differences calmly
50 **depart**: go your separate ways

54 **livery**: servant's uniform (i.e. he isn't your servant)
55 **go ... field**: walk in front of him to the duelling field
56 **'man'**: i.e. a man of honour (willing to fight a duel)
58 **thou ... villain**: a direct insult that would lead to a duel

BENVOLIO And I were so apt to quarrel as thou art, any man should 30
buy the fee-simple of my life for an hour and a quarter.

(handwritten: If I were in the habit of fighting the way you are, my life insurance rates would be sky high)

MERCUTIO The fee-simple? O, simple!

(handwritten: Your life insurance?)

Enter Tybalt, with other Capulets and servants.

BENVOLIO By my head, here come the Capulets!

MERCUTIO By my heel, I care not. *(handwritten: I don't care)*

TYBALT (*To his men*) Follow me close, for I will speak to them. 35
(*To Mercutio and Benvolio*) Gentlemen, good e'en: a
word with one of you.

MERCUTIO And but one word with one of us? Couple it with
something. Make it a word and a blow.

(handwritten: You just want one word with one of us? Put it together with something else. Make it a word + a slap)

TYBALT You shall find me apt enough to that, sir, an you will
give me occasion. 40

(handwritten: if you give me a reason)

MERCUTIO Could you not take some occasion without giving?

(handwritten: Can't you find a reason without my giving you one?)

TYBALT Mercutio, thou consortest with Romeo –

(handwritten: You hang out with Romeo)

MERCUTIO Consort? What, dost thou make us minstrels? And thou
make minstrels of us, look to hear nothing but discords.
Here's *my* fiddlestick! (*Moving his hand to his sword*) 45
– Here's that shall make you dance. Zounds, consort!

(handwritten: Group of musicians)
(handwritten: sword)

BENVOLIO We talk here in the public haunt of men!
Either withdraw unto some private place,
Or reason coldly of your grievances,
Or else depart. Here, all eyes gaze on us. 50

(handwritten: We're talking here in a public place)
(handwritten: Since everybody can see, let's private, settle it out)
(handwritten: rationally, or else just go away. Here everybody can see us.)
(handwritten: Goddammit)

MERCUTIO Men's eyes were made to look, and let them gaze.
I will not budge for no man's pleasure, I.

(handwritten: I won't move to please anybody)

Enter Romeo.

TYBALT Well, peace be with you, sir. Here comes my man.

(handwritten: Here comes my man the man I'm looking for)

MERCUTIO But I'll be hanged, sir, if he wear your livery.
Marry, go before to field, he'll be your follower – 55
Your worship in that sense may call him 'man'.

(handwritten: He isn't your manservant.)
(handwritten: Alright walk out in a field + he'll chase you.)
(handwritten: In that sense you can call him man. Your man!)

TYBALT Romeo, the love I bear thee can afford
No better term than this: thou art a villain.

(handwritten: direct insult that would lead to a duel)

117

Romeo responds calmly to Tybalt's insults and tries to make peace with him. Mercutio disapproves of Romeo's attitude and challenges Tybalt. They fight and Mercutio is wounded.

60–1 **Doth … greeting**: excuses me for not displaying the anger appropriate to your greeting

63 **Boy**: another serious insult

65 **protest**: promise / declare
66 **devise**: understand

68 **tender**: value

71 **Alla stoccata**: At the thrust (a fencing term)
carries it away: has won (i.e. is the right thing to say now)
72 **rat-catcher**: i.e. he is 'King of Cats'
will you walk: a challenge to a duel
74 **nine lives**: Cats are said to have nine lives.
75 **make bold withal**: do what I want with
75–6 **as you … eight**: depending how you behave to me afterwards, I'll thrash the other eight
77 **his pilcher**: its sheath (insulting)
by the ears: forcefully
78 **about your ears**: attacking you
80 **put … up**: put your sword away
81 **passado**: lunge
83 **forbear**: stop

85 **bandying**: exchanging blows

THINK ABOUT *for* GCSE

Performance and staging

- There are different ways in which Tybalt could try to provoke Romeo. In the Luhrmann film, for example, Tybalt kicks him to the ground and injures him. What would you have Tybalt do if you were the director?

- In what tone should Romeo reply to Tybalt? How might an actor underline Romeo's intentions at this point through his gestures and movements?

ROMEO
Tybalt, the reason that I have to love thee
Doth much excuse the appertaining rage   60
To such a greeting. Villain am I none.
Therefore, farewell. I see thou know'st me not.

[handwritten: So goodbye. I can tell you that you don't know who I am.]

TYBALT
[handwritten: another insult →] Boy, this shall not excuse the injuries
That thou hast done me. Therefore turn, and draw!

[handwritten: your words can't excuse the harm you've done to me.]
[handwritten: Now turn + draw your sword.]

ROMEO
I do protest I never injured thee,   65
But love thee better than thou canst devise –
Till thou shalt know the reason of my love.
And so, good Capulet – which name I tender
As dearly as mine own – be satisfied.

[handwritten: I disagree. I've never done you harm]
[handwritten: I love you more than you can understand]
[handwritten: Until you know the reason why I love you.]
[handwritten: And so, good Capulet – which is a name I love like my own name]
[handwritten: – you should be satisfied with what I say.]

MERCUTIO
O calm, dishonourable, vile submission!   70
'Alla stoccata' carries it away! (***Drawing his sword***)
Tybalt, you rat-catcher, will you walk?

[handwritten: all he has]

TYBALT
What wouldst thou have with me?

[handwritten: what do you want from me?]

MERCUTIO
Good King of Cats, nothing but one of your nine lives
that I mean to make bold withal – and, as you shall use   75
me hereafter, dry-beat the rest of the eight. Will you
pluck your sword out of his pilcher by the ears? Make
haste, lest mine be about your ears ere it be out.

[handwritten: Pull your sword out of its sheath – hurry up!]
[handwritten: smack you on the ears with my sword before you have drawn yours.]

TYBALT
(***Drawing his sword***) I am for you!

[handwritten: I'll fight you!]

ROMEO
Gentle Mercutio, put thy rapier up.   80

[handwritten: your sword away]

MERCUTIO
(***To*** TYBALT) Come, sir, your passado!

[handwritten: fencing move]

MERCUTIO *and* TYBALT *fight.*

ROMEO
[handwritten: Draw your sword]
Draw, Benvolio! Beat down their weapons!
Gentlemen, for shame, forbear this outrage!
Tybalt! Mercutio! The Prince expressly hath
Forbid this bandying in Verona streets.   85
Hold, Tybalt! Good Mercutio!

[handwritten: Gentleman, stop this disgraceful fight]
[handwritten: against Prince's wishes]

ROMEO *comes between them, obstructing the fight.* TYBALT
makes a hidden thrust past ROMEO*'s body, and wounds*
MERCUTIO.

Exit TYBALT, *running, with his followers.*

The dying Mercutio curses
the families for their feud. Left
alone, Romeo feels ashamed
that he did not respond
to Tybalt's insults himself.
Benvolio returns to announce
that Mercutio is dead.

THINK ABOUT for GCSE

Performance and staging

• In the Luhrmann film,
Mercutio realises that he is
seriously wounded after line
94, but in the 1983 RSC
production it was not until
line 98. Where do you think
is the most effective point?

Themes and issues

• Does Mercutio seem to
blame Tybalt, Romeo,
or the feud between the
familes the most for his
death? Where do you think
the blame lies?

Context

• Many people in
Shakespeare's time believed
that a dying man's curse
was certain to be fulfilled.
Why is that superstition
significant here?

87 **houses**: families
sped: finished (i.e. fatally wounded)
88 **and hath nothing**: without being wounded in return
89 **a scratch**: i.e. it was inflicted by the 'King of Cats'

93 **'twill serve**: it'll do / it will be enough (i.e. to kill me)
94 **grave**: 1 serious (unusual for him); 2 buried in a grave
94–5 **peppered ... world**: finished as far as this world is concerned
96 **Zounds**: God's wounds
97 **braggart**: boaster
98 **book of arithmetic**: rule book
103 **worms' meat**: a corpse (only fit to be eaten by worms)
103–4 **I have ... too**: I am wounded, and fatally

105 **near ally**: close relative
106 **very**: true

108 **slander**: insulting words

110 **effeminate**: lacking manly virtues
111 **temper**: 1 character; 2 hardening of steel
softened ... steel: weakened my courage
113 **aspired**: soared up to
114 **untimely**: early / prematurely

MERCUTIO   I am hurt.
May A plague o' both your houses! I am sped. [*May a plague curse both your families. I'm finished.*]
Is he gone, and hath nothing? [*Did he get away clean?*]

BENVOLIO   What, art thou hurt?

MERCUTIO   Ay, ay, a scratch, a scratch. Marry, 'tis enough. [*But it's enough*]
Where is my page? Go, villain, fetch a surgeon.   90

Exit the page, running.

ROMEO   Courage, man: the hurt cannot be much. [*It can't be that bad*]

MERCUTIO   No, 'tis not so deep as a well, nor so wide as a church
door – but 'tis enough, 'twill serve. [*to kill me*] Ask for me tomorrow
grave (i) serious – (ii) in a grave and you shall find me a grave man. I am peppered, I [*in this world*]
warrant, for this world. A plague, o' both your houses! [*I am done for in this world*]_ 95 [*Curse*]
Zounds! A dog, a rat, a mouse, a cat – to scratch a man
to death! A braggart, a rogue, a villain that fights by the [*rule book*]
rem. R. by the book book of arithmetic! Why the devil came you between [*hell*]
kissed by the book us? I was hurt under your arm. [*He struck me from under your arm*]

ROMEO   I thought all for the best.   100

MERCUTIO   Help me into some house, Benvolio,
Or I shall faint. A plague o' both your houses!
They have made worms' meat of me. I have it,
And soundly too. – Your houses! – *Curse your families*

Exit, supported by BENVOLIO,

ROMEO   *+ my dear friend,* This gentleman, the Prince's near ally, [*This gentleman Mercutio, a close relative of the Prince*]   105
My very friend, hath got this mortal hurt [*was killed while defending*]
In my behalf: my reputation stained [*me from Tybalt's insulting*]
With Tybalt's slander. – Tybalt! – that an hour [*words – Tybalt who has been my cousin*]
Hath been my cousin. O sweet Juliet – [*for a whole hour.*]
Thy beauty hath made me effeminate, [*Your beauty has made me weak like a woman*]   110
+ softened And in my temper softened valour's steel! [*and softened my bravery, which before was as hard as steel*]

Re-enter BENVOLIO.

BENVOLIO   O Romeo, Romeo! Brave Mercutio is dead! [*– Mercutio*]
That gallant spirit hath aspired the clouds, [*– dead*]
Which too untimely here did scorn the earth.

his spirit has floated up to heaven

When Tybalt returns, Romeo kills him. He flees before the Prince arrives with the Montagues and Capulets.

115 on more … depend: i.e. threatens the future with more unhappiness

119 respective lenity: gentleness which comes from respect (perhaps for the Prince's laws, or his new relationship with Tybalt)

120 be my conduct: guide my actions

124 Staying: waiting

126 consort: accompany

129 up: raised up and in arms

130 amazed: in a daze

doom thee death: sentence you to death

131 taken: arrested

132 fortune's fool: i.e. a plaything or helpless victim of the goddess Fortune

136 charge: order

THINK ABOUT for GCSE

Performance and staging

- In what ways should the fight between Romeo and Tybalt be different from the earlier one between Mercutio and Tybalt? Think about the differences between Romeo's and Mercutio's moods as they approach their fights, for example.

Themes and issues

- **Fate**: What does Romeo mean by 'O, I am fortune's fool' (line 132)? What might he be thinking or feeling at this moment?

The future will be affected by today's terrible events

ROMEO   This day's black fate on more days doth depend: ✗   115
Today is the start of a terror that will
         This but begins the woe others must end.
end in the days ahead.

Re-enter TYBALT.

BENVOLIO Here comes the furious Tybalt back again.

He's alive + victorious, + Mercutio's dead?

ROMEO   Alive – in triumph! And Mercutio slain!
Enough with mercy + consideration.
         Away to heaven, respective lenity,
It's time for rage to guide my actions.
         And fire-eyed fury be my conduct now!   120
Now, Tybalt, you can call me 'villain' no way
         Now, Tybalt, take the 'villain' back again
you died before   Mercutio's soul is
explain That late thou gavest me – for Mercutio's soul
fleeting above our heads.
         Is but a little way above our heads,
He's waiting for you to keep him company on way
         Staying for thine to keep him company.   *to heaven*
Either thou or I or both of us need to go   with him
         Either thou or I, or both, must go with him.   125

TYBALT   Thou, wretched boy, that didst consort him here,
         Shalt with him hence! *You're going to heaven with him*

This fight will decide who dies

ROMEO   (*Drawing his sword*) This shall determine that.

They fight. ROMEO *kills* TYBALT.

Romeo, get out of here
BENVOLIO Romeo, away, be gone! *, and Tybalt is dead.*
The citizens are around,
         The citizens are up, and Tybalt slain.
Don't stand here shocked, the prince will give you the death
         Stand not amazed! The Prince will doom thee death   130
if you get caught, so get out of here.   penalty
         If thou art taken. Hence, be gone, away!

I am a plaything / victim of Goddess Fortune. —
ROMEO   O, I am fortune's fool!

BENVOLIO   *why are you waiting?*   Why dost thou stay?

                                   Exit ROMEO.

Enter an OFFICER, *and armed citizens.*

OFFICER Which way ran he that killed Mercutio?
         Tybalt, that murderer, which way ran he?

BENVOLIO There lies that Tybalt.

OFFICER   Up, sir, go with me.   135
         I charge thee in the Prince's name, obey.

Enter PRINCE ESCALUS, MONTAGUE *and* CAPULET, *their* LADIES,
servants and attendants.

PRINCE   Where are the vile beginners of this fray?
where are the evil men that started this fight?

Lady Capulet calls upon the Prince to punish the Montagues for Tybalt's death. Benvolio reports how Mercutio and Tybalt came to be killed.

138 **discover**: reveal
139 **manage**: sequence of events

144 **true**: fair and just

149 **spoke him fair**: spoke politely to him
    bid him bethink: asked him to consider
150 **nice**: trivial
    urged withal: also stressed
153 **take truce with**: pacify / calm
    unruly spleen: uncontrolled temper
154 **tilts**: thrusts
156 **all as hot**: just as angry
157 **martial scorn**: aggressive contempt

159 **dexterity**: skill
160 **Retorts it**: turns it back

163 **'twixt**: between
164 **envious**: intending harm
165 **stout**: brave
166 **by and by**: almost at once
167 **but newly entertained**: just at that moment thought about

173 **Affection ... false**: i.e. he is lying because he is a Montague
174 **black strife**: fatal conflict

THINK ABOUT for GCSE

Themes and issues

- There are always different perspectives on a **conflict**. What differences do you notice between Benvolio's account of the fight (lines 148 to 171) and what actually happened? Is his version of the story biased in favour of the Montagues as Lady Capulet claims?

BENVOLIO O noble Prince, I can discover all
I can tell you everything
The unlucky manage of this fatal brawl.
I can tell you everything about the unfortunate circumstances of this deadly fight.
There lies the man, slain by young Romeo,   **140**
over here Tybalt is lying dead, he killed your relative, brave Mercutio
That slew thy kinsman, brave Mercutio.
+ then young Romeo killed him.

LADY CAPULET Tybalt, my cousin? O, my brother's child!
O Prince! O husband! O, the blood is spilled
Of my dear kinsman! Prince, as thou art true,
For blood of ours, shed blood of Montague!   **145**
revenge for his murder by killing someone from the Montague family.
O cousin, cousin!

PRINCE Benvolio, who began this bloody fray?
started bloody fight?

BENVOLIO Tybalt, here slain, whom Romeo's hand did slay.
Tybalt started the fight before he was killed by Romeo
Romeo, that spoke him fair, bid him bethink
Romeo spoke to him politely + told him
How nice the quarrel was, and urged withal   **150**
How silly the argument was, He remembered that you
Your high displeasure. All this, uttered
would not approve the fight. He said all of this gently +
With gentle breath, calm look, knees humbly bowed,
calmly kneeling down, out of respect.
Could not take truce with the unruly spleen
But he could not make peace with Tybalt
Of Tybalt, deaf to peace, but that he tilts
explain   he thrusts
With piercing steel at bold Mercutio's breast –   **155**
his sword at Mercutio's breast
Who, all as hot, turns deadly point to point,
they begin fighting each other
And, with a martial scorn, with one hand beats
Cold death aside, and with the other sends
It back to Tybalt, whose dexterity
Retorts it. Romeo he cries aloud,   **160**
Romeo cried out
'Hold, friends! Friends part!' – and, swifter than his
stop, my friends. Break it up
   tongue,
His agile arm beats down their fatal points,
He then jumped in between them + forced them
And 'twixt them rushes, underneath whose arm
to put their swords down, But Tybalt reached
An envious thrust from Tybalt hit the life
underneath Romeo's arms + thrust his sword into brave
Of stout Mercutio, and then Tybalt fled –   **165**
But very soon he came back to Romeo, Mercutio. Then Tybalt
But by and by comes back to Romeo,
who had thoughts of revenge   fled.
Who had but newly entertained revenge,
And to 't they go like lightning: for, ere I
+ start fighting. Before I
Could draw to part them, was stout Tybalt slain,
Could break up the fight, Tybalt was killed.
And as he fell did Romeo turn and fly.   **170**
Romeo ran away when Tybalt fell dead.
This is the truth, or let Benvolio die.

LADY CAPULET He is a kinsman to the Montague.
Benvolio is part of the Montague family
Affection makes him false! He speaks not true.
His loyalty to the Montagues make him tell lies.
He's not telling the truth here
Some twenty of them fought in this black strife,
were 20 Montagues fighting in this violent

125

Lady Capulet demands Romeo's death. Instead the Prince banishes Romeo from Verona.

179 **Who ... owe**: Who is now to pay for shedding Mercutio's precious blood

181 **His fault ... end**: His crime has simply put into effect what the law would have demanded

183 **exile**: banish (from Verona)

184 **have an interest**: am personally concerned

185 **My blood**: i.e. Mercutio, his kinsman

186 **amerce**: punish

189 **purchase out abuses**: buy a pardon for crimes

190 **Let Romeo hence**: Romeo must leave here

192 **attend our will**: come with me to hear what I intend to do

193 **Mercy ... kill**: Mercy will only cause more murders, if killers are pardoned

THINK ABOUT for GCSE

Themes and issues

• **Authority:** In Act 1 Scene 1 the Prince said that death would be the penalty for any future fighting. How fair is his punishment of Romeo here, in your opinion? How effective is it likely to be in ending the feud? How good a ruler does it show him to be?

• Which statements are made at the end of this scene by Lady Capulet and by Montague that suggest that the **conflict** will continue?

[handwritten: and together those 20 could only kill one man]
And all those twenty could but kill one life.   175
I beg for justice, which thou, Prince, must give:
[handwritten: Romeo killed Tybalt, Romeo must die.]
Romeo slew Tybalt. Romeo must not live.

PRINCE *[handwritten: Romeo killed Tybalt, Tybalt killed Mercutio]*
Romeo slew him; *he* slew Mercutio.
[handwritten: Who now should pay the price for Mercutio's life?]
Who now the price of his dear blood doth owe?

MONTAGUE Not Romeo, Prince – he was Mercutio's friend.   180
[handwritten: His crime did justice's job by taking Tybalt's life]
His fault concludes but what the law should end –
The life of Tybalt.

PRINCE   And for that offence
[handwritten: Romeo is hereby exiled from Verona]
Immediately we do exile him hence!
[handwritten: I am involved in your rivalry]
I have an interest in your hate's proceedings:
[handwritten: Mercutio was my relative, & he lies dead because of your bloody feud]
My blood for your rude brawls doth lie a-bleeding.   185
[handwritten: I'll punish you so harshly]
But I'll amerce you with so strong a fine
[handwritten: That you shall regret causing me his loss]
That you shall all repent the loss of mine.
[handwritten: I won't listen to your pleas or excuses]
I will be deaf to pleading and excuses –
Nor tears, nor prayers shall purchase out abuses.
[handwritten: These if he is told Romeo leave my city immediately]
Therefore use none. Let Romeo hence in haste: 190
[handwritten: else if he is found he will be killed]
Else, when he is found, that hour is his last.
[handwritten: take away this body & do what I say]
Bear hence this body, and attend our will.
[handwritten: showing mercy by pardoning killers]
Mercy but murders, pardoning those that kill.
[handwritten: only causes more murders]

                                                        Exeunt.

[handwritten annotations:]

Contrast of mood

Act 2 scene 6 – joyous – light
            – love – lives joining
            – triumphant together

Act 3 scene 1 – murder / death – lives being
            – darkness   taken
            – violence   away

Deliberate contrast

antithesis

127

In this scene ...

- Juliet is longing for night and Romeo's arrival, when the Nurse enters, grieving at Tybalt's death.
- When Juliet realises that Romeo killed Tybalt, her feelings are at first confused. Then it sinks in that Romeo is banished and she becomes desperate.
- The Nurse offers comfort, promising to bring Romeo to Juliet that night.

As Juliet is wishing for night and Romeo's arrival, the Nurse enters.

THINK ABOUT for GCSE

Language

- What does Juliet's language tell us about her mood? Think about (a) her use of words to do with night; and (b) her use of commands, like 'Gallop' and 'Come'.

Themes and issues

- **Love:** Much of Juliet's language in this speech has a sexual meaning, some of which is open (e.g. 'true love acted' in line 16) and some which is hidden (e.g. 'die' in line 21). How important is sexual attraction in Romeo and Juliet's relationship?

1 **apace**: quickly
2 **Phoebus' lodging**: the sun-god's home (i.e. the West – where the sun sets)
  waggoner: chariot-driver
3 **Phaeton**: Phoebus's son, who drove the sun-god's chariot
5 **close**: concealing
  love-performing: when acts of love take place
6 **runaway's ... wink**: any night-wanderer may sleep
8 **amorous rites**: sacred acts of love
10 **civil**: respectable
12 **learn ... match**: teach me how to lose my virginity but win a husband
13 **a pair ... maidenhoods**: i.e. they will both lose their virginity
14 **Hood ... cheeks**: i.e. cover up my blushes
  unmanned: 1 untamed; 2 with no sexual experience of men
15 **black mantle**: dark covering of night
  strange: 1 new to me; 2 shy
16 **Think ... modesty**: will consider the physical act of love to be chastity
25 **garish**: crudely bright
26 **mansion**: house
28 **tedious**: long drawn-out

Act 3 Scene 2

In the Capulet house.

Enter JULIET, *alone.*

JULIET

Gallop apace, you fiery-footed steeds,
Towards Phoebus' lodging! Such a waggoner
As Phaeton would whip you to the west,
And bring in cloudy night immediately.
Spread thy close curtain, love-performing night – 5
That runaway's eyes may wink, and Romeo
Leap to these arms untalked of and unseen!
Lovers can see to do their amorous rites
By their own beauties – or, if love be blind
It best agrees with night. Come, civil night, 10
Thou sober-suited matron all in black,
And learn me how to lose a winning match,
Played for a pair of stainless maidenhoods.
Hood my unmanned blood, bating in my cheeks,
With thy black mantle – till strange love, grown bold, 15
Think true love acted simple modesty.
Come night – come Romeo! Come, thou day in night –
For thou wilt lie upon the wings of night,
Whiter than new snow upon a raven's back.
Come, gentle night: come loving, black-browed night – 20
Give me my Romeo! And when I shall die,
Take him and cut him out in little stars –
And he will make the face of heaven so fine
That all the world will be in love with night
And pay no worship to the garish sun. 25
O, I have bought the mansion of a love,
But not possessed it – and though I am sold,
Not yet enjoyed. So tedious is this day
As is the night before some festival
To an impatient child that hath new robes 30
And may not wear them. O, here comes my Nurse –

Enter the NURSE, *with the rope-ladder.*

And she brings news – and every tongue that speaks

Seeing the Nurse's grief, Juliet is desperate, thinking at first that it is Romeo who has died.

33 **eloquence**: beautifully expressed language
34 **cords**: rope-ladder

38 **undone**: ruined

40 **envious**: intending harm / spiteful

45–50 **Ay**: 1 yes; 2 the pronoun 'I'; 3 'eye'
47 **cockatrice**: mythical creature whose look could kill
49 **those eyes shut**: i.e. Romeo's eyes closed in death
51 **determine ... woe**: will decide my happiness or misery
53 **God ... mark**: forgive me for saying something so awful
54 **corse**: corpse
55 **bedaubed**: spattered with
56 **gore**: clotted
swounded: fainted
57 **bankrupt**: someone who has lost all their money and will be imprisoned for their debts
break: become 'broke' (wordplay)
59 **Vile ... here**: Body, surrender to the grave and end activity
60 **And thou ... bier**: both my corpse and Romeo's lie on the same sad funeral carriage

THINK ABOUT for GCSE

Characterisation

- Why do you think the Nurse does not tell Juliet straight away that it is Tybalt who has died?
- Why might the Nurse refer to Tybalt as 'the best friend I had' (line 61)?

But Romeo's name, speaks heavenly eloquence.
Now, Nurse, what news? What hast thou there? The
    cords
That Romeo bid thee fetch?

NURSE   Ay, ay, the cords.   35

She drops the rope-ladder on the floor.

JULIET   Ay me, what news? Why dost thou wring thy hands?

NURSE   Ah, well-a-day! He's dead, he's dead, he's dead!
            We are undone, lady, we are undone.
            Alack the day! He's gone, he's killed, he's dead!

JULIET   Can heaven be so envious?

NURSE   Romeo can –   40
            Though heaven cannot. O Romeo, Romeo!
            Whoever would have thought it? Romeo!

JULIET   What devil art thou dost torment me thus?
            This torture should be roared in dismal hell!
            Hath Romeo slain himself? Say thou but 'Ay',   45
            And that bare vowel 'I' shall poison more
            Than the death-darting eye of cockatrice.
            I am not I, if there be such an 'I',
            Or those eyes shut that makes thee answer 'Ay'.
            If he be slain, say 'Ay', or if not, 'No'.   50
            Brief sounds determine of my weal or woe.

NURSE   I saw the wound, I saw it with mine eyes –
            God save the mark! – here on his manly breast.
            A piteous corse – a bloody, piteous corse,
            Pale, pale as ashes! – All bedaubed in blood,   55
            All in gore blood! I swounded at the sight!

JULIET   O break, my heart! Poor bankrupt, break at once!
            To prison, eyes: ne'er look on liberty!
            Vile earth, to earth resign, end motion here
            And thou and Romeo press one heavy bier!   60

NURSE   O Tybalt, Tybalt, the best friend I had!
            O courteous Tybalt, honest gentleman,
            That ever I should live to see thee dead!

131

When Juliet realises that Romeo has killed Tybalt, she bitterly accuses Romeo of hiding wickedness behind a beautiful appearance. But when the Nurse criticises Romeo, Juliet is angry and defends him.

64 so contrary: first in one direction, then in the other

67 dreadful ... doom: blow, trumpet, to signal Judgement Day

73 serpent heart: Romeo is compared with the serpent which tempted Eve in the Garden of Eden in the Bible.
flowering: youthful and fair
74 keep: live in
76 wolvish-ravening: ravenous as a wolf
77 Despisèd: detested
divinest: most holy
78 Just: exactly
81 bower: beautifully enclose

86–7 All ... forsworn: They all lie and break their promises
87 naught: sinful
dissemblers: cheats / deceivers
88 aqua-vitae: strong drink (brandy)

THINK ABOUT for GCSE

Language

- Which oxymorons (expressions that seem to contradict themselves while still making sense) best express the conflict between Juliet's anger at Romeo and her relief that he is alive?

95 chide at: speak harshly of

JULIET	What storm is this that blows so contrary?
	Is Romeo slaughtered, and is Tybalt dead?	65
	My dearest cousin *and* my dearer lord?
	Then, dreadful trumpet, sound the general doom! –
	For who is living if those two are gone?

| NURSE | Tybalt is gone – and Romeo banishèd. |
| | Romeo that killed him – *he* is banishèd! | 70 |

| JULIET | O God! Did Romeo's hand shed Tybalt's blood? |

| NURSE | It did, it did! Alas the day, it did! |

JULIET	O serpent heart, hid with a flowering face!
	Did ever dragon keep so fair a cave?
	Beautiful tyrant, fiend angelical! –	75
	Dove-feathered raven, wolvish-ravening lamb! –
	Despised substance of divinest show –
	Just opposite to what thou justly seem'st,
	A damnèd saint, an honourable villain!
	O nature, what hadst thou to do in hell	80
	When thou didst bower the spirit of a fiend
	In mortal paradise of such sweet flesh?
	Was ever book containing such vile matter
	So fairly bound? O, that deceit should dwell
	In such a gorgeous palace!

NURSE	There's no trust,	85
	No faith, no honesty in men. – All perjured,
	All forsworn, all naught, all dissemblers!
	Ah, where's my man? Give me some aqua-vitae.
	These griefs, these woes, these sorrows make me old.
	Shame come to Romeo!

JULIET	Blistered be thy tongue	90
	For such a wish! He was not born to shame!
	Upon his brow shame is ashamed to sit,
	For 'tis a throne where honour may be crowned
	Sole monarch of the universal earth.
	O, what a beast was I to chide at him!	95

| NURSE | Will you speak well of him that killed your cousin? |

Confused by what has happened, Juliet tries to sort out her true feelings. She becomes desperate as it gradually sinks in that Romeo has been banished from Verona.

98 **smooth thy name**: speak well of you

100 **wherefore**: why

102 **native spring**: source
103 **tributary drops**: i.e. tears
104 **mistaking**: having made a mistake

109 **fain**: gladly

114 **Hath slain**: i.e. is as bad as the deaths of
116 **delights in fellowship**: likes company
117 **needly ... ranked**: has to be included

120 **modern ... moved**: might have caused an ordinary kind of grief
121 **rear-ward**: rearguard (i.e. following up behind)

125 **bound**: limit
126 **sound**: 1 give expression to; 2 measure the depth of

128 **corse**: corpse

130 **spent**: shed

132 **beguiled**: cheated

THINK ABOUT for GCSE

Themes and issues

• Actor Niamh Cusack said 'this scene is where Juliet really grows up: she understands what commitment and depth of **love** are.' What does Juliet say here which supports this view?

JULIET

Shall I speak ill of him that is my husband?
Ah, poor my lord, what tongue shall smooth thy name,
When I, thy three-hours' wife, have mangled it?
But wherefore, villain, didst thou kill my cousin?   100
That villain cousin would have killed my husband.
Back, foolish tears, back to your native spring –
Your tributary drops belong to woe,
Which you, mistaking, offer up to joy.
My husband lives, that Tybalt would have slain,   105
And Tybalt's dead that would have slain my husband.
All this is comfort. Wherefore weep I then?
Some word there was, worser than Tybalt's death,
That murdered me. I would forget it fain,
But O, it presses to my memory   110
Like damnèd guilty deeds to sinners' minds:
'Tybalt is dead, and Romeo banishèd.'
That 'banishèd', that one word 'banishèd',
Hath slain ten thousand Tybalts! Tybalt's death
Was woe enough if it had ended there –   115
Or, if sour woe delights in fellowship
And needly will be ranked with other griefs,
Why followed not, when she said, 'Tybalt's dead',
'Thy father', or 'thy mother', nay, or both,
Which modern lamentation might have moved?   120
But with a rear-ward following Tybalt's death,
'Romeo is banishèd'! To speak that word
Is father, mother, Tybalt, Romeo, Juliet –
All slain, all dead! 'Romeo is banishèd'.
There is no end, no limit, measure, bound,   125
In that word's death. No words can that woe sound.
Where is my father and my mother, Nurse?

NURSE

Weeping and wailing over Tybalt's corse.
Will you go to them? I will bring you thither.

JULIET

Wash they his wounds with tears? Mine shall be spent   130
When theirs are dry, for Romeo's banishment.
Take up those cords. Poor ropes, you are beguiled,
Both you and I, for Romeo is exiled.
He made you for a highway to my bed,

The Nurse knows that Romeo is hiding at the Friar's cell. She promises to bring him to Juliet.

137   **maidenhead**: virginity

138   **Hie**: Hurry

139   **wot**: know

THINK ABOUT
for **GCSE**

Characterisation

• Juliet experiences some dramatic changes of emotion in this scene. Look at the following lines and decide what feelings she might be experiencing at each point: 1, 31, 36, 43, 57, 64, 71, 73, 90, 100 to 101, 106, 112 to 113, and 142 to 143.

	But I, a maid, die maiden-widowèd.	135
	Come cords – come Nurse. I'll to my wedding-bed –	
	And death, not Romeo, take my maidenhead!	

NURSE   (*Gathering up the rope-ladder*) Hie to your chamber.
            I'll find Romeo
         To comfort you. I wot well where he is.
         Hark ye, your Romeo will be here at night: 140
         I'll to him – he is hid at Lawrence' cell.

JULIET   O, find him! Give this ring to my true knight,
         And bid him come to take his last farewell.

Exeunt.

In this scene ...

• Romeo is desperate when he hears that he has been banished from Verona, and the Friar cannot comfort him.

• The Nurse arrives. Fearing that Juliet must now hate him and imagining her grief, Romeo threatens to kill himself, but is prevented by the Friar and the Nurse.

• The Friar instructs Romeo to leave for Mantua by dawn at the latest, after he has spent the night with Juliet.

The Friar tells Romeo the Prince's sentence: that he is banished from Verona. He is angry with Romeo for not being grateful to have avoided a death sentence.

1 **fearful**: frightened
2 **Affliction ... parts**: You seem to be attracting suffering
3 **calamity**: great misfortune
4 **doom**: judgement / sentence
5 **craves ... hand**: wants to be introduced to me
6–7 **Too ... company**: i.e. You already know it too well

9 **doomsday**: Judgement Day (i.e. death)

10 **vanished from**: came out of

THINK ABOUT
for **GCSE**

Characterisation

• Given that Romeo expected the death sentence (line 9), why does he react so badly to the news that he is to be banished? How sympathetic are you to his reactions here?

17 **without**: outside
18 **purgatory**: where souls had to wait and suffer for their sins before being allowed into heaven
20 **world's exile**: exile from the world
21 **mis-termed**: given the wrong name

24 **deadly**: that will lead to damnation
25 **Thy fault ... death**: Your crime is punishable by death
26 **rushed**: pushed
28 **dear**: unusual and precious

Act 3 Scene 3

Friar Lawrence's cell.

Enter FRIAR LAWRENCE.

FR. LAWRENCE Romeo, come forth! Come forth, thou fearful man.
Affliction is enamoured of thy parts,
And thou art wedded to calamity.

Enter ROMEO, *from an inner room.*

ROMEO Father, what news? What is the Prince's doom?
What sorrow craves acquaintance at my hand   5
That I yet know not?

FR. LAWRENCE   Too familiar
Is my dear son with such sour company!
I bring thee tidings of the Prince's doom.

ROMEO What less than doomsday is the Prince's doom?

FR. LAWRENCE A gentler judgement vanished from his lips: 10
Not body's death, but body's banishment.

ROMEO Ha! Banishment? Be merciful – say 'death' –
For exile hath more terror in his look,
Much more than death. Do not say 'banishment'!

FR. LAWRENCE Hence from Verona art thou banishèd.   15
Be patient, for the world is broad and wide.

ROMEO There is no world without Verona walls,
But purgatory, torture, hell itself!
Hence 'banishèd' is banished from the world,
And world's exile is death. Then 'banishèd'   20
Is death mis-termed. Calling death 'banishèd',
Thou cut'st my head off with a golden axe,
And smilest upon the stroke that murders me!

FR. LAWRENCE O deadly sin! O rude unthankfulness!
Thy fault our law calls death. But the kind Prince,   25
Taking thy part, hath rushed aside the law,
And turned that black word 'death' to 'banishment'.
This is dear mercy, and thou seest it not.

Romeo is devastated because banishment means that he will be separated from Juliet. He refuses to listen to the Friar's words of comfort.

33 **validity**: value
34 **courtship**: 1 courtly behaviour;
    2 opportunity for wooing
35 **carrion flies**: flies which live off rotting
    flesh
38 **vestal**: virginal

43 **say'st thou yet**: do you still say

45 **mean**: means
    though … mean: however
    dishonourable
48 **attends**: accompanies
49 **divine**: holy man
    ghostly: spiritual
50 **my friend professed**: someone who
    claims to be my friend
51 **mangle**: destroy
52 **fond**: foolish

THINK ABOUT *for* GCSE

Language

• How does Romeo's language convey his insistence on seeing the worst of his situation and his refusal to accept the Friar's words of consolation? Look, for example, at the repeated words and language he uses to convey the unfairness of being removed from Juliet.

55 **Adversity**: misfortune
    philosophy: the ability to understand
    and accept what happens

59 **Displant**: transplant / move to another
    place
60 **prevails not**: is of no effect / is no use

63 **dispute … estate**: discuss your
    situation with you

ROMEO	'Tis torture and not mercy. Heaven is here	
	Where Juliet lives! – and every cat and dog	30
	And little mouse, every unworthy thing,	
	Live here in heaven and may look on her,	
	But Romeo may not. More validity,	
	More honourable state, more courtship, lives	
	In carrion flies than Romeo: they may seize	35
	On the white wonder of dear Juliet's hand,	
	And steal immortal blessing from her lips,	
	Who even in pure and vestal modesty	
	Still blush, as thinking their own kisses sin.	
	But Romeo may not: he is banishèd!	40
	Flies may do this, but I from this must fly:	
	They are free men, but I am banishèd.	
	And say'st thou yet that exile is not death?	
	Hadst thou no poison mixed, no sharp-ground knife,	
	No sudden mean of death, though ne'er so mean,	45
	But 'banishèd' to kill me? 'Banishèd'!	
	O Friar, the damnèd use that word in hell.	
	Howling attends it! How hast thou the heart,	
	Being a divine, a ghostly confessor,	
	A sin-absolver, and my friend professed,	50
	To mangle me with that word 'banishèd'?	

FR. LAWRENCE	Thou fond mad man! – Hear me a little speak.

ROMEO	O, thou wilt speak again of banishment.

FR. LAWRENCE	I'll give thee armour to keep off that word –	
	Adversity's sweet milk, philosophy,	55
	To comfort thee though thou art banishèd.	

ROMEO	Yet 'banishèd'? Hang up philosophy!	
	Unless philosophy can make a Juliet,	
	Displant a town, reverse a Prince's doom,	
	It helps not, it prevails not! Talk no more.	60

FR. LAWRENCE	O, then I see that madmen have no ears.

ROMEO	How should they, when that wise men have no eyes?

FR. LAWRENCE	Let me dispute with thee of thy estate.

Romeo is overcome with emotion and flings himself to the floor. He refuses to move, even when someone knocks at the door. It is the Nurse.

67 **Doting**: being deeply in love

70 **Taking … of**: measuring out / taking the space of

73 **infold**: wrap me up and hide me

THINK ABOUT for GCSE

Structure and form

- How does the way Romeo reacts to the word 'banishèd' here (line 67), compare with Juliet's reaction to the word in Act 3 Scene 2?

Performance and staging

- If you were the director, how would you stage lines 70 to 88? Think about (a) how the characters are feeling and what their reactions will be; (b) where they should be positioned on stage; and (c) when and how the characters should move.

75 **taken**: caught / arrested
    Stay: Wait
76 **By and by**: I'll be with you straight away
77 **simpleness**: foolishness

84 **even … case**: in exactly the same state as my mistress ('case' could also sometimes mean pregnancy)
85 **woeful sympathy**: they're feeling the same grief

ROMEO	Thou canst not speak of that thou dost not feel!
	Wert thou as young as I, Juliet thy love,	65
	An hour but married, Tybalt murderèd,
	Doting like me, and like me banishèd,
	Then mightst thou speak! – then mightst thou tear thy hair,
	And fall upon the ground as I do now,
	Taking the measure of an unmade grave!	70

He flings himself down on the floor. A knocking is heard.

| FR. LAWRENCE | Arise! One knocks. Good Romeo, hide thyself. |

| ROMEO | Not I – unless the breath of heartsick groans |
| | Mist-like infold me from the search of eyes. |

More knocking heard.

FR. LAWRENCE	Hark how they knock! – (*Calling*) Who's there? – Romeo, arise!
	Thou wilt be taken. – (*Calling*) Stay a while! – Stand up!	75
	Run to my study. – (*Calling*) By and by! – God's will! –
	What simpleness is this? – (*Calling*) I come, I come!

Louder knocking from the door.

| | Who knocks so hard? Whence come you? What's your will? |

| NURSE | (*Calling from outside*) Let me come in and you shall know my errand! |
| | I come from Lady Juliet. |

| FR. LAWRENCE | (*Opening the door*) Welcome then. | 80 |

| NURSE | (*Entering*) O holy Friar – O tell me, holy Friar, |
| | Where's my lady's lord? Where's Romeo? |

| FR. LAWRENCE | There on the ground, with his own tears made drunk. |

NURSE	O, he is even in my mistress' case,
	Just in her case! O woeful sympathy!	85
	Piteous predicament! Even so lies she,
	Blubbering and weeping, weeping and blubbering.
	Stand up, stand up! Stand, and you be a man!

Romeo fears that Juliet must now hate him for having killed her cousin, Tybalt. He draws a dagger to kill himself, but the Friar prevents him, furious at Romeo's behaviour.

89 **rise and stand**: both words can also mean 'have an erection'
90 **an O**: 1 a fit of groaning; 2 the vagina

93 **old**: hardened / great

95 **removed but little**: closely related (Tybalt was Juliet's cousin)
97 **concealed**: i.e. she is secretly his wife

99 **now**: one minute

102 **level**: aim

105 **anatomy**: body
106 **sack**: destroy

THINK ABOUT for GCSE

Language

* The Nurse's language (lines 84 to 90) includes several examples of sexual innuendo (double-meanings). Does she intend them? What effect do they have on an audience here (a) if she intends them; and (b) if she does not realise what she is saying?

Characterisation

* What seems to be the Nurse's intentions in the way she deals with Romeo and describes Juliet's behaviour to him?

108 **form**: physical shape
109 **denote**: are the sign of
110 **unreasonable**: lacking human reason
111 **Unseemly**: behaving inappropriately
112 **ill-beseeming**: unnatural and wrong

114 **disposition**: personality / character
better tempered: was more stable

117 **damnèd hate**: i.e. suicide
118 **rail'st thou on**: curse

121 **shape**: (manly) physical appearance
wit: intellect

For Juliet's sake – for her sake rise and stand!
Why should you fall into so deep an O?   90

ROMEO   (*Getting up*) Nurse!

NURSE   Ah, sir! Ah, sir! Death's the end of all.

ROMEO   Spak'st thou of Juliet? How is it with her?
Doth she not think me an old murderer,
Now I have stained the childhood of our joy
With blood removed but little from her own?   95
Where is she? And how doth she? And what says
My concealed lady to our cancelled love?

NURSE   O, she says nothing, sir – but weeps and weeps,
And now falls on her bed, and then starts up,
And Tybalt calls, and then on Romeo cries,   100
And then down falls again!

ROMEO   As if that name,
Shot from the deadly level of a gun,
Did murder her, as that name's cursèd hand
Murdered her kinsman. O, tell me, Friar, tell me,
In what vile part of this anatomy   105
Doth my name lodge? Tell me! – that I may sack
The hateful mansion!

He draws his dagger as if to stab himself.

FR. LAWRENCE   Hold thy desperate hand!
Art thou a man? Thy form cries out thou art:
Thy tears are womanish – thy wild acts denote
The unreasonable fury of a beast!   110
Unseemly woman in a seeming man,
And ill-beseeming beast in seeming both!
Thou hast amazed me! By my holy order,
I thought thy disposition better tempered.
Hast thou slain Tybalt? Wilt thou slay thyself?   115
And slay thy lady, that in thy life lives,
By doing damnèd hate upon thyself?
Why rail'st thou on thy birth, the heaven, and earth,
Since birth, and heaven, and earth, all three, do meet
In thee at once, which thou at once wouldst lose?   120
Fie, fie! Thou sham'st thy shape, thy love, thy wit,

145

The Friar tells Romeo to count his blessings and instructs him to visit Juliet as planned, but to leave for Mantua by dawn at the latest. The Friar will try to find an opportunity to explain to everyone in Verona what has happened.

122 **usurer**: money-lender
abound'st: are wealthy
123 **usest ... use**: do not spend your wealth properly
124 **bedeck**: be an ornament to
125 **form of wax**: i.e. poor copy
126 **Digressing**: deviating
127 **hollow perjury**: empty lies
130 **Misshapen ... both**: leading both (i.e. manliness and love) astray
131 **powder**: gunpowder
skilless: i.e. careless
133 **dismembered**: blown limb from limb
with ... defence: by the very thing that should protect you
135 **but lately dead**: only a few minutes ago as good as dead
136 **There ... happy**: in that you are fortunate
140 **light**: alight / land
141 **best array**: finest clothes
145 **decreed**: arranged
147 **look ... set**: take care you don't stay until the night-patrol goes on duty
148 **pass**: get through the city gates
Mantua: the nearest city to Verona

150 **blaze**: make publicly known
reconcile your friends: bring your two families together
153 **lamentation**: grieving

156 **heavy ... unto**: grief over Tybalt will make them ready for

159 **counsel**: advice

THINK ABOUT for GCSE

Characterisation

• What are the main points that the Friar makes in his speech to Romeo? For example, what does he say (a) to express his anger at Romeo (lines 108 to 133); and (b) to try to cheer him up (lines 134 to 153)?

Which like a usurer abound'st in all,
And usest none in that true use indeed
Which should bedeck thy shape, thy love, thy wit.
Thy noble shape is but a form of wax,   125
Digressing from the valour of a man –
Thy dear love sworn but hollow perjury,
Killing that love which thou hast vowed to cherish!
Thy wit, that ornament to shape and love,
Misshapen in the conduct of them both,   130
Like powder in a skilless soldier's flask,
Is set afire by thine own ignorance,
And thou dismembered with thine own defence.
What? Rouse thee, man! Thy Juliet is alive,
For whose dear sake thou wast but lately dead: 135
There art thou happy. Tybalt would kill thee,
But thou slew'st Tybalt. There art thou happy.
The law that threatened death becomes thy friend,
And turns it to exile. There art thou happy too.
A pack of blessings light upon thy back;   140
Happiness courts thee in her best array –
But like a misbehaved and sullen wench
Thou frown'st upon thy fortune and thy love.
Take heed, take heed! – for such die miserable.
Go – get thee to thy love, as was decreed.   145
Ascend her chamber: hence, and comfort her –
But look thou stay not till the watch be set,
For then thou canst not pass to Mantua,
Where thou shalt live till we can find a time
To blaze your marriage, reconcile your friends,   150
Beg pardon of the Prince, and call thee back
With twenty hundred thousand times more joy
Than thou went'st forth in lamentation.
Go before, Nurse. Commend me to thy lady,
And bid her hasten all the house to bed –   155
Which heavy sorrow makes them apt unto.
Romeo is coming.

NURSE   O Lord, I could have stayed here all the night
To hear good counsel! O, what learning is!
My lord, I'll tell my lady you will come.   160

147

Romeo is comforted when the Nurse gives him Juliet's ring. The Friar promises to send messages to Romeo in Mantua, and Romeo goes to meet Juliet.

161 **chide**: rebuke me / tell me off

164 **comfort**: happiness

165 **here ... state**: your future happiness depends on this (i.e. on following my instructions)

168 **Sojourn**: Stay for the time being

169 **signify**: report

170 **good hap**: fortunate thing
      chances: happens

172 **But ... me**: Were it not that I am called away by the greatest of joys (i.e. of being with Juliet)

173 **It were ... thee**: I would be very sad to leave you in such a hurry

THINK ABOUT for **GCSE**

Characterisation

• Romeo's mood seems to change strikingly at the end of this scene. What causes him to cheer up? What does this mood-swing suggest about him?

ROMEO	Do so, and bid my sweet prepare to chide.

NURSE	(*Leaving, but turning back again to* ROMEO) Here, sir – a ring she bid me give you, sir. Hie you, make haste – for it grows very late.

Exit.

ROMEO	How well my comfort is revived by this.

FR. LAWRENCE	Go hence – good night – and here stands all your state: 165 Either be gone before the watch be set, Or by the break of day disguised from hence. Sojourn in Mantua. I'll find out your man, And he shall signify from time to time Every good hap to you that chances here. 170 Give me thy hand. 'Tis late. Farewell, good night.

ROMEO	But that a joy past joy calls out on me, It were a grief so brief to part with thee. Farewell.

Exeunt.

In this scene ...

- Capulet arranges with Paris that his wedding to Juliet will take place in a few days' time.
- He sends Lady Capulet to inform Juliet.

Capulet explains to Paris that Juliet cannot see him as she is mourning the death of her cousin, Tybalt. But he then tells Paris that he can marry Juliet the following Thursday.

1   **fallen out**: happened
2   **move**: persuade (i.e. to marry Paris)
3   **Look you**: You have to understand that

8   **afford**: allow
9   **Commend me**: Give my regards
10 **mind**: views (i.e. about the marriage)
11 **mewed ... heaviness**: shut away with sadness

12 **desperate tender**: bold offer

16 **son**: i.e. Capulet already sees Paris as a son-in-law
18 **soft**: wait a minute

20 **O'**: On

23 **keep ... ado**: won't make a great fuss
24 **late**: recently
25 **held him carelessly**: did not care much about him
26 **kinsman**: relative
    revel much: have a big celebration

THINK ABOUT for GCSE

Characterisation

- Do you have any sympathy for Paris and the situation he is in? Has he behaved badly either in this scene or in Act 1 Scene 2, in your opinion?

Themes and issues

- How far do you **blame** him for being an obstacle in the way of Romeo and Juliet's happiness?

The Capulet house.

Enter CAPULET, LADY CAPULET, *and Count* PARIS.

CAPULET	Things have fallen out, sir, so unluckily
	That we have had no time to move our daughter.
	Look you, she loved her kinsman Tybalt dearly,
	And so did I. Well, we were born to die.
	'Tis very late. She'll not come down tonight.

5

I promise you, but for your company,
I would have been a-bed an hour ago.

PARIS   These times of woe afford no time to woo.
         Madam, good night. Commend me to your daughter.

LADY CAPULET   I will, and know her mind early tomorrow.   10
                Tonight she's mewed up to her heaviness.

PARIS *goes, but* CAPULET *calls him back.*

CAPULET   Sir Paris! – I will make a desperate tender
           Of my child's love. I think she will be ruled
           In all respects by me – nay more, I doubt it not.
           Wife, go you to her ere you go to bed.   15
           Acquaint her here of my son Paris' love,
           And bid her – mark you me? – on Wednesday next –
           But soft, what day is this?

PARIS   Monday, my lord.

CAPULET   Monday, ah ha! Well, Wednesday is too soon.
           O' Thursday let it be. O' Thursday, tell her,   20
           She shall be married to this noble earl.
           Will you be ready? Do you like this haste?
           We'll keep no great ado – a friend or two.
           For hark you, Tybalt being slain so late,
           It may be thought we held him carelessly,   25
           Being our kinsman, if we revel much.
           Therefore we'll have some half a dozen friends,
           And there an end. (*To* PARIS) But what say you to
              Thursday?

151

Capulet instructs his wife to tell
Juliet of the wedding plans, and
goes to bed.

29 **would**: wish

32 **against**: for

34 **Afore me**: My goodness
35 **by and by**: almost immediately

THINK ABOUT
for GCSE

Relationships

• What does this short scene
tell us about Capulet as a
father? Think about how
concerned he is for his
daughter's happiness and
whether he understands her
feelings. Look back at what
he says in Act 1 Scene 2,
lines 8 to 19, for example.

Performance and staging

• What do you think about
Lady Capulet's silence
throughout this scene? How
would you direct the actor
to play her here?

PARIS   My lord, I would that Thursday were tomorrow!

CAPULET   Well, get you gone. O' Thursday be it then.   30
           (*To* LADY CAPULET) Go you to Juliet ere you go to bed.
           Prepare her, wife, against this wedding day.
           Farewell, my lord. (***Calling for a servant***) Light to my
              chamber, ho!
           Afore me! – 'tis so very late that we
           May call it early by and by. Good night.   35

                                                    Exeunt.

In this scene ...

- Having spent the night with Juliet, Romeo leaves for Mantua.
- Lady Capulet tells Juliet that she is to marry Paris, but she refuses.
- Capulet is furious with Juliet for her disobedience and threatens her.
- The Nurse advises Juliet to marry Paris. Juliet pretends to accept her advice, but privately plans to seek help from the Friar.

As their night together comes to an end, Juliet at first tries to persuade Romeo to stay longer. But she then fears for his safety and reluctantly encourages him to go.

2 **nightingale ... lark**: Nightingales are heard singing at night; larks begin at dawn.

7 **envious**: harmfully jealous
8 **severing**: parting
9 **Night's candles**: i.e. the stars
   jocund: cheerful

13 **exhales**: breathes out

17 **ta'en**: arrested
18 **so thou ... so**: so long as that is what you want
20 **reflex ... brow**: reflection of the moon's face (Cynthia was another name for Diana, the moon goddess.)
22 **vaulty**: arched
23 **care**: concern / desire

THINK ABOUT for GCSE

Performance and staging

- According to the opening stage direction here, where might this scene have taken place in Shakespeare's theatre? If you were staging it or filming it today, where would you place the two lovers?

28 **sharps**: sharp notes
29 **division**: 1 melody; 2 separation (of the lovers)
31 **change**: exchanged (In folk-lore, the lark has dull eyes, and the toad remarkable ones.)

The Capulet garden, and Juliet's window-balcony.

Enter ROMEO *and* JULIET *above, at the window.*

JULIET

Wilt thou be gone? It is not yet near day.
It was the nightingale, and not the lark,
That pierced the fearful hollow of thine ear.
Nightly she sings on yond pomegranate tree.
Believe me, love, it was the nightingale.   5

ROMEO

It was the lark, the herald of the morn –
No nightingale. Look, love, what envious streaks
Do lace the severing clouds in yonder east.
Night's candles are burnt out, and jocund day
Stands tiptoe on the misty mountain tops.   10
I must be gone and live, or stay and die.

JULIET

Yond light is not daylight – I know it, I.
It is some meteor that the sun exhales
To be to thee this night a torch-bearer
And light thee on thy way to Mantua.   15
Therefore stay yet. Thou need'st not to be gone.

ROMEO

Let me be ta'en, let me be put to death –
I am content, so thou wilt have it so.
I'll say yon grey is not the morning's eye –
'Tis but the pale reflex of Cynthia's brow;   20
Nor that is not the lark whose notes do beat
The vaulty heaven so high above our heads.
I have more care to stay than will to go.
Come, death, and welcome! – Juliet wills it so.
How is't, my soul? Let's talk – it is not day.   25

JULIET

It is, it is! Hie hence, be gone! Away!
It is the lark that sings so out of tune,
Straining harsh discords and unpleasing sharps.
Some say the lark makes sweet division:
This doth not so, for she divideth us.   30
Some say the lark and loathèd toad change eyes.
O, now I would they had changed voices too! –

When the Nurse tells Juliet that Lady Capulet is on her way, Romeo climbs down the ladder. As they part, Juliet experiences a sense that something bad will happen.

33 **arm from … affray**: the lark's song frightens us out of each other's arms
34 **hunt's-up**: a song to waken hunters

40 **wary**: careful

43 **ay**: for ever
   friend: lover

46 **count**: method of counting
   much in years: very old

52 **discourses**: conversations
53 **ill-divining**: prophesying bad things

58 **Dry**: Thirsty (It was believed that sorrow exhausted the blood.)

THINK ABOUT for GCSE

Language

• Both Romeo and Juliet describe their situation using strong images. What pictures form in your mind at line 36, and at lines 54 to 55?

	Since arm from arm that voice doth us affray,	
	Hunting thee hence with hunt's-up to the day.	
	O now be gone! – more light and light it grows.	35

| ROMEO | More light and light, more dark and dark our woes. |

Enter the NURSE, *hurriedly.*

| NURSE | Madam! |

| JULIET | Nurse? |

| NURSE | Your lady mother is coming to your chamber! |
| | The day is broke. Be wary, look about! | 40 |

Exit NURSE.

| JULIET | Then, window, let day in, and let life out. |

| ROMEO | Farewell, farewell. One kiss and I'll descend. |

He goes down the rope-ladder, to the garden.

JULIET	Art thou gone so, love? – lord, ay husband, friend!
	I must hear from thee every day in the hour,
	For in a minute there are many days.	45
	O, by this count I shall be much in years
	Ere I again behold my Romeo!

ROMEO	(*From the garden below*) Farewell! I will omit no
	opportunity
	That may convey my greetings, love, to thee.

| JULIET | O, think'st thou we shall ever meet again? | 50 |

| ROMEO | I doubt it not. And all these woes shall serve |
| | For sweet discourses in our time to come. |

JULIET	O God, I have an ill-divining soul!
	Methinks I see thee, now thou art so low,
	As one dead in the bottom of a tomb.	55
	Either my eyesight fails, or thou look'st pale.

| ROMEO | And trust me, love, in my eye so do you. |
| | Dry sorrow drinks our blood. Adieu, adieu! |

Exit ROMEO.

Lady Capulet believes that Juliet is still weeping for Tybalt's death, and says how angry she is that his killer, Romeo, is still alive.

59 **fickle**: changeable
60 **what dost thou**: what business have you

65 **Is she ... late**: Has she not yet gone to bed
66 **procures**: brings

67 **how now**: what's the matter

71 **Some**: A moderate amount of
72 **still**: always
   want of wit: lack of common sense
73 **feeling**: deeply felt

THINK ABOUT for GCSE

Performance and staging

• If you were performing this play in Shakespeare's Globe Theatre, how would you stage the opening of this scene (up to Lady Capulet's entrance at line 67)? Think about the positions of characters on the stage, furniture, and entrances and exits, for example.

76 **friend**: can mean 'lover' (Juliet's private meaning)

80 **asunder**: apart

82 **like**: so much as

JULIET *pulls up the rope-ladder.*

JULIET   O, Fortune, Fortune! All men call thee fickle.
                 If thou art fickle, what dost thou with him   **60**
                 That is renowned for faith? *Be* fickle, Fortune –
                 For then I hope thou wilt not keep him long,
                 But send him back.

LADY CAPULET   (*From inside the house*) Ho, daughter, are you up?

JULIET   Who is't that calls? It is my lady mother.
                 Is she not down so late, or up so early?   **65**
                 What unaccustomed cause procures her hither?

        Enter LADY CAPULET, *below.* JULIET *comes down from her
        window and enters to meet her mother.*

LADY CAPULET   Why, how now, Juliet?

JULIET   Madam, I am not well.

LADY CAPULET   Evermore weeping for your cousin's death?
                 What, wilt thou wash him from his grave with tears?
                 And if thou couldst, thou couldst not make him live – **70**
                 Therefore have done. Some grief shows much of love,
                 But much of grief shows still some want of wit.

JULIET   Yet let me weep for such a feeling loss.

LADY CAPULET   So shall you feel the loss, but not the friend
                 Which you weep for.

JULIET   Feeling so the loss,   **75**
                 I cannot choose but ever weep the friend.

LADY CAPULET   Well, girl, thou weep'st not so much for his death
                 As that the villain lives which slaughtered him.

JULIET   What villain, madam?

LADY CAPULET   That same villain, Romeo.

JULIET   (*Aside*) Villain and he be many miles asunder. –   **80**
                 (*To her mother*) God pardon him! I do, with all my
                    heart –
                 And yet no man like he doth grieve my heart.

LADY CAPULET   That is because the traitor murderer lives.

Lady Capulet promises that they will take revenge on Romeo by having him killed. But when she tells Juliet that she is to marry Paris on Thursday, Juliet forcefully refuses.

THINK ABOUT for GCSE

Relationships

- Look at the exchange between Lady Capulet and Juliet (lines 67 to 101). For each of the following lines, decide (a) what Lady Capulet thinks Juliet means; and (b) what Juliet actually means: 67, 73, 75 to 76, 81, 82, 84, 85, 92 to 93, 95 to 98, 98 to 99, and 100 to 101.

Language

- What do you notice about the language Juliet uses in her reply to her father (lines 115 to 122)? Look particularly at the oath with which she opens, the heavy use of monosyllables throughout, and the reference to Romeo at the end. What effects does each of these have? What aspect of her character does Juliet reveal here?

85 **venge**: get revenge for

88 **runagate**: fugitive villain
89 **unaccustomed dram**: strange dose (of poison)

94 **vexed**: angered

96 **temper**: 1 mix; 2 weaken / dilute

98 **abhors**: hates

100 **wreak the love**: 1 get revenge for my love (for Tybalt); 2 physically express my love (for Romeo)

104 **in such … time**: when we most need it

106 **careful**: considerate / who wants the best for you
107 **heaviness**: sadness
108 **sorted out**: chosen
     sudden: soon to come
109 **nor … for**: and which I did not expect either
110 **in happy time**: it has come just at the right time

117 **wonder at**: am amazed at
118 **should be**: wants to be

JULIET	Ay, madam – from the reach of these my hands.
	Would none but I might venge my cousin's death! **85**
LADY CAPULET	We will have vengeance for it, fear thou not.
	Then weep no more. I'll send to one in Mantua,
	Where that same banished runagate doth live,
	Shall give him such an unaccustomed dram
	That he shall soon keep Tybalt company – **90**
	And then I hope thou wilt be satisfied.
JULIET	Indeed, I never shall be satisfied
	With Romeo till I behold him – dead –
	Is my poor heart, so for a kinsman vexed.
	Madam, if you could find out but a man **95**
	To bear a poison, I would temper it
	That Romeo should upon receipt thereof
	Soon sleep in quiet. O, how my heart abhors
	To hear him named and cannot come to him –
	To wreak the love I bore my cousin **100**
	Upon his body that hath slaughtered him!
LADY CAPULET	Find thou the means, and I'll find such a man.
	But now I'll tell thee joyful tidings, girl.
JULIET	And joy comes well in such a needy time.
	What are they, I beseech your ladyship? **105**
LADY CAPULET	Well, well, thou hast a careful father, child –
	One who, to put thee from thy heaviness,
	Hath sorted out a sudden day of joy
	That thou expects not, nor I looked not for.
JULIET	Madam, in happy time! What day is that? **110**
LADY CAPULET	Marry, my child, early next Thursday morn,
	The gallant, young, and noble gentleman,
	The County Paris, at Saint Peter's Church,
	Shall happily make thee there a joyful bride.
JULIET	Now, by Saint Peter's Church, and Peter too, **115**
	He shall *not* make me there a joyful bride!
	I wonder at this haste, that I must wed
	Ere he that should be husband comes to woo!
	I pray you tell my lord and father, madam,

Capulet enters and finds Juliet in tears. He explodes with anger when he is told that Juliet is refusing to marry Paris.

THINK ABOUT for GCSE

Language

• Capulet compares Juliet's mood to a ship at sea in stormy weather. Decide what particular comparisons he is making in the following lines, and how effective they are, in your opinion: 125 to 127, 128, 129, and 129 to 136.

Characterisation

• What do you think this language reveals about Capulet? Is he genuinely upset or is he selfishly thinking about his own interest in Juliet marrying Paris? Which of these interpretations would you choose to show on stage, if you were acting the part?

124 **at your hands**: from you yourself

126 **sunset ... son**: i.e. Tybalt's death

128 **conduit**: street-fountain

130 **counterfeits**: are imitating
bark: ship
131 **still**: always / constantly

135 **Without**: unless there is
sudden calm: i.e. in the winds
overset: capsize
137 **decree**: decision

138 **will none**: refuses / will have none of it

140 **Soft ... you**: Wait a minute, I don't understand, say that again
142 **count her**: consider herself
143 **wrought**: arranged / secured
144 **bride**: bridegroom
147 **hate ... love**: a hateful action which was intended to be a loving one
148 **How ... chop-logic**: What do you mean, arguing like this
150 **minion**: spoilt brat
152 **fettle ... joints**: i.e. get yourself ready
'gainst: in preparation for
154 **hurdle**: wooden rack used for dragging criminals to their execution
155 **green-sickness carrion**: pale corpse
156 **tallow-face**: i.e. a face as white as candle-wax

	I will not marry yet. And when I do, I swear	120
	It shall be Romeo, whom you know I hate,	
	Rather than Paris. These are news indeed!	

Lady Capulet Here comes your father. Tell him so yourself,
And see how he will take it at your hands.

Enter Capulet, *and the* Nurse.

Capulet When the sun sets, the earth doth drizzle dew –   125
But for the sunset of my brother's son
It rains downright.
How now – a conduit, girl? What, still in tears?
Evermore showering? In one little body
Thou counterfeits a bark, a sea, a wind –   130
For still thy eyes, which I may call the sea,
Do ebb and flow with tears. The bark thy body is,
Sailing in this salt flood – the winds thy sighs,
Who raging with thy tears, and they with them,
Without a sudden calm will overset   135
Thy tempest-tossèd body. How now, wife?
Have you delivered to her our decree?

Lady Capulet Ay, sir – but she will none, she gives you thanks.
I would the fool were married to her grave!

Capulet Soft! – take me with you, take me with you, wife.   140
How will she none? Doth she not give us thanks?
Is she not proud? Doth she not count her blest,
Unworthy as she is, that we have wrought
So worthy a gentleman to be her bride?

Juliet Not proud you have, but thankful that you have.   145
Proud can I never be of what I hate –
But thankful, even for hate that is meant love.

Capulet How, now! How, now – chop-logic? What is this?
'Proud', and 'I thank you', and 'I thank you not' –
And yet 'Not proud'? – mistress minion, you!   150
Thank me no thankings, nor proud me no prouds! –
But fettle your fine joints 'gainst Thursday next,
To go with Paris to Saint Peter's Church –
Or I will drag thee on a hurdle thither.
Out, you green-sickness carrion! Out, you baggage!   155
You tallow-face!

163

Maddened at Juliet's disobedience, Capulet threatens and insults her, ignoring the attempts by his wife and the Nurse to calm him down.

Themes and issues

• **Conflict**: In this scene Capulet abuses Juliet verbally (and, in some productions, physically too). What do you think he means by the insults in the following lines: 150, 155, 156, 159, 167, 183, and 184? How do you react to Capulet's violence?

Relationships

• What features of Juliet's character and behaviour seem to be angering Capulet most here? What does this reveal about their father–daughter relationship?

Context

• What shows us here that daughters were regarded as a father's property in Elizabethan England?

156 **Fie**: For shame

163 **My fingers itch**: i.e. I'm tempted to hit you

167 **Out ... hilding**: Away with her, the worthless creature
168 **rate**: verbally attack

170 **Good Prudence**: Madam Wisdom
Smatter ... gossips: Natter with your women-friends
171 **God ... e'en**: i.e. for God's sake

173 **Utter ... bowl**: Save your serious words for when you're having a drink with your women-friends
174 **hot**: angry
175 **God's bread**: a powerful oath (referring to the bread used in the holy mass)
177 **still ... been**: the one thing I have always been concerned with
178 **have her matched**: provide a husband for her
180 **fair demesnes**: good estates
181 **parts**: qualities
182 **Proportioned ... man**: with as good a physique as you could hope for
183 **puling**: whimpering / whingeing
184 **whining mammet**: crying doll
in her fortune's tender: when good fortune is offered to her

LADY CAPULET	(*To her husband*) Fie, fie! What, are you mad?
JULIET	(*Kneeling*) Good father, I beseech you on my knees –
	Hear me with patience but to speak a word.
CAPULET	Hang thee, young baggage! Disobedient wretch!

CAPULET
Hang thee, young baggage! Disobedient wretch!
I tell thee what: get thee to church o' Thursday,   160
Or never after look me in the face!
Speak not, reply not, do not answer me!
My fingers itch. Wife, we scarce thought us blest
That God had lent us but this only child –
But now I see this one is one too much,   165
And that we have a curse in having her.
Out on her, hilding!

NURSE   God in heaven bless her!
You are to blame, my lord, to rate her so.

CAPULET   And why, my Lady Wisdom? Hold your tongue,
Good Prudence! Smatter with your gossips. Go!   170

NURSE   I speak no treason.

CAPULET   O, God gi' good e'en!

NURSE   May not one speak?

CAPULET   Peace, you mumbling fool!
Utter your gravity o'er a gossip's bowl,
For here we need it not.

LADY CAPULET   You are too hot.

CAPULET   God's bread! It makes me mad!   175
Day, night, hour, tide, time, work, play,
Alone, in company – still my care hath been
To have her matched! And having now provided
A gentleman of noble parentage,
Of fair demesnes, youthful and nobly trained,   180
Stuffed, as they say, with honourable parts,
Proportioned as one's thought would wish a man –
And then to have a wretched puling fool,
A whining mammet, in her fortune's tender,
To answer 'I'll not wed. I cannot love.   185
I am too young, I pray you pardon me'!

Capulet threatens to throw Juliet out of the house and to disown her unless she agrees to marry Paris. When her mother rejects her too, Juliet turns to the Nurse for comfort and advice.

187 **and**: if

188 **Graze**: Feed
house with me: live in my house

189 **do … jest**: am not in the habit of making jokes

190 **Advise**: Give it some careful thought

194 **what … good**: i.e. you will inherit none of my wealth

195 **be forsworn**: break my word

201 **monument**: tomb

205 **my … heaven**: i.e. she has made marriage vows before God

206 **How … earth**: How can I take my vows back

208 **By leaving earth**: i.e. by dying

209 **practise stratagems**: play deceitful tricks

210 **soft**: easy

213 **all … nothing**: i.e. it's a perfectly safe bet

214 **challenge you**: claim you as his wife

219 **dishclout**: dishcloth
to: compared with

220 **green … quick**: beautiful … alive

THINK ABOUT for GCSE

Characterisation

• What does Lady Capulet reveal about herself in this scene? Look particularly at lines 67 to 102, 103 to 114, 123 to 124, 156, and 174. How far does she mean what she says in lines 139 and 203?

But, and you will not wed, I'll pardon you!
Graze where you will – you shall not house with me!
Look to 't, think on't! I do not use to jest.
Thursday is near. Lay hand on heart. Advise.   190
And you be mine, I'll give you to my friend:
And you be not, hang, beg, starve, die in the streets! –
For, by my soul, I'll ne'er acknowledge thee,
Nor what is mine shall never do thee good.
Trust to't, bethink you! I'll not be forsworn.   195

Exit.

JULIET   Is there no pity sitting in the clouds
                That sees into the bottom of my grief?
                O sweet my mother, cast me not away!
                Delay this marriage for a month, a week –
                Or, if you do not, make the bridal bed   200
                In that dim monument where Tybalt lies!

LADY CAPULET   Talk not to me, for I'll not speak a word.
                Do as thou wilt, for I have done with thee.

Exit.

JULIET   O God! – O Nurse, how shall this be prevented?
                My husband is on earth, my faith in heaven.   205
                How shall that faith return again to earth,
                Unless that husband send it me from heaven
                By leaving earth? Comfort me, counsel me.
                Alack, alack, that heaven should practise stratagems
                Upon so soft a subject as myself!   210
                What say'st thou? Hast thou not a word of joy?
                Some comfort, Nurse?

NURSE   Faith, here it is:
                Romeo is banishèd – and all the world to nothing
                That he dares ne'er come back to challenge you.
                Or, if he do, it needs must be by stealth.   215
                Then, since the case so stands as now it doth,
                I think it best you married with the County.
                O, he's a lovely gentleman!
                Romeo's a dishclout to him. An eagle, madam,
                Hath not so green, so quick, so fair an eye   220

When the Nurse advises her to marry Paris, Juliet tells the Nurse to say that she has gone to Friar Lawrence for confession. In reality she goes, deperately, to seek the Friar's help.

THINK ABOUT for GCSE

Performance and staging

- How might an actor playing Juliet say 'Amen' (line 228)?

- How would you advise an actor playing the Nurse to deliver her advice to Juliet (lines 212 to 227)? For example, should the audience get the impression that she means what she says about Juliet's second marriage ('it excels your first') or not? Should we feel that the Nurse fully understands that she is advising Juliet to commit bigamy, or not?

Characterisation

- How do you feel about the Nurse by the end of this scene? Have your views about her changed?

221 **Beshrew**: Curse
222 **match**: marriage

224 **'twere … were**: he might as well be
225 **here**: i.e. on earth / alive
    no use of him: without being able to enjoy him as a husband

228 **Amen**: So be it

233 **absolved**: forgiven for my sins

235 **Ancient damnation**: Damned old woman
236 **wish … forsworn**: want me to break my marriage vows
237 **dispraise**: criticise / speak ill of
238 **with above compare**: as being beyond comparison
240 **bosom**: private thoughts
    twain: separated

	As Paris hath. Beshrew my very heart,	
	I think you are happy in this second match,	
	For it excels your first – or if it did not,	
	Your first is dead, or 'twere as good he were,	
	As living here, and you no use of him.	225

| JULIET | Speak'st thou from thy heart? | |

| NURSE | And from my soul too – else beshrew them both. | |

| JULIET | Amen! | |

| NURSE | What? | |

JULIET	Well, thou hast comforted me marvellous much.	230
	Go in, and tell my lady I am gone,	
	Having displeased my father, to Lawrence' cell –	
	To make confession and to be absolved.	

| NURSE | Marry, I will; and this is wisely done. | |

Exit.

JULIET	Ancient damnation! O most wicked fiend!	235
	Is it more sin to wish me thus forsworn,	
	Or to dispraise my lord with that same tongue	
	Which she hath praised him with above compare	
	So many thousand times? Go, counsellor! –	
	Thou and my bosom henceforth shall be twain.	240
	I'll to the Friar, to know his remedy.	
	If all else fail, myself have power to die.	

Exit.

In this scene ...

- Juliet arrives at the Friar's cell. After a brief conversation with Paris, she asks the Friar for help.
- Seeing how desperate Juliet is, the Friar suggests a plan. Juliet is to take a potion which will make it appear as though she is dead. She will be laid in the Capulet tomb. The Friar will write to Romeo, who can then come and collect her secretly. She eagerly agrees.

Juliet arrives at the Friar's cell just as Paris is discussing arrangements for the wedding.

THINK ABOUT for GCSE

Structure and form

- What have the Friar and Paris been talking about before the scene begins? What might have been in the Friar's mind when Paris arrived?

Themes and issues

- What do Juliet and the Friar mean by 'What must be shall be. / That's a certain text.' (line 21)? How do their words tie in with the theme of **fate** running through the play?

2 **father**: i.e. father-in-law to be

3 **nothing ... haste**: very keen not to slow him down

5 **Uneven ... course**: This is an irregular way of going about things

8 **Venus ... tears**: i.e. people in mourning do not want to think about love

9 **counts**: considers

10 **do give ... sway**: gives way to her sorrow so much

12 **inundation**: flood

13 **minded**: thought about

14 **put ... society**: driven away by company

16 **would**: wish

18 **Happily**: Fortunately

21 **certain text**: true saying

Friar Lawrence's cell.

Enter FRIAR LAWRENCE, *with Count* PARIS.

FR. LAWRENCE On Thursday, sir? The time is very short.

PARIS My father Capulet will have it so,
And I am nothing slow to slack his haste.

[handwritten: very keen, not to slow him down]

FR. LAWRENCE You say you do not know the lady's mind?
Uneven is the course: I like it not.   5

[handwritten: You say you don't know what the girl thinks.]
[handwritten: That's a rocky road to be riding. I don't like it.]

PARIS Immoderately she weeps for Tybalt's death,
And therefore have I little talked of love,
For Venus smiles not in a house of tears.
Now, sir, her father counts it dangerous
That she do give her sorrow so much sway,   10
And in his wisdom hastes our marriage,
To stop the inundation of her tears –
Which, too much minded by herself alone,
May be put from her by society.
Now do you know the reason of this haste.   15

[handwritten: She's grieving too much over the death of Tybalt.]
[handwritten: So I haven't had the chance to talk of love.]
[handwritten: Romantic love doesn't happen when people are in mourning.]
[handwritten: Now, sir, her father thinks it's dangerous]
[handwritten: that she allows herself to become so sad.]
[handwritten: He's being smart by rushing our marriage to stop her from crying]
[handwritten: She cries too much by herself.]
[handwritten: If she had someone to be with her, she would stop crying.]
[handwritten: Now you know the reason for the rush.]

FR. LAWRENCE (*Aside*) I would I knew not why it should be slowed. –
Look, sir, here comes the lady toward my cell.

[handwritten: I wish I didn't know the reason why the marriage should be slowed down.]
[handwritten: Look, sir, here comes Juliet.]

Enter JULIET.

PARIS Happily met, my lady and my wife!

[handwritten: Fortunately met,]

JULIET That may be, sir, when I may be a wife.

[handwritten: That may be the case sir, after I'm married]

PARIS That 'may be' must be, love, on Thursday next.   20

JULIET What must be shall be.

[handwritten: will be]

FR. LAWRENCE   That's a certain text.

[handwritten: That's a true saying]

PARIS Come you to make confession to this father?

[handwritten: Have you come to make confession to this father?]

JULIET To answer that, I should confess to you.

[handwritten: If I answered that question, I'd be making confession to you.]

PARIS Do not deny to him that you love me.

JULIET I will confess to you that I love him.   25

[handwritten: Friar   Romeo]

171

Juliet responds coldly to Paris's words of love. When Paris leaves, she begs the Friar's help, threatening to kill herself immediately if all else fails.

THINK ABOUT for GCSE

Relationships

- What is your opinion of Paris's behaviour with Juliet? Think about whether he seems over-possessive, for example, or if he is simply behaving as a fiancé should.

Characterisation

- How do you think Paris might feel when he thinks back to this meeting with the Friar and Juliet? How might he interpret Juliet's behaviour?

Structure and form

- In what ways does Paris's arrival at the Friar's cell add tension at this point, making us realise how urgent it is that some solution to Juliet's predicament should be found?

27 **price**: value

29 **abused**: spoiled

31 **spite**: meanness in harming it

33 **slander**: unfair criticism
34 **to my face**: 1 about my face; 2 openly

39 **My leisure serves me**: I am free
   pensive: 1 thoughtful; 2 sad
40 **entreat**: ask for
41 **shield**: forbid

46 **thy grief**: the cause of your grief
47 **It strains ... wits**: I have racked my brains without success
48 **prorogue**: postpone

53 **resolution**: determination
54 **presently**: at once

56 **ere**: before
   sealed: joined

PARIS	So will ye, I am sure, that you love me.
JULIET	If I do so, it will be of more price,
	Being spoke behind your back, than to your face.

that I do so, it will mean more if I say it behind
your back than if I say it to your face.

PARIS	Poor soul, thy face is much abused with tears.

You poor soul your face has suffered many tears.

JULIET	The tears have got small victory by that, 30
	For it was bad enough before their spite.

The tears haven't done much because my face was/looks
bad enough before I started to cry

PARIS	Thou wrong'st it more than tears with that report.

You're wrecking your face even worse by saying that.

JULIET	That is no slander, sir, which is a truth,
	And what I spake, I spake it to my face.

And what I said, I said to my face (openly)

PARIS	Thy face is mine, and thou hast slandered it. 35

Your face is mine, and you have unfairly criticised it

JULIET	It may be so, for it is not mine own. –
	Are you at leisure, holy Father, now,
	Or shall I come to you at evening mass?

That may be the case, because my face doesn't belong
to me
Do you have time for me now, Father, or
should I come to you at evening mass?

FR. LAWRENCE	My leisure serves me, pensive daughter, now.
	My lord, we must entreat the time alone. 40

I'm free, my sad daughter
My lord we must ask you to leave us alone.

PARIS	God shield I should disturb devotion.
	Juliet, on Thursday early will I rouse ye –
	Till then, adieu, and keep this holy kiss.

God forbid I should prevent sacred devotion.

He kisses her.

Exit.

JULIET	O, shut the door, and when thou hast done so,
②	Come weep with me – past hope, past cure, past help! 45

This mess is beyond hope, beyond
cure, beyond help

FR. LAWRENCE	O Juliet, I already know thy grief –
	It strains me past the compass of my wits.
	I hear thou must – and nothing may prorogue it –
	On Thursday next be married to this County.

It's a problem too hard for me to solve.
I hear that you must – and nobody can delay it –
marry the Count on next Thursday

JULIET	Tell me not, Friar, that thou hearest of this, 50
	Unless thou tell me how I may prevent it.
	If in thy wisdom thou canst give no help,
	Do thou but call my resolution wise,
	And with this knife I'll help it presently.
	God joined my heart and Romeo's, thou our hands. 55
	And ere this hand, by thee to Romeo's sealed,

Don't tell me that you've heard about this marriage
Friar, unless you can tell me how to prevent it.
If you who are so wise can't help, please be kind
enough to call my solution wise
And with this knife I'll solve the problem
You joined our hands

And this hand, by you sealed to Romeo's
before

173

Juliet declares that she will go along with any plan of the Friar's, however desperate. He gives her a potion.

THINK ABOUT *for* **GCSE**

Performance and staging

- How could the actor playing Juliet perform lines 44 to 88? In particular, what could she do at line 62?

Characterisation

- What might the Friar be thinking as Juliet speaks? Think about how he arrives at the plan he tells Juliet about from line 89, for example.

57 **label ... deed**: seal to another marriage contract

59 **this**: i.e. the knife

60 **time**: life

61 **present counsel**: immediate advice

62 **'Twixt ... me**: between me and the desperate situation I am in

63 **arbitrating**: making a final decision about

64 **commission**: authority
   art: skill

65 **issue ... honour**: honourable conclusion

68 **Hold**: Wait

69 **craves ... execution**: requires you to do something as desperate

70 **that ... prevent**: i.e. killing yourself or committing bigamy

74 **chide away**: i.e. drive off

75 **cop'st with**: i.e. are prepared to face
   scape from it: escape from the disgrace of marrying Paris

79 **thievish ways**: places where you find thieves

81 **charnel house**: building in which old skulls and bones were stored when new graves were being dug in the churchyard

83 **reeky shanks**: stinking shin-bones
   chapless: with lower jaws missing

85 **shroud**: sheet in which the corpse was wrapped

88 **unstained**: pure / chaste

91 **look ... lie**: make sure you sleep

93 **vial**: small bottle / flask

94 **distilling**: refined into a spirit

95 **presently**: immediately

And before I am married to another man

Shall be the label to another deed,

my heart will revolt

Or my true heart with treacherous revolt

Turn to another, this shall slay them both!

You are wise and you have so much experience.

Therefore, out of thy long-experienced time,   60

Give me some advice about the current situation, or watch

Give me some present counsel – or, behold,

caught between these two difficulties I'll act
like a judge with my bloody knife

'Twixt my extremes and me, this bloody knife

I will truly and honestly resolve me

Shall play the umpire, arbitrating that

situation that you can't fix, despite your experience.

Which the commission of thy years and art

Could to no issue of true honour bring.   65

Don't wait long to speak. I want to die.

Be not so long to speak. I long to die –

if what you say isn't another solution

If what thou speak'st speak not of remedy.

FR. LAWRENCE Hold, daughter. – I do spy a kind of hope,

But we must act boldly because the situation is so
desperate

Which craves as desperate an execution

As that is desperate which we would prevent.   70

If you have made up your mind to kill yourself

If, rather than to marry County Paris,

instead of marrying County Paris

Thou hast the strength of will to slay thyself,

Then you'll probably be willing to my
same time... the death to solve this shameful problem

Then is it likely thou wilt undertake

A thing *like* death to chide away this shame –

you are prepared to face death to escape from it. from
the disgrace of

That cop'st with death himself to scape from it.   75

And if you dare to do it I'll give you the solution marrying Paris

And, if thou dar'st, I'll give thee remedy.

JULIET *oh you can tell me to jump off the battle posts of*
any tower than marry Paris

O, bid me leap, rather than marry Paris,

From off the battlements of any tower –

Or in walk down crime-ridden streets or tell me to

Or walk in thievish ways, or bid me lurk

Stay Where serpents are! Chain me with roaring bears,   80

morgue – place were dead bodies were
stored

Or hide me nightly in a charnel house,

shrinking ship bones shanks without lever jaws

O'ercovered quite with dead men's rattling bones,

With reeky shanks and yellow chapless skulls!

death sheet

Or bid me go into a new-made grave,

And hide me with a dead man in his shroud! –   85

Things that, to hear them told, have made me tremble –

love death

And I will do it, without fear or doubt,

Pure wife to my sweet love

To live an unstained wife to my sweet love.

FR. LAWRENCE Hold, then. Go home, be merry, give consent

tell them you agree to marry Paris

To marry Paris. Wednesday is tomorrow.   90

Tomorrow night make sure that you are alone.

Tomorrow night look that thou lie alone.

Don't let the Nurse stay with you in your bedroom

Let not the Nurse lie with thee in thy chamber.

small flask

Take thou this *vial*, being then in bed,

mix vial into liquor & drink.

And this distilling liquor drink thou off –

When presently through all thy veins shall run   95

A cold, sleep-inducing drug will run through your veins

175

The potion will cause Juliet to seem dead. She will be placed in the Capulet tomb and, when she wakes, can go with Romeo to Mantua. Juliet readily agrees and the Friar promises to send letters to tell Romeo what is going on.

96 **humour**: fluid
97 **native progress**: natural rate
    surcease: stop
98 **testify**: give evidence that
100 **wanny**: pale
    windows: shutters (i.e. lids)
102 **supple government**: control of movement
104 **borrowed likeness**: imitation

108 **there ... dead**: they will find you (apparently) dead
109 **manner**: custom
110 **uncovered**: with your face uncovered
    bier: funeral carriage
113 **against**: in preparation for the time when
114 **drift**: intentions
116 **watch thy waking**: watch over you until you wake up
117 **bear thee hence**: carry you off
119 **inconstant toy**: whim making you change your mind
120 **Abate**: lessen
    valour: courage
122 **prosperous**: fortunate

125 **afford**: provide

THINK ABOUT for GCSE

Characterisation

• What are the strengths and weaknesses of the Friar's plan? How far is he protecting himself, do you think?

• What does Juliet's reaction to the plan at line 121 reveal about her?

176

And your pulse will stop
A cold and drowsy humour: for no pulse
Shall keep his native progress, but surcease.
Your flesh will be cold, and you'll stop breathing
No warmth, no breath, shall testify thou livest.
turn pale
The roses in thy lips and cheeks shall fade
and your eyes' windows will shut
To wanny ashes, thy eyes' windows fall   **100**
It will seem like you're dead
Like death when he shuts up the day of life.
and your body will be stiff like a corpse.   *won't be able to move*
Each part, deprived of supple government,
Shall, stiff and stark and cold, appear like death,
You'll remain in this death-like state for
And in this borrowed likeness of shrunk death
42 hours, and then you'll
Thou shalt continue two and forty hours –   **105**
wake up as if from a pleasant sleep.
And then awake as from a pleasant sleep.
Now, when the bridegroom in the morning comes
you'll seem dead
To rouse thee from thy bed, there art thou, dead.
Then, as tradition demands, you'll be dressed up,
Then, as the manner of our country is,
in your best clothes, put in an open coffin,
In thy best robes, uncovered on the bier,   **110**
and carried to the Capulet family tomb.
Thou shalt be borne to that same ancient vault
Where all the kindred of the Capulets lie.
Meanwhile, I'll send Romeo word of our plan.
In the meantime, against thou shalt awake,
Shall Romeo by my letters know our drift,
He'll come here, and we'll both watch for when you
And hither shall he come. And he and I   **115**
wake up.
Will watch thy waking, and that very night
That night, Romeo will take you away to Mantua.
Shall Romeo bear thee hence to Mantua.
This plan will free you from the shameful situation
And this shall free thee from this present shame,
that troubles you now as long as   you don't change your
If no inconstant toy nor womanish fear   *mind, or ruin*
(as long as a silly weakness +
before scared like
Abate thy valour in the acting it.   *your brave effort*   **120**

(list her fears
→ JULIET ✐   *Give me the vial! Don't talk to me about fear!*
             Give me, give me! O, tell not me of fear!

FR. LAWRENCE Hold. Get you gone. Be strong and prosperous
             In this resolve. I'll send a friar with speed
             To Mantua, with my letters to thy *Romeo* lord.

JULIET   Love give me strength! – and strength shall help afford!   **125**
             Farewell, dear Father!

                                                         Exeunt.

In this scene ...

- Juliet returns home and tells her father that she has seen the Friar and is now sorry for her disobedience.
- Capulet excitedly gives instructions that the wedding will now take place the following day and goes to inform Paris.

Juliet returns home to find her father making preparations for the wedding. She says that, after speaking to the Friar, she wishes to ask forgiveness for her earlier disobedience.

2 **cunning**: skilful

3 **none ill**: no bad ones
   try: test

6–7 **lick ... fingers**: i.e. it shows that they are confident in their own cooking

10 **much unfurnished**: extremely unprepared

12 **Ay, forsooth**: She certainly has

14 **A peevish ... is**: She is a moody, stubborn little good-for-nothing

15 **shrift**: confession

16 **gadding**: running around enjoying yourself

19 **behests**: commands
    enjoined: instructed

Structure and form

- What does Capulet's dialogue with the servants (lines 1 to 9) add to the beginning of this scene? In productions it is often cut. What would be gained and lost by cutting it?

178

The Capulet house.

Enter CAPULET, LADY CAPULET, *the* NURSE, *and three* SERVANTS.

CAPULET	*(Giving a paper to a servant)* So many guests invite as here are writ.

Invite all the guests on this list

Exit SERVANT.

(To another SERVANT*)* Sirrah, go hire me twenty cunning cooks.

Boy, go hire 20 skilled cooks

SERVANT   You shall have none ill, sir, for I'll try if they can lick their fingers.

You won't get any bad cooks from me. I'll test them by making them lick their fingers

CAPULET   How canst thou try them so?   5

How can you test them like that?

SERVANT   Marry, sir, 'tis an ill cook that cannot lick his own fingers! Therefore he that cannot lick his own fingers goes not with me.

Easy sir, it's a bad cook who can't lick his own fingers! Some cooks who can't lick their fingers aren't hired.

CAPULET   Go, be gone.

Exit SERVANT.

We shall be much unfurnished for this time.   10
What, is my daughter gone to Friar Lawrence?

We're unprepared for this wedding celebration
What, has my daughter gone to see Friar Lawrence.

NURSE   Ay, forsooth.

She certainly has

CAPULET   Well, he may chance to do some good on her. | *Is this*
A peevish, self-willed harlotry it is! | *She's a stubborn moody little brat.* | *true?*

Enter JULIET.

NURSE   See where she comes from shrift with merry look.   15

Look, she's come home from confession with a happy look.

CAPULET   How now, my headstrong? Where have you been gadding?

So, my headstrong daughter, where have you been?

JULIET   *(Kneeling to her father)* Where I have learnt me to repent the sin
Of disobedient opposition
To you and your behests, and am enjoined

I went somewhere where I learned that being disobedient to my father is a sin
Holy Friar Lawrence instructed me to fall on my knees and beg your forgiveness

real?
why
does she do this?

Capulet is so delighted at Juliet's change of heart that he gives orders for the wedding to take place the following day. He joyfully promises to oversee the wedding preparations himself and bustles off to inform Paris.

20 **fall prostrate**: i.e. kneel down

22 **am ever … you**: will always do as you say

24 **this knot**: i.e. the 'marriage-knot'

26 **becomèd**: appropriate
27 **stepping … modesty**: doing anything improper

32 **is … to him**: owes him a great debt

33 **closet**: private room
34 **sort**: select
    needful: necessary
35 **to furnish me**: for me to wear

38 **be … provision**: not have enough food ready

39 **Tush**: Nonsense
    stir about: stay up and get things done
40 **warrant**: assure
41 **deck up**: dress
42 **Let me alone**: Leave everything to me

44 **forth**: out of the house

46 **Against**: for
47 **reclaimed**: i.e. obedient once again

THINK ABOUT for GCSE

Performance and staging

• What advice would you give to the actor playing Capulet on how he should (a) behave with the servants (lines 1 to 9); (b) talk about Juliet before she enters (lines 11 to 14); (c) address Juliet (line 16); and (d) react to her (lines 23 to 24, 28 to 32, and 37)?

	By holy Lawrence to fall prostrate here	20
	To beg your pardon. Pardon, I beseech you!	
	Henceforward I am ever ruled by you.	
CAPULET	Send for the County! Go, tell him of this.	
	I'll have this knot knit up tomorrow morning!	
JULIET	I met the youthful lord at Lawrence' cell,	25
	And gave him what becomèd love I might,	
	Not stepping o'er the bounds of modesty.	
CAPULET	Why, I am glad on't! This is well. Stand up.	
	This is as 't should be. Let me see the County! –	
	Ay, marry, go, I say, and fetch him hither.	30
	Now, afore God, this reverend holy Friar –	
	All our whole city is much bound to him!	
JULIET	Nurse, will you go with me into my closet	
	To help me sort such needful ornaments	
	As you think fit to furnish me tomorrow?	35
LADY CAPULET	No, not till Thursday. There is time enough.	
CAPULET	Go, Nurse, go with her. We'll to church tomorrow.	

Exit JULIET, **with the** NURSE.

LADY CAPULET	We shall be short in our provision.	
	'Tis now near night.	
CAPULET	Tush, I will stir about,	
	And all things shall be well, I warrant thee, wife.	40
	Go thou to Juliet. Help to deck up her.	
	I'll not to bed tonight. Let me alone –	
	I'll play the housewife for this once! (*Calling for the servants*) What ho! –	
	They are all forth. – Well, I will walk myself	
	To County Paris, to prepare up him	45
	Against tomorrow. My heart is wondrous light	
	Since this same wayward girl is so reclaimed!	

Exeunt.

In this scene ...

- Juliet prepares for bed and says goodnight to her mother and the Nurse.
- Juliet overcomes her fears and drinks the potion.

Juliet says goodnight to her mother and the Nurse. Left alone, she anxiously thinks about what might happen if the potion does not work. It occurs to her that the Friar might be trying to poison her, to avoid having to marry her a second time, illegally.

THINK ABOUT for GCSE

Characterisation

- The Nurse thinks that Juliet is going to marry Paris even though she is already married to Romeo, committing both a serious crime and a sin. Shakespeare gives her no lines here, but what might she be thinking?

Relationships

- Lady Capulet says very little, but how should she behave towards Juliet, and how should her daughter react to her? Think about their earlier behaviour.

1   **attires**: clothes

3   **orisons**: prayers
4   **move**: persuade
     state: situation
5   **cross**: wrong

7   **culled such necessaries**: selected what we need
8   **behoveful**: suitable and needed
     state: wedding ceremony

12   **sudden**: unexpectedly quick

15   **faint cold**: causing faintness and chill
     thrills: shivers

19   **dismal**: dreadful
20   **vial**: small bottle / flask (containing the potion)

25   **Subtly hath ministered**: has cunningly prescribed for me
26   **Lest ... dishonoured**: for fear of his being disgraced by this wedding

ACT 4 SCENE 3

Juliet's bedroom.

Enter JULIET *and the* NURSE.

JULIET   Ay, those attires are best. But, gentle Nurse,
                I pray thee leave me to myself tonight,
                For I have need of many orisons   *prayers*
                To move the heavens to smile upon my state,
You know that my life is troubled + full of sin Which well thou knowest is cross and full of sin.   5

Enter LADY CAPULET.

LADY CAPULET   What, are you busy, ho? Need you my help?
                                we have selected what we need for tomoro
JULIET   No, madam – we have culled such necessaries
                As are behoveful for our state tomorrow.
                So please you, let me now be left alone,
let the nurse sit up with you tonight And let the Nurse this night sit up with you –   10
                For I am sure you have your hands full all
                In this so sudden business.

LADY CAPULET   Good night.
                Get thee to bed and rest, for thou hast need.

                                        Exit, with the NURSE.

                        only God knows when we'll meet again
JULIET   Farewell. – God knows when we shall meet again.
There is a slight cold fear cutting through my veins. I have a faint cold fear thrills through my veins,   15
J. Lavins   That almost freezes up the heat of life. *It almost freezes the heat of life.*
2nd *I'll call them back here to comfort me.* I'll call them back again to comfort me.
maybe   *oh what good would she do here?*
                (*She calls*) Nurse! – What should she do here?
from desperate situation, I have to act alone My dismal scene I needs must act alone.
                Come, vial.   20
                What if this mixture do not work at all?
                Shall I be married then tomorrow morning?
                No, no. – (*Taking out her knife*) This shall forbid it.
                    (*Placing the knife inside the curtain by her bed*)
                Lie thou there. *what if the Friar mixed the potion to kill me?*
                What if it be a poison which the Friar
                Subtly hath ministered to have me dead,   25
                Lest in this marriage he should be dishonoured
Is he worried that he will be disgraced if

183

Juliet is terrified at the thought of suffocating in the tomb, or going mad with fear when she wakes to find herself surrounded by bones. Imagining Tybalt's ghost looking for Romeo, she drinks the potion.

29 **still been tried**: always proved to be

32 **redeem**: rescue
33 **stifled**: suffocated
34 **healthsome**: fresh / wholesome
35 **strangled ere**: choked before

37 **conceit**: thoughts / idea

39 **receptacle**: collecting place

42 **green in earth**: newly buried
43 **shroud**: burial sheet
44 **resort**: gather

47 **mandrakes**: roots shaped like a man (It was believed that, if someone pulled one out of the ground, it would scream and the person would go mad.)
49 **distraught**: driven mad
50 **Environed with**: surrounded by
53 **rage**: madness

56 **spit**: pierce / skewer
57 **Stay**: Stop

THINK ABOUT for GCSE

Language

- Juliet's fears seem like nightmares. Which of her descriptions do you find most effective here?

- How is language used to (a) describe the terrifying scenes she is imagining; and (b) convey her fear? Look, for example, at verb tenses, the repetition of 'I', choice of vocabulary, and her description of imagined situations.

I am to marry Paris after he married me to Romeo?
Because he married me before to Romeo?
I'm afraid that it's poison
I fear it is. And yet methinks it should not,
Friar is a trustworthy + holy man.
For he hath still been tried a holy man.
when when I am put in the tomb, I
How if, when I am laid into the tomb,
wake up before Romeo comes to save me?
I wake before the time that Romeo   **30**
That's a frightening idea!
Come to redeem me? There's a fearful point!
Won't I suffocate in the tomb?
Shall I not then be stifled in the vault,
There's no healthy air to breathe in here.
To whose foul mouth no healthsome air breathes in,
will I die of suffocation (choked) before Romeo
And there die strangled ere my Romeo comes?   **35**
comes?
or will I live
Or, if I live, is it not very like
I'll be surrounded by thoughts of death + darkness
The horrible conceit of death and night,
It will be terrible
Together with the terror of the place –
As in a vault, an ancient receptacle,
Where, for this many hundred years, the bones   **40**
Of all my buried ancestors are packed –
Tybalt's body will be in here freshly entombed,
Where bloody Tybalt, yet but green in earth,
his corpse will be rotting. They say that
Lies festering in his shroud – where, as they say,
during the night, the spirits are in tombs.
At some hours in the night spirits resort –
Alack, alack! – Is it not like that I,   **45**
I'll wake up + smell awful odors.
So early waking – what with loathsome smells,
I'll hear screams that would drive people crazy
And shrieks like mandrakes torn out of the earth,
That living mortals, hearing them run mad –
If I wake too early, won't I go insane
O! – If I wake, shall I not be distraught,
with all these horrible, frightening things around me.
Environed with all these hideous fears,   **50**
Start playing with my ancestors's bones, +
And madly play with my forefathers' joints,
pulling Tybalt's corpse out of his death shroud?
And pluck the mangled Tybalt from his shroud! –
will I grab one of my dead ancestor's bones +
And in this rage, with some great kinsman's bone,
bash in my own skull?
As with a club, dash out my desperate brains?
I think I see my cousin's Tybalt's
O look! – Methinks I see my cousin's ghost,   **55**
ghost.
He's looking for Romeo because
Seeking out Romeo that did spit his body
Romeo killed him with his sword.
Upon a rapier's point. Stay, Tybalt! Stay! –
Romeo! Romeo, Romeo! Here's drink! – I drink to thee!

She drinks the drug and falls onto her bed.

① – Describe how J. feels.
② – Lang-lang of nightmares (ll. 30 – 58)
③ What's nightmares / things she fears happening to her
    which is most effective + why

④ why is it imp. that Shakespeare includes this scene
                                    – build up tension/suspense
                      – Juliet fears of:
                      – determined to be with
                                                      Romeo

In this scene ...

- Early next morning the household is busy preparing for the wedding when music is heard outside: Paris has arrived to take Juliet to church.

At three o'clock in the morning, Capulet is fussily supervising last-minute preparations for the wedding.

2 **pastry**: pastry-room in the kitchen

3 **stir**: get a move on
4 **curfew bell**: bell rung when the watch patrol went on or off duty
5 **baked meats**: pies
   Angelica: probably the Nurse's name
6 **cot-quean**: man who interferes with household matters (a woman's job in those days)
8 **watching**: staying awake
9 **not a whit**: not at all

11 **mouse-hunt**: i.e. woman-chaser
12 **watch you**: keep an eye on you

13 **jealous-hood**: jealous woman

THINK ABOUT for GCSE

Relationships

- What does the exchange between Capulet and the Nurse (lines 5 to 10) suggest about their relationship?

Performance and staging

- How would you direct the actor playing Lady Capulet to say lines 11 to 12? Is she joking, bitter, threatening, or something else?

The great hall of the Capulet house.

Enter LADY CAPULET *with the* NURSE *(carrying a basket of herbs).*

hustle/bustle

nervous energy

Morning of wedding. — *imagine atmosphere* — *excitement* — *preparation taking place* — *business* — *tension*

LADY CAPULET	Hold, take these keys and fetch more spices, Nurse.

Take these keys + get more spices

NURSE	They call for dates and quinces in the pastry.

Enter CAPULET.

CAPULET	Come, stir, stir, stir! The second cock hath crowed,	
	The curfew bell hath rung, 'tis three o'clock.	
	Look to the baked meats, good Angelica! –	5
	Spare not for cost.	

get a move on!

Don't worry about the cost.

NURSE	Go, you cot-quean, go!
	Get you to bed. Faith, you'll be sick to-morrow
	For this night's watching.

you old housewife, go?

staying up all night

CAPULET	No, not a whit. What! I have watched ere now	
	All night for lesser cause and ne'er been sick.	10

Not at all. I have stayed up all night many times, before, for less important matters, + I've never gotten sick.

LADY CAPULET	Ay, you have been a mouse-hunt in your time,
	But I will watch you from such watching now.

you've been a ladies' man in your time, I'll make sure you don't stay up any later now.

Exit, with the NURSE.

CAPULET	A jealous-hood, a jealous-hood!

jealous woman

Enter three SERVANTS, *carrying cooking-spits, firewood, and baskets.*

Now, fellow, what is there?

SERVANT	Things for the cook, sir, but I know not what.

CAPULET	Make haste, make haste, sirrah! Fetch drier logs.	15
	Call Peter – he will show thee where they are.	

Exit SERVANT. *Another follows.*

SERVANT	I have a head, sir, that will find out logs –
	And never trouble Peter for the matter.

I'm smart enough to find the logs myself without bothering Peter.

187

Hearing Paris approach with the musicians, Capulet tells the Nurse to hurry off and wake Juliet up.

19 **Mass**: By the mass (a common oath)
    whoreson: rogue
20 **loggerhead**: blockhead
21 **straight**: straight away

24 **trim her up**: get her ready

THINK ABOUT for GCSE

Structure and form

- Very little happens in this scene, so what are its purposes? Compare it with the scenes which come before and after it, for example.

CAPULET   Mass, and well said! – a merry whoreson, ha!
           Sweet, + well said!   *A funny rogue, ha!*
           Thou shalt be loggerhead! (*Exit* SERVANT) – Good faith,
           He's a lock head
           'tis day!   20
           The County will be here with music straight,
           Count   *head full of logs - joke*   *strings on way*
           For so he said he would. (*Faint sounds of music are
               heard*) – I hear him near.
           Nurse! Wife! What ho! What, Nurse, I say!

Enter the NURSE.

           Go waken Juliet! – go, and trim her up.
                                    get her ready
           I'll go and chat with Paris. Hie, make haste,   25
           Make haste! The bridegroom he is come already.
           Make haste, I say!

                                                            Exit.

           The NURSE *goes directly to Juliet's bedroom.*

- what purpose of scene - build up tension
          - Show preparations in
            advance of wedding day
        - Show how happy + excited
Film director   J's parents are that she
- Should film scene   is going to be marrying
- 2 reasons why to   Paris
  cut it
                    - Does it suggest they are
- 2 reasons why to   selfish + only want their
  keep it   own wishes fulfilled or do
                      they really feel Paris is
                      best for J ?

189

In this scene ...

- When the Nurse goes to wake Juliet, she finds her apparently dead.
- Paris and the Friar enter to find the Capulets grief-stricken over Juliet's death.
- As the family go off to prepare for a funeral, Peter jokes with the musicians.

The Nurse comes to wake Juliet, but the potion has worked and Juliet appears to be dead.

1   **Fast**: Fast asleep

4   **pennyworths**: small quantities (i.e. what little sleep you can get)
6   **set up his rest**: made up his mind

10 **take you**: 1 find you; 2 have sex with you
11 **fright you up**: frighten you into getting up
12 **down again**: lying down on your bed again
13 **I must needs**: I'll have to
15 **well-a-day**: an expression of grief
16 **aqua-vitae**: strong spirits (brandy)

THINK ABOUT for **GCSE**

Performance and staging

- On stage there are many ways in which the Nurse can come to realise that Juliet is 'dead'. Do you think she should realise gradually or suddenly? When does she know for certain?

20 **look up**: open your eyes

Juliet's bedroom.

NURSE	(*Going in and calling*) Mistress! What, mistress! – Fast,
	I warrant her, she.
	Why, lamb! Why, lady! Fie, you slug-a-bed!
	Why, love, I say! Madam! Sweetheart! Why, bride!
	What, not a word? You take your pennyworths now.
	Sleep for a week – for the next night, I warrant, 5
	The County Paris hath set up his rest
	That you shall rest but little. – God forgive me!
	Marry, and amen! How sound is she asleep!
	I needs must wake her. Madam, madam, madam!
	Ay – let the County take you in your bed – 10
	He'll fright you up, i' faith. Will it not be?

She pulls aside the bed-curtain.

	What, dressed, and in your clothes, and down again?
	I must needs wake you. Lady, lady, lady!
	Alas, alas! Help, help! My lady's dead!
	O well-a-day that ever I was born! 15
	Some aqua-vitae, ho! My lord! My lady!

Enter LADY CAPULET.

LADY CAPULET	What noise is here?
NURSE	O lamentable day!
LADY CAPULET	What is the matter?
NURSE	Look, look! O heavy day!
LADY CAPULET	O me, O me! My child, my only life!
	Revive, look up, or I will die with thee! 20
	Help, help! Call help!

Enter CAPULET.

CAPULET	For shame, bring Juliet forth. Her lord is come.
NURSE	She's dead, deceased! She's dead, alack the day!
LADY CAPULET	Alack the day, she's dead, she's dead, she's dead!

Paris arrives with the Friar, to find Juliet's parents grieving at their daughter's death.

26 is settled: has stopped flowing

28 untimely: out of season (i.e. too early)

36 lain with: had sex with
37 deflowerèd by him: lost her virginity to him (i.e. death)

40 living: property
41 thought long: i.e. been impatient

THINK ABOUT *for* **GCSE**

Characterisation

• What might each of the following characters be thinking at the moment the Friar enters with Paris (line 32): Capulet, Lady Capulet, the Nurse, the Friar, and Paris?

Language

• What picture of Death does Capulet seem to have formed? Look at lines 28 to 29, and 31 to 40.

45 lasting … pilgrimage: the unending toil of his journey
46 But one: I had only one
47 solace: find comfort
48 catched: snatched

Capulet	Ha, let me see her! Out, alas! She's cold! –	25

Capulet Ha, let me see her! Out, alas! She's cold! – 25
Her blood is settled, and her joints are stiff.
Life and these lips have long been separated.
Death lies on her like an untimely frost
Upon the sweetest flower of all the field.

Nurse O lamentable day!

Lady Capulet O woeful time! 30

Capulet Death, that hath ta'en her hence to make me wail,
Ties up my tongue and will not let me speak.

Enter Friar Lawrence *and Count* Paris, *followed by* Musicians, *for the wedding.*

Fr. Lawrence Come, is the bride ready to go to church?

Capulet Ready to go, but never to return.
O son, the night before thy wedding day 35
Hath Death lain with thy wife. There she lies,
Flower as she was, deflowerèd by him.
Death is my son-in-law, Death is my heir.
My daughter he hath wedded. I will die
And leave him all. Life, living – all is Death's! 40

Paris Have I thought long to see this morning's face,
And doth it give me such a sight as this?

Lady Capulet Accursed, unhappy, wretched, hateful day!
Most miserable hour that e'er time saw
In lasting labour of his pilgrimage. 45
But one, poor one, one poor and loving child –
But one thing to rejoice and solace in,
And cruel Death hath catched it from my sight!

Nurse O woe! O woeful, woeful, woeful day!
Most lamentable day, most woeful day 50
That ever, ever I did yet behold!
O day, O day, O day, O hateful day!
Never was seen so black a day as this.
O woeful day, O woeful day!

The Friar tries to stop people grieving, offering them the comfort that Juliet is now in heaven. Capulet prepares for a funeral rather than the expected wedding.

55 **Beguiled**: Cheated

59 **martyred**: punished by death
60 **Uncomfortable**: Pitiless
61 **murder our solemnity**: ruin our wedding feast with death

65 **Confusion's cure**: The cure for your great loss
66 **confusions**: wild cries of grief
67 **part**: a share
70 **his part**: i.e. her soul
71 **promotion**: moving up in the world (by marrying Paris)
72 **heaven**: i.e. greatest happiness
    be advanced: move higher up in society
75 **this love**: i.e. the love that mourns her death
76 **well**: happy (often used of those who are dead)
77–8 **She's not … young** : i.e. a woman who dies young is best 'married' to heaven
79 **rosemary**: the herb of remembrance, used at weddings and funerals
80 **corse**: corpse
81 **array**: clothes
82 **fond … lament**: foolish (and too affectionate) natural feelings cause us to grieve
83 **nature's … merriment**: i.e. it is natural to cry but not sensible, as she is in heaven
84 **ordainèd festival**: i.e. the wedding plans
85 **office**: usual function
87 **cheer**: banquet
88 **sullen dirges**: mournful funeral hymns
90 **contrary**: opposite

THINK ABOUT for GCSE

Context

• What do the Friar's words of consolation (lines 65 to 83) reveal about attitudes to death in Shakespeare's time?

Characterisation

• The commonest words in Capulet's two speeches (lines 59 to 64, and 84 to 90) are 'my' and 'our'. What might that suggest about his reaction to Juliet's supposed death?

Paris	Beguiled, divorcèd, wrongèd, spited, slain! 55
	Most detestable Death, by thee beguiled –
	By cruel, cruel thee quite overthrown!
	O love! O life! – Not life, but love in death!

Capulet   Despised, distressèd, hated, martyred, killed!
Uncomfortable time, why cam'st thou now   60
To murder, murder our solemnity?
O child, O child! My soul, and not my child!
Dead art thou. Alack, my child is dead,
And with my child my joys are burièd.

Fr. Lawrence   Peace, ho, for shame! Confusion's cure lives not   65
In these confusions. Heaven and yourself
Had part in this fair maid: now heaven hath all,
And all the better is it for the maid.
Your part in her you could not keep from death,
But heaven keeps his part in eternal life.   70
The most you sought was her promotion,
For 'twas your heaven she should be advanced.
And weep ye now, seeing she is advanced
Above the clouds, as high as heaven itself?
O, in this love you love your child so ill   75
That you run mad, seeing that she is well.
She's not well married that lives married long,
But she's best married that dies married young.
Dry up your tears, and stick your rosemary
On this fair corse, and, as the custom is,   80
In all her best array bear her to church.
For though fond nature bids us all lament,
Yet nature's tears are reason's merriment.

Capulet   All things that we ordainèd festival
Turn from their office to black funeral: 85
Our instruments to melancholy bells,
Our wedding cheer to a sad burial feast,
Our solemn hymns to sullen dirges change,
Our bridal flowers serve for a buried corse,
And all things change them to the contrary.   90

As the family leave, Peter asks the musicians to play something to console him. He then engages in some wordplay with them.

94 **lour**: look angrily
   ill: sin
95 **Move**: anger
   crossing: defying / going against

96 **may ... gone**: might as well pack up

98 **case**: state of affairs

99 **case may be amended**: 1 things could be better; 2 my instrument case needs repairing

100 **Heart's ease**: a popular song of the time
101 **and**: if

104 **dump**: sad tune
105 **Not ... we**: We're not playing a sad tune
108 **give ... soundly**: pay you out in full
110 **gleek**: gibe / jeer
110–11 **give ... minstrel**: call you worthless wandering musicians (an insult)
112 **serving-creature**: more insulting than 'serving-man'
114 **pate**: head
   carry no crotchets: not put up with any of your games (crotchets are musical notes)
   re ... fa: musical notes
114–15 **Do you note me**: Are you paying attention

THINK ABOUT for GCSE

Performance and staging

- In lines 100 to 104 Peter seems to be sad at Juliet's death, but he soon switches to wordplay with the musicians. How should the actor play this scene, do you think? Should he be sad, but attempting to cover it, for example, or not really affected at all?

196

FR. LAWRENCE   Sir, go you in. And, madam, go with him;
And go, Sir Paris. Everyone prepare
To follow this fair corse unto her grave.
The heavens do lour upon you for some ill:
Move them no more by crossing their high will.   95

They sadly scatter rosemary around JULIET*'s body, and close
the bed-curtain.*

All exit, except the NURSE, *and the* MUSICIANS,
who remain by the door.

MUSICIAN 1   Faith, we may put up our pipes and be gone.

NURSE   Honest good fellows – ah, put up, put up –
For well you know this is a pitiful case.

MUSICIAN 1   Ay, by my troth, the case may be amended.

Exit the NURSE.

Enter PETER.

PETER   Musicians, O musicians, 'Heart's ease', 'Heart's ease'! 100
O, and you will have me live, play 'Heart's ease'!

MUSICIAN 1   Why 'Heart's ease'?

PETER   O musicians, because my heart itself plays 'My heart is
full'. O, play me some merry dump to comfort me.

MUSICIAN 1   Not a dump, we. 'Tis no time to play now.   105

PETER   You will not then?

MUSICIAN 1   No.

PETER   I will then give it you soundly.

MUSICIAN 1   What will you give us?

PETER   No money, on my faith, but the gleek. I will give you 110
the minstrel.

MUSICIAN 1   Then will I give *you* the serving-creature.

PETER   Then will I lay the serving-creature's dagger on your
pate. I will carry no crotchets. I'll re you, I'll fa you! Do
you note me?   115

Peter continues to joke with the musicians. They decide to wait for the mourners to return from the funeral and then join them for dinner.

116 **note us**: 1 pay attention to us; 2 set us to music
117 **put up**: put away
put out: display
118 **dry-beat you**: beat you up without drawing blood
119 **iron wit**: i.e. 'killing', merciless wit
121–3 **When … sound**: the last few lines of a poem in praise of music

125 **Catling**: lute-string (made of cat-gut)

127 **Pretty**: Nice answer
Rebeck: three-stringed fiddle
128 **sound for silver**: play for money
129 **Soundpost**: support inside a stringed instrument

131 **cry you mercy**: beg your pardon
You … singer: i.e. you aren't much of a speaker
133 **for sounding**: 1 as payment for playing; 2 to jingle in their purses
135 **lend redress**: put things right

136 **pestilent knave**: wretched nuisance
137 **Jack**: rogue
tarry: linger
138 **stay**: wait for

THINK ABOUT for GCSE

Structure and form

• In most productions this section with the musicians (lines 96 to 138) is cut. What purpose does it serve? What is gained and lost by cutting it?

MUSICIAN 1	And you re us and fa us, you note us.
MUSICIAN 2	Pray you, put up your dagger, and put out your wit.
PETER	Then have at you with my wit! I will dry-beat you with an iron wit, and put up my iron dagger. Answer me like men:

    'When griping grief the heart doth wound,
    And doleful dumps the mind oppress,
    Then music with her silver sound –'
Why 'silver sound'? Why 'music with her silver sound'?
What say you, Simon Catling?

MUSICIAN 1	Marry, sir, because silver hath a sweet sound.
PETER	Pretty! What say you, Hugh Rebeck?
MUSICIAN 2	I say 'silver sound' because musicians sound for silver.
PETER	Pretty too! What say you, James Soundpost?
MUSICIAN 3	Faith, I know not what to say.
PETER	O, I cry you mercy! You are the singer. I will say for you. It is 'music with her *silver* sound' because musicians have no gold for sounding!

    '– Then music with her silver sound
    With speedy help doth lend redress.'

Exit PETER.

MUSICIAN 1	What a pestilent knave is this same!
MUSICIAN 2	Hang him, Jack! Come, we'll in here, tarry for the mourners, and stay dinner.

Exeunt.

Line numbers: 120, 125, 130, 135

In this scene ...

- Balthasar brings news to Romeo in Mantua that Juliet is dead.
- In desperation, Romeo vows to be with Juliet that night.
- He buys poison from an Apothecary and leaves for Verona.

In Mantua, Romeo thinks about a dream which has made him feel happier. But he is devastated when Balthasar brings news that Juliet is dead, her body lying in the Capulet tomb.

THINK ABOUT for GCSE

Themes and issues

- **Fate:** What do you think Romeo means by 'Then I defy you, stars!' (line 24)? What is he thinking about? Why does he express himself in this way?

- What attitude does Romeo seem to have towards **fate**? Look back at Act 3 Scene 1, line 132 (O, I am fortune's fool!), for example.

1 **flattering**: i.e. because dreams often tell us what we want to believe
2 **presage**: foretell
3 **My bosom's ... throne**: i.e. my heart is full of love
4 **unaccustomed spirit**: unusual feeling
7 **leave**: permission

10 **itself possessed**: enjoyed in reality
11 **love's shadows**: dreams of love

17 **well**: happy (often used of those who are dead)
18 **Capel's monument**: the Capulet tomb
19 **immortal part**: soul
20 **kindred**: family
21 **presently took post**: rode here straight away
23 **for my office**: as my duty
24 **Is it e'en so**: Is that the way things are
26 **post-horses**: the fastest means of transport
28–9 **import ... misadventure**: suggest some future disaster

A street in Mantua.

Enter ROMEO*.*

ROMEO	If I may trust the flattering truth of sleep,
	My dreams presage some joyful news at hand.
	My bosom's lord sits lightly in his throne,
	And all this day an unaccustomed spirit
	Lifts me above the ground with cheerful thoughts. 5
	I dreamt my lady came and found me dead –
	Strange dream, that gives a dead man leave to think! –
	And breathed such life with kisses in my lips
	That I revived and was an emperor.
	Ah me! How sweet is love itself possessed, 10
	When but love's shadows are so rich in joy!

Enter BALTHASAR *(**Romeo's servant), in riding-boots.***

	News from Verona! How now, Balthasar?
	Dost thou not bring me letters from the Friar?
	How doth my lady? Is my father well?
	How fares my Juliet? That I ask again, 15
	For nothing can be ill if she be well.
BALTHASAR	Then she is well, and nothing can be ill.
	Her body sleeps in Capel's monument,
	And her immortal part with angels lives.
	I saw her laid low in her kindred's vault, 20
	And presently took post to tell it you.
	O pardon me for bringing these ill news,
	Since you did leave it for my office, sir.
ROMEO	Is it e'en so? Then I defy you, stars!
	Thou know'st my lodging. Get me ink and paper – 25
	And hire post-horses. I will hence tonight.
BALTHASAR	I do beseech you, sir, have patience.
	Your looks are pale and wild, and do import
	Some misadventure.

Balthasar confirms that he has not brought a letter from the Friar, and leaves on Romeo's orders. Romeo is determined to be with Juliet that night and calls on an Apothecary who can sell him poison.

29 **Tush … deceived**: Nonsense, you're mistaken

34 **lie with**: 1 sleep beside; 2 be with as a lover
35 **Let's … means**: How am I going to do it
37 **apothecary**: pharmacist, who makes up medicines
38 **hereabouts 'a dwells**: he lives somewhere around here
late I noted: I recently spotted
39 **tattered weeds**: ragged clothes
overwhelming brows: overhanging eyebrows
40 **Culling of simples**: gathering herbs for medicine
Meagre … looks: He was thin-looking
42 **needy**: poor
45 **beggarly account**: wretchedly small number
46 **bladders**: used as containers for liquids
47 **Remnants of packthread**: bits of string
cakes of roses: compressed rose petals used as perfume
49 **penury**: poverty
50 **An if**: If
51 **Whose … death**: the sale of which is punishable by immediate execution
52 **caitiff wretch**: wretched creature
53 **forerun**: anticipate
56 **holiday**: a saint's day
59 **ducats**: gold coins
60 **dram**: small quantity
soon-speeding gear: fast-acting stuff

THINK ABOUT for GCSE

Structure and form

- What do you think are the purposes of the detailed description of the Apothecary's shop in lines 37 to 48?

Performance and staging

- If you were staging a production set today, what would your Apothecary and his shop look like?

| ROMEO | Tush, thou art deceived. |
| | Leave me, and do the thing I bid thee do. |

Leave me, and do the thing I bid thee do.   30
Hast thou no letters to me from the Friar?

BALTHASAR   No, my good lord.

ROMEO   No matter. Get thee gone,
And hire those horses. I'll be with thee straight.

Exit BALTHASAR.

Well, Juliet, I will lie with thee tonight.
Let's see for means. O mischief, thou art swift   35
To enter in the thoughts of desperate men!
I do remember an apothecary,
And hereabouts 'a dwells, which late I noted
In tattered weeds, with overwhelming brows,
Culling of simples. Meagre were his looks.   40
Sharp misery had worn him to the bones.
And in his needy shop a tortoise hung,
An alligator stuffed, and other skins
Of ill-shaped fishes – and about his shelves
A beggarly account of empty boxes,   45
Green earthen pots, bladders, and musty seeds,
Remnants of packthread, and old cakes of roses,
Were thinly scattered to make up a show.
Noting this penury, to myself I said:
'An if a man did need a poison now,   50
Whose sale is present death in Mantua,
Here lives a caitiff wretch would sell it him.'
O, this same thought did but forerun my need –
And this same needy man must sell it me.
As I remember, this should be the house.   55
Being holiday, the beggar's shop is shut.
What ho! Apothecary!

Enter the APOTHECARY.

APOTHECARY   Who calls so loud?

ROMEO   Come hither, man. I see that thou art poor.
Hold, there is forty ducats. (***Showing a bag of gold
coins***) Let me have
A dram of poison – such soon-speeding gear   60

203

The Apothecary is poor and so sells Romeo the deadly poison even though the penalty for doing so is death. Romeo leaves for Verona.

61   **disperse**: spread

63   **trunk ... breath**: body will stop breathing
64   **hasty powder**: explosive gunpowder
65   **womb**: belly (i.e. interior)
66   **mortal**: deadly / lethal
67   **he**: man
       utters: makes available / sells
68   **bare**: poor
69   **fear'st**: are afraid
70   **Need and oppression**: i.e. poverty that has ground you down
       starveth: produce the effects of hunger
71   **Contempt ... back**: your clothes show how poor you are, and the way the world despises you for it
73   **affords**: provides
74   **break it**: 1 break the law; 2 break out of your poverty

79   **dispatch you straight**: kill you instantly

82   **compounds**: mixtures

84   **get ... flesh**: fatten yourself up

THINK ABOUT *for* **GCSE**

Characterisation

85   **cordial**: healing medicine

- Look at what Romeo says to the Apothecary. What is Romeo's attitude to life and the world at this point in the play? How has he changed since the begining of the play?

As will disperse itself through all the veins,
That the life-weary taker may fall dead,
And that the trunk may be discharged of breath
As violently as hasty powder fired
Doth hurry from the fatal cannon's womb.   **65**

APOTHECARY   Such mortal drugs I have. But Mantua's law
Is death to any he that utters them.

ROMEO   Art thou so bare and full of wretchedness,
And fear'st to die? Famine is in thy cheeks –
Need and oppression starveth in thy eyes,   **70**
Contempt and beggary hangs upon thy back.
The world is not thy friend, nor the world's law.
The world affords no law to make thee rich –
Then be not poor, but break it, and take this.

APOTHECARY   My poverty, but not my will consents.   **75**

ROMEO   I pay thy poverty and not thy will.

APOTHECARY   (*Giving him the poison*) Put this in any liquid thing you
will
And drink it off – and if you had the strength
Of twenty men, it would dispatch you straight.

ROMEO   (*Giving him the money*) There is thy gold – worse
poison to men's souls,   **80**
Doing more murder in this loathsome world,
Than these poor compounds that thou mayst not sell.
I sell *thee* poison: thou hast sold me none.
Farewell. Buy food, and get thyself in flesh.

Exit the APOTHECARY.

Come, cordial, and not poison – go with me   **85**
To Juliet's grave, for there must I use thee.

Exit.

In this scene ...

- Friar Lawrence is shocked to hear that Friar John has been unable to deliver his letter to Romeo.
- He rushes off to collect Juliet from the tomb, knowing that she will soon be awake.

Friar John reports to Friar Lawrence that he has been unable to deliver his letter to Romeo. He has been shut up in a house containing people suspected of having the plague.

4 **his mind be writ**: he has written down his thoughts

5 **barefoot brother**: i.e. another Franciscan friar

6 **order**: religious order / community
   associate: accompany

8 **searchers**: city health inspectors

10 **pestilence**: plague

11 **forth**: out

12 **my speed ... stayed**: I was held up there and could not get to Mantua

13 **bare**: delivered

14 **here ... again**: i.e. I have brought it back to you

18 **nice**: trivial / unimportant
   charge: serious matters

19 **Of dear import**: extremely important

21 **crow**: crow-bar
   straight: straight away

THINK ABOUT for GCSE

Context

- What does Friar John's explanation tell us about life in Shakespeare's time? Think about friars and their way of life, the plague, and methods of communication. Why are these facts important for the plot?

Friar Lawrence's cell.

Enter FRIAR JOHN.

FRIAR JOHN	Holy Franciscan! Friar! Brother, ho!

Enter FRIAR LAWRENCE, *from his inner room.*

FR. LAWRENCE This same should be the voice of Friar John.
Welcome from Mantua! What says Romeo?
Or, if his mind be writ, give me his letter.

FRIAR JOHN Going to find a barefoot brother out,   5
One of our order, to associate me,
Here in this city visiting the sick,
And finding him, the searchers of the town –
Suspecting that we both were in a house
Where the infectious pestilence did reign –   10
Sealed up the doors, and would not let us forth,
So that my speed to Mantua there was stayed.

FR. LAWRENCE Who bare my letter then to Romeo?

FRIAR JOHN I could not send it – here it is again –
Nor get a messenger to bring it thee,   15
So fearful were they of infection.

FR. LAWRENCE Unhappy fortune! By my brotherhood,
The letter was not nice, but full of charge,
Of dear import – and the neglecting it
May do much danger! Friar John, go hence –   20
Get me an iron crow, and bring it straight
Unto my cell.

FRIAR JOHN Brother, I'll go and bring it thee.

Exit.

Friar Lawrence anxiously prepares to break into the Capulet monument, knowing that Juliet is about to wake up. He plans to keep her at his cell until Romeo can collect her.

24 **monument**: tomb

26 **beshrew me much**: be very angry with me

27 **notice ... accidents**: report about what has happened

30 **corse**: corpse

THINK ABOUT for GCSE

Structure and form

• Some films represent this scene without dialogue. In the Luhrmann film, a mailman delivers a note to Romeo's caravan which he never finds. In the Zeffirelli film, Balthasar sees Juliet's 'funeral' and gets to Romeo before Friar John does. Do you think these versions are more or less convincing than Shakespeare's?

FR. LAWRENCE   Now must I to the monument alone.
Within this three hours will fair Juliet wake.   25
She will beshrew me much that Romeo
Hath had no notice of these accidents.
But I will write again to Mantua,
And keep her at my cell till Romeo come.
Poor living corse, closed in a dead man's tomb!   30

Exit.

In this scene ...

- Romeo kills Paris when he tries to stop him entering the tomb.
- To be with Juliet again, Romeo drinks the poison and dies.
- When the Friar arrives, Juliet wakes up. He tries to hustle her away, but she is determined to stay by Romeo and the Friar flees. Taking Romeo's dagger, Juliet kills herself.
- The Prince, the Capulets and Montague find their children and Paris dead.
- The Friar explains what has happened and the two fathers make peace.

Paris arrives outside the Capulet tomb. When his page signals that someone is coming, he hides.

1   **aloof**: some way off

3   **lay ... along**: lie flat on the ground
4   **hollow**: because of the graves

6   **Being**: i.e. since the soil is
7   **But ... hear**: without you hearing

10   **stand**: stay
11   **adventure**: take the risk

12   **strew**: scatter
13   **canopy**: covering (of her 'bed', the tomb)
14   **sweet water**: perfume
     dew: sprinkle
15   **wanting**: lacking
     distilled by: made out of (like distilled spirits)
16   **obsequies**: funeral rituals

20   **cross**: disturb / interfere with
     rite: rituals

THINK ABOUT *for* **GCSE**

Performance and staging

- How might these opening moments have been staged in Shakespeare's Globe theatre? Think about where Juliet should be placed, where Paris's page should hide, and where Paris should hide.

Verona: a churchyard, with the family tomb of the Capulets.

Enter Count PARIS *and his* PAGE, *with a torch burning to light their way. (The* PAGE *brings flowers, and* PARIS *a flask of perfumed water.)*

PARIS	Give me thy torch, boy. Hence, and stand aloof.
	Yet put it out – for I would not be seen.
	Under yond yew trees lay thee all along,
	Holding thy ear close to the hollow ground –
	So shall no foot upon the churchyard tread, 5
	Being loose, unfirm with digging up of graves,
	But thou shalt hear it. Whistle then to me,
	As signal that thou hear'st something approach.
	Give me those flowers. Do as I bid thee, go.
PAGE	(*Aside*) I am almost afraid to stand alone 10
	Here in the churchyard, yet I will adventure.

The PAGE *moves away and hides.*

Paris scatters his flowers and perfumed water at the entrance of the tomb, in which JULIET *now lies.*

PARIS	Sweet flower, with flowers thy bridal bed I strew –
	O woe, thy canopy is dust and stones! –
	Which with sweet water nightly I will dew,
	Or, wanting that, with tears distilled by moans. 15
	The obsequies that I for thee will keep,
	Nightly shall be to strew thy grave and weep.

The PAGE *whistles.*

	The boy gives warning! Something doth approach.
	What cursèd foot wanders this way tonight,
	To cross my obsequies and true love's rite? 20
	What, with a torch? Muffle me, night, a while.

Paris hides himself near the tomb.

As they enter, Romeo orders Balthasar to leave and not interrupt him, but Balthasar hides nearby. As Romeo tries to get into the tomb, Paris decides to try to arrest him, convinced that he has come to dishonour the bodies lying in the tomb.

22 **mattock**: pick
    wrenching iron: crow-bar
23 **Hold**: Wait
24 **See**: make sure
25 **charge**: order
26 **all aloof**: well out of the way
27 **my course**: what I am doing
28 **Why**: The reason why

32 **In dear employment**: for a very personal purpose
33 **jealous**: suspicious

36 **hungry**: because death has a great appetite
38 **inexorable**: relentless
39 **empty**: hungry

THINK ABOUT for GCSE

Characterisation

• Look at lines 23 to 48. What is Romeo thinking and what is he planning to do? Think about why he lies to Balthasar (lines 28 to 32) and speaks so harshly to him.

Language

• What differences do you notice in the way Paris and Romeo speak about the tomb and their purpose in being there? Look at lines 12 to 17, and 45 to 48.

44 **his … doubt**: I am worried and suspicious about his intentions

45 **maw … womb**: both can mean 'stomach'

48 **more food**: i.e. Romeo's own body

53 **apprehend**: arrest

Enter Romeo *and* Balthasar, *with a torch burning, carrying a pick and a crow-bar.*

Romeo	Give me that mattock and the wrenching iron.
	Hold, take this letter. Early in the morning
	See thou deliver it to my lord and father.
	Give me the light. Upon thy life I charge thee,

25

	Whate'er thou hear'st or seest, stand all aloof,
	And do not interrupt me in my course.
	Why I descend into this bed of death
	Is partly to behold my lady's face,
	But chiefly to take thence from her dead finger

30

	A precious ring, a ring that I must use
	In dear employment. Therefore hence, be gone.
	But if thou, jealous, dost return to pry
	In what I farther shall intend to do,
	By heaven, I will tear thee joint by joint,

35

	And strew this hungry churchyard with thy limbs!
	The time and my intents are savage-wild,
	More fierce and more inexorable far
	Than empty tigers or the roaring sea.

Balthasar	I will be gone, sir, and not trouble ye.

40

Romeo	So shalt thou show me friendship. (*Gives him money*)
	Take thou that.
	Live and be prosperous – and farewell, good fellow.

Balthasar	(*Aside*) For all this same, I'll hide me hereabout.
	His looks I fear, and his intents I doubt.

Balthasar *goes, but hides further off in the churchyard.* Romeo *uses the crow-bar to force open the entrance of the tomb.*

Romeo	Thou detestable maw! – Thou womb of death! –

45

	Gorged with the dearest morsel of the earth! –
	Thus I enforce thy rotten jaws to open,
	And in despite I'll cram thee with more food.

Paris	(*Aside*) This is that banished haughty Montague
	That murdered my love's cousin, with which grief

50

	It is supposèd the fair creature died –
	And here is come to do some villainous shame
	To the dead bodies. I will apprehend him!

Resisting arrest, Romeo fights Paris and kills him, not knowing who he is. When he recognises the dead man, Romeo grants Paris his dying wish and lays his body next to Juliet's.

54   **unhallowed**: unholy / wicked

58   **therefore … hither**: that's why I came here
59   **tempt**: provoke
60   **these gone**: i.e. the dead

65   **armed against myself**: i.e. with the poison for my suicide

68   **defy thy conjurations**: reject your wishes and warnings
69   **felon**: criminal

THINK ABOUT *for* GCSE

Structure and form

• The confrontation between Romeo and Paris is cut in both the Zeffirelli and Luhrmann films. What is its purpose? What effect does Romeo killing Paris have on the way we view the story?

Characterisation

• Think about what we learn about Romeo from his reaction to fighting and killing Paris, and the way he treats the dead man.

74   **peruse**: examine / look closely at

76   **betossèd soul**: tormented mind
77   **attend**: listen to
78   **should have**: was supposed to have

82   **writ … book**: i.e. who shares my unhappy fate

He comes forward to challenge Romeo.

Stop thy unhallowed toil, vile Montague!
Can vengeance be pursued further than death?   55
Condemnèd villain, I do apprehend thee!
Obey, and go with me, for thou must die.

Romeo   I must indeed – and therefore came I hither.
Good gentle youth, tempt not a desperate man.
Fly hence and leave me. Think upon these gone –   60
Let them affright thee. I beseech thee, youth,
Put not another sin upon my head
By urging me to fury. O, be gone!
By heaven, I love thee better than myself
For I come hither armed against myself.   65
Stay not, be gone! Live – and hereafter say
A madman's mercy bid thee run away.

Paris   (*Drawing his sword*) I do defy thy conjurations
And apprehend thee for a felon here!

Romeo   Wilt thou provoke me? Then have at thee, boy!   70

They fight.

Page   O Lord, they fight! I will go call the Watch.

Exit, running.

Paris   (*Falling, mortally wounded*) O, I am slain! If thou be
merciful,
Open the tomb. Lay me with Juliet.

He dies.

Romeo   In faith, I will. Let me peruse this face.
Mercutio's kinsman, noble County Paris!   75
What said my man, when my betossèd soul
Did not attend him as we rode? I think
He told me Paris should have married Juliet.
Said he not so? Or did I dream it so?
Or am I mad, hearing him talk of Juliet,   80
To think it was so? O, give me thy hand,
One writ with me in sour misfortune's book!
I'll bury thee in a triumphant grave. –

215

Romeo admires Juliet's beauty and, drinking the poison, he kisses her and dies.

84 **lantern**: building designed with many windows to let in light
86 **feasting presence**: chamber for receiving party guests
87 **interred**: buried

89 **keepers**: jailers
90 **lightning**: sudden light-heartedness

92 **honey**: sweetness

94 **ensign**: flag

96 **is not advancèd**: has not reached there yet

99 **cut … twain**: i.e. killed you when you were young
100 **sunder … enemy**: i.e. to kill the person who was your enemy (himself)
101 **cousin**: i.e. Tybalt (his cousin by marriage)
103 **unsubstantial**: without a physical body
   amorous: in love
104 **abhorrèd**: revolting / repulsive
105 **paramour**: lover
106 **still**: forever
111 **shake … stars**: shake off the oppressive weight of my unlucky fortune
115 **dateless bargain**: a contract which will never expire
   engrossing: that consumes everything
116 **conduct**: guide (i.e. the poison)
117 **pilot**: navigator
   run on: run aground on
118 **seasick weary bark**: ship, tired of voyaging (i.e. his body, tired of life)

THINK ABOUT for GCSE

Language

• What kind of person does Romeo imagine Death to be in lines 102 to 105?

Themes and issues

• **Fate**: Earlier in the play Romeo compared life to a course sailed by a ship (Act 1 Scene 4, lines 113 to 114, and Act 2 Scene 2, lines 82 to 84). How does he develop that idea here? Who is the 'pilot' directing his course (lines 116 to 118)?

He wrenches the tomb-entrance wide open, and drags PARIS's
body inside, where JULIET *already lies.*

      – A grave? – O, no – a lantern, slaughtered youth! –
      For here lies Juliet, and her beauty makes   85
      This vault a feasting presence full of light.
      Death, lie thou there, by a dead man interred.

He lays PARIS's *body down, and turns towards* JULIET.

      How oft when men are at the point of death
      Have they been merry, which their keepers call
      A lightning before death! O, how may I   90
      Call this a lightning? O my love, my wife!
      Death, that hath sucked the honey of thy breath,
      Hath had no power yet upon thy beauty.
      Thou art not conquered. Beauty's ensign yet
      Is crimson in thy lips and in thy cheeks,   95
      And death's pale flag is not advancèd there.
      Tybalt, liest thou there in thy bloody sheet?
      O, what more favour can I do to thee
      Than with that hand that cut thy youth in twain
      To sunder his that was thine enemy?   100
      Forgive me, cousin. Ah, dear Juliet,
      Why art thou yet so fair? Shall I believe
      That unsubstantial Death is amorous,
      And that the lean abhorrèd monster keeps
      Thee here in dark to be his paramour?   105
      For fear of that I still will stay with thee,
      And never from this palace of dim night
      Depart again. Here, here will I remain,
      With worms that are thy chambermaids. O, here
      Will I set up my everlasting rest,   110
      And shake the yoke of inauspicious stars
      From this world-wearied flesh. Eyes, look your last.
      Arms, take your last embrace! – And lips, O you,
      The doors of breath, seal with a righteous kiss
      A dateless bargain to engrossing Death!   115
      Come, bitter conduct – come, unsavoury guide! –
      Thou desperate pilot – now at once run on
      The dashing rocks thy seasick weary bark!

Moments too late, Friar Lawrence arrives in the graveyard. Balthasar tells the Friar that Romeo has been in the tomb for some time.

119 apothecary: the person who sold him the poison
120 quick: 1 rapid; 2 lively

121 speed: aid

125 yond: over there
vainly: uselessly
126 discern: make out
127 Capels': Capulets'

THINK ABOUT *for* **GCSE**

Performance and staging

* In the text, Juliet wakes just after Romeo's death. In the Luhrmann film, he remains alive just long enough to realise that Juliet is not dead and then she sees him die. Which version do you prefer and why?

132 My master ... but: As far as my master is aware
133 menace: threaten

136 ill unthrifty thing: evil and unlucky happening

Here's to my love! (***Drinks the poison***) O true
   apothecary!
Thy drugs are quick. Thus with a kiss I die.   120

He dies, falling beside JULIET.

Enter FRIAR LAWRENCE, *in the churchyard, with a lantern,*
crow-bar and spade.

FR. LAWRENCE   Saint Francis be my speed! How oft tonight
Have my old feet stumbled at graves! Who's there?

BALTHASAR   (***Coming forward***) Here's one, a friend, and one that
   knows you well.

FR. LAWRENCE   Bliss be upon you! Tell me, good my friend,
What torch is yond that vainly lends his light   125
To grubs and eyeless skulls? As I discern
It burneth in the Capels' monument.

BALTHASAR   It doth so, holy sir – and there's my master,
One that you love.

FR. LAWRENCE   Who is it?

BALTHASAR   Romeo.

FR. LAWRENCE   How long hath he been there?

BALTHASAR   Full half an hour.   130

FR. LAWRENCE   Go with me to the vault.

BALTHASAR   I dare not, sir.
My master knows not but I am gone hence,
And fearfully did menace me with death
If I did stay to look on his intents.

FR. LAWRENCE   Stay then – I'll go alone. Fear comes upon me.   135
O, much I fear some ill unthrifty thing!

BALTHASAR   As I did sleep under this yew tree here,
I dreamt my master and another fought,
And that my master slew him.

Anxious when he sees blood on the ground, Friar Lawrence enters the tomb. As he finds the bodies of Romeo and Paris, Juliet awakes and asks him where Romeo is. He tries to explain, but, hearing voices approaching, wants to hurry her away. When she realises that Romeo is dead, she refuses to go. Friar Lawrence flees without her.

141 **sepulchre**: tomb
142 **masterless**: abandoned by their owners
     gory: bloody

145 **unkind**: cruel and unnatural
146 **guilty … chance**: responsible for this tragic happening

148 **comfortable**: comforting / reassuring

THINK ABOUT for GCSE

Performance and staging

- Actor Niamh Cusack played the moment when Juliet wakes very happily: she believed that everything had gone to plan. What effect might a happy Juliet at that moment have on the audience?

Characterisation

- What is your opinion of the Friar's words and behaviour after Juliet awakes? What motivates him to run away (line 159)?

152 **contagion**: disease
153 **contradict**: argue against
154 **thwarted our intents**: prevented us from doing what we wanted to do
155 **thy bosom**: your arms
156–7 **dispose … Among**: find you a place with

162 **timeless**: 1 everlasting; 2 untimely
163 **churl**: ill-mannered person
164 **after**: come after / follow
165 **Haply**: Perhaps
166 **restorative**: 1 cure; 2 something to restore her to him

FR. LAWRENCE	Romeo! –	
	(*Approaching the tomb, and stooping to examine the ground*) – Alack, alack! – What blood is this which stains	140
	The stony entrance of this sepulchre?	
	What mean these masterless and gory swords	
	To lie discoloured by this place of peace?	

He enters the tomb.

Romeo! O pale! Who else? What, Paris too? –
And steeped in blood? Ah, what an unkind hour 145
Is guilty of this lamentable chance!

JULIET *wakes, and begins to sit up.*

The lady stirs.

JULIET	O comfortable Friar! – Where is my lord?	
	I do remember well where I should be,	
	And there I am. Where is my Romeo?	150

Voices are heard in the churchyard.

FR. LAWRENCE	I hear some noise, lady. Come from that nest	
	Of death, contagion, and unnatural sleep.	
	A greater power than we can contradict	
	Hath thwarted our intents. Come, come away!	
	Thy husband in thy bosom there lies dead –	155
	And Paris too. Come, I'll dispose of thee	
	Among a sisterhood of holy nuns.	
	Stay not to question, for the Watch is coming.	
	Come, go, good Juliet! – I dare no longer stay.	

| JULIET | Go, get thee hence – for I will not away. | 160 |

Exit FRIAR LAWRENCE.

What's here? A cup closed in my true love's hand?
Poison, I see, hath been his timeless end.
O churl! – drunk all, and left no friendly drop
To help me after? I will kiss thy lips.
Haply some poison yet doth hang on them 165
To make me die with a restorative.
(*Kissing him*) Thy lips are warm.

Juliet kills herself with Romeo's dagger. The Watchmen enter the tomb and discover the bodies. As the Friar and Balthasar are detained and brought in, the Prince arrives.

169 **brief**: quick
     happy: found at the right time

170 **This**: i.e. her breast

173 **attach**: arrest

THINK ABOUT *for* **GCSE**

Structure and form

• What purposes do the Watchmen fulfil here? What are the arguments for and against cutting their dialogue (lines 171 to 201) and having no gap between Juliet's death and the entrance of the main characters, who could all begin to arrive at line 202?

179 **woes**: miserable creatures (i.e. the three dead bodies)
180 **ground**: 1 underlying reason for; 2 earth (wordplay)
     woes: unhappy events
181 **cannot ... descry**: cannot discover without further details
183 **in safety**: securely

185 **mattock**: pick

187 **A great suspicion**: That looks extremely suspicious
     Stay: Hold

Enter Paris's PAGE, *with the men of the* WATCH, *approaching the tomb.*

WATCHMAN 1   Lead, boy. Which way?

JULIET   Yea, noise? Then I'll be brief! –
               (*She snatches Romeo's dagger from his belt.*)
                                    O happy dagger!
               This is thy sheath! (*Stabbing herself*) – There rust, and
                   let me die.   170

She falls across ROMEO'*s body, and dies.*

PAGE   This is the place – there, where the torch doth burn!

WATCHMAN 1   The ground is bloody. Search about the churchyard.
               Go, some of you. Whoe'er you find, attach.

                                    WATCHMEN *go out searching.*

The FIRST WATCHMAN *enters the tomb, then comes out again.*

               Pitiful sight! Here lies the County slain,
               And Juliet bleeding, warm and newly dead,   175
               Who here hath lain this two days burièd!
               Go, tell the Prince, run to the Capulets!
               Raise up the Montagues! Some others search.

                                    More WATCHMEN *go off.*

               We see the ground whereon these woes do lie,
               But the true ground of all these piteous woes   180
               We cannot without circumstance descry.

Re-enter a WATCHMAN, *bringing* BALTHASAR.

WATCHMAN 2   Here's Romeo's man. We found him in the churchyard.

WATCHMAN 1   Hold him in safety till the Prince come hither.

Re-enter another WATCHMAN, *with* FRIAR LAWRENCE.

WATCHMAN 3   Here is a Friar that trembles, sighs, and weeps.
               We took this mattock and this spade from him,   185
               As he was coming from this churchyard's side.

WATCHMAN 1   A great suspicion! Stay the Friar too.

Juliet's parents arrive and find their daughter dead. Montague arrives and sadly reports that his wife has died from grief at Romeo's banishment. He is stunned to find his son dead in the tomb.

188   **misadventure ... up**: dreadful event has happened so early in the day

190   **shrieked abroad**: screamed out in the streets

194   **fear ... ears**: is this fearful event you are hearing about

200   **instruments**: tools

203   **has mista'en**: is in the wrong place
      house: sheath
204   **Montague**: i.e. Romeo

207   **warns ... sepulchre**: summons me to my grave

209   **more early down**: already dead

210   **liege**: sovereign
      is dead to-night: died during the night

214   **thou untaught**: you ill-mannered boy

215   **press before**: push in front of

THINK ABOUT for **GCSE**

Language

• The Prince's wordplay with Montague (lines 208 to 209) can seem inappropriate at such a sad moment, yet Montague himself plays with imagery (lines 214 to 215). What effect does wordplay have at this point?

Enter PRINCE ESCALUS, *with attendants.*

PRINCE	What misadventure is so early up,
	That calls our person from our morning rest?

Enter CAPULET, *and* LADY CAPULET.

CAPULET	What should it be that is so shrieked abroad?	190
LADY CAPULET	The people in the streets cry 'Romeo!' –	
	Some 'Juliet!', and some 'Paris!', and all run	
	With open outcry toward our monument.	
PRINCE	What fear is this which startles in your ears?	
WATCHMAN 1	Sovereign, here lies the County Paris slain;	195
	And Romeo dead; and Juliet, dead before –	
	Warm and new killed.	
PRINCE	Search, seek, and know how this foul murder comes!	
WATCHMAN 1	Here is a Friar, and slaughtered Romeo's man,	
	With instruments upon them fit to open	200
	These dead men's tombs.	
CAPULET	(*Seeing the bodies*) O heavens! O wife, look how our	
	daughter bleeds!	
	This dagger has mista'en, for lo, his house	
	Is empty on the back of Montague,	
	And is mis-sheathèd in my daughter's bosom.	205
LADY CAPULET	O me! This sight of death is as a bell	
	That warns my old age to a sepulchre!	

Enter MONTAGUE, *with servants.*

PRINCE	Come, Montague – for thou art early up	
	To see thy son and heir more early down.	
MONTAGUE	Alas, my liege, my wife is dead tonight.	210
	Grief of my son's exile hath stopped her breath.	
	What further woe conspires against mine age?	
PRINCE	Look, and thou shalt see.	
MONTAGUE	(*Seeing* ROMEO's *body*) O thou untaught! What	
	manners is in this,	
	To press before thy father to a grave?	215

Friar Lawrence tells what he knows about the events that have led to the tragic deaths.

216 **Seal ... outrage**: Stop your expressions of passionate grief
217 **clear ... ambiguities**: clear up these mysteries
218 **spring ... descent**: origin, cause and true sequence of events
219 **be ... woes**: lead you in mourning
220 **even to death**: i.e. the death of the guilty
   forbear: control your feelings
221 **let mischance ... patience**: allow your patience to keep a hold on your misfortunes
222 **parties of suspicion**: suspects
223 **the greatest**: most liable to be suspected
225 **Doth ... me**: throws suspicion on me
   direful: terrible
226–7 **impeach ... excused**: accuse myself and be found guilty, and to make excuses and be pardoned
228 **in**: of
229 **date of breath**: time I have to live
233 **stol'n**: secret
234 **doomsday**: day of death
237 **remove ... her**: relieve her of the grief possessing her
238 **Betrothed**: promised her in marriage
   perforce: forcibly
240 **devise some mean**: think up some way
243 **tutored by my art**: guided by my special knowledge
245–6 **wrought ... form**: gave her the appearance
247 **as**: on
   dire: terrible
248 **borrowed**: temporary
249 **force should cease**: effect should wear off
251 **stayed**: delayed

THINK ABOUT for GCSE

Structure and form

- As the audience has already seen the events the Friar describes, what purpose does his speech serve?

Performance and staging

- How would you direct the other main characters to behave during the Friar's speech?

PRINCE	Seal up the mouth of outrage for a while,
	Till we can clear these ambiguities –
	And know their spring, their head, their true descent.
	And then will I be general of your woes,
	And lead you even to death. Meantime forbear,	220
	And let mischance be slave to patience.
	Bring forth the parties of suspicion.

FRIAR LAWRENCE *and* BALTHASAR *are brought forward.*

FR. LAWRENCE	I am the greatest – able to do least,
	Yet most suspected, as the time and place
	Doth make against me, of this direful murder.	225
	And here I stand, both to impeach and purge,
	Myself condemnèd and myself excused.

| PRINCE | Then say at once what thou dost know in this. |

FR. LAWRENCE	I will be brief, for my short date of breath
	Is not so long as is a tedious tale.	230
	Romeo, there dead, was husband to that Juliet –
	And she, there dead, that Romeo's faithful wife.
	I married them. And their stol'n marriage day
	Was Tybalt's doomsday, whose untimely death
	Banished the new-made bridegroom from this city –	235
	For whom, and not for Tybalt, Juliet pined.
	You, to remove that siege of grief from her,
	Betrothed and would have married her perforce
	To County Paris. Then comes she to me,
	And with wild looks bid me devise some mean	240
	To rid her from this second marriage –
	Or in my cell there would she kill herself.
	Then gave I her, so tutored by my art,
	A sleeping potion, which so took effect
	As I intended, for it wrought on her	245
	The form of death. Meantime I writ to Romeo
	That he should hither come as this dire night
	To help to take her from her borrowed grave,
	Being the time the potion's force should cease.
	But he which bore my letter, Friar John,	250
	Was stayed by accident, and yesternight
	Returned my letter back. Then all alone,

Balthasar and Paris's page also tell the Prince what they know.

253 prefixèd: pre-arranged

255 closely: secretly

257 ere: before

260 entreated: begged

266 is privy: shares the secret
aught: anything
267 Miscarried: went wrong
268 hour ... time: time before I might have been expected to die
269 Unto ... law: in line with the strictest interpretation of the law
270 still: always
273 post: a great hurry

275 early: as soon as I could
276 going in: as he was going into
277 If I departed not: unless I went away

THINK ABOUT for GCSE

Structure and form

- There are other points in the play where characters report what has happened. Look at Act 3 Scene 1, lines 148 to 171, and Act 5 Scene 3, lines 137 to 139. How are these reports different from the Friar's? Think about the way they describe the events they have been involved in.

280 made your master: was your master doing
282 aloof: out of the way
283 Anon: Straight afterwards
284 by and by: almost at once

286 make ... words: back up what the Friar said

	At the prefixèd hour of her waking,	
	Came I to take her from her kindred's vault –	
	Meaning to keep her closely at my cell	255
	Till I conveniently could send to Romeo.	
	But when I came, some minute ere the time	
	Of her awakening, here untimely lay	
	The noble Paris and true Romeo dead.	
	She wakes – and I entreated her come forth	260
	And bear this work of heaven with patience.	
	But then a noise did scare me from the tomb,	
	And she, too desperate, would not go with me –	
	But, as it seems, did violence on herself.	
	All this I know, and to the marriage	265
	Her Nurse is privy. And if aught in this	
	Miscarried by my fault, let my old life	
	Be sacrificed some hour before his time	
	Unto the rigour of severest law.	
PRINCE	We still have known thee for a holy man.	270
	Where's Romeo's man? What can he say to this?	
BALTHASAR	I brought my master news of Juliet's death,	
	And then in post he came from Mantua	
	To this same place, to this same monument.	
	This letter he early bid me give his father,	275
	And threatened me with death, going in the vault,	
	If I departed not and left him there.	
PRINCE	Give me the letter. I will look on it.	
	Where is the County's page that raised the watch?	

The PAGE *comes forward.*

	Sirrah, what made your master in this place?	280
PAGE	He came with flowers to strew his lady's grave,	
	And bid me stand aloof, and so I did.	
	Anon comes one with light to ope the tomb,	
	And by and by my master drew on him,	
	And then I ran away to call the Watch.	285
PRINCE	This letter doth make good the Friar's words,	
	Their course of love, the tidings of her death.	
	And here he writes that he did buy a poison	

The Prince summons the two fathers to look at the terrible results of their hatred. Montague and Capulet make peace, each one promising to set up a golden statue as a monument to the other man's child. The Prince declares that some people will be punished and some pardoned, and concludes the story of Romeo and Juliet.

289 therewithal: i.e. with the poison
292 scourge: i.e. punishment
293 kill ... love: i.e. use love to kill your children
294 winking ... discords: shutting my eyes to your quarrels
295 brace: pair (i.e. Mercutio and Paris)
297 jointure: marriage-settlement (the dowry which the father of the bride would be expected to pay)

301 figure: statue / image
    at such ... set: be valued so highly

304 Poor sacrifices of: 1 sad victims of; 2 inadequate compensation / payment for
    enmity: hatred
305 glooming: cloudy

THINK ABOUT *for* GCSE

Themes and issues

- The Prince says that some will be pardoned and some punished. Who do you think should be pardoned, and who punished?

- **Conflict**: Will there now be peace or will the feud start up again, in your opinion?

Performance and staging

- In what different ways could you stage the ending to bring out these contrasting interpretations?

Of a poor 'pothecary, and therewithal
Came to this vault, to die and lie with Juliet.   290
Where be these enemies? Capulet, Montague?
See what a scourge is laid upon your hate,
That heaven finds means to kill your joys with love!
And I, for winking at your discords too,
Have lost a brace of kinsmen. All are punished.   295

Capulet O brother Montague, give me thy hand.
This is my daughter's jointure – for no more
Can I demand.

Montague   But I can give thee more –
For I will raise her statue in pure gold,
That whiles Verona by that name is known,   300
There shall no figure at such rate be set
As that of true and faithful Juliet.

Capulet As rich shall Romeo's by his lady's lie –
Poor sacrifices of our enmity!

Prince A glooming peace this morning with it brings.   305
The sun for sorrow will not show his head.
Go hence, to have more talk of these sad things.
Some shall be pardoned, and some punishèd.
– For never was a story of more woe
Than this of Juliet and her Romeo.   310

Exeunt.

We do not know exactly when Shakespeare wrote *Romeo and Juliet*, but it was probably around 1595. He did not invent the story of the two young lovers; it had been popular throughout Europe for fifty years. But Shakespeare did convert it into a tragedy about love, honour and fate, which remains one of his most popular plays.

LOVE AND COURTSHIP

In Shakespeare's time it was not always possible for a girl and boy simply to fall in love and get married. Wealthy families, like the Capulets, would arrange marriages for their children for any number of reasons that had nothing to do with love. They might want their child to marry into a wealthy family, for example, or into one with a noble title like Count Paris's.

Courtship in powerful or noble families followed certain rules. Paris has to ask Juliet's father for permission to woo her. Fathers were especially powerful figures and their children were expected to do as they were told. In England the law said that a daughter was legally her father's property until she got married, when she became the property of her husband. Capulet is confident that Juliet will be 'ruled in all respects' by him and seems to think that he can give her away to whichever husband he chooses.

HONOUR

An individual's personal pride and reputation were extremely important as a person would feel very proud to have a famous and respected family name, such as Capulet or Montague. If one family felt insulted or injured by another, they might seek revenge, and a family feud would have begun which could continue for generations. Shakespeare's audience would have associated Italy, where the story is set, with violent passions: a place where a strong sense of family honour could often lead to violent acts of revenge and feuds.

When Tybalt finally meets up with Romeo, he calls him a 'villain'. In Shakespeare's time, this was an insult to a man's birth and his behaviour. It suggested that he was both low-born and of bad character. It would be enough to provoke a duel, which is what

Tybalt wants. Mercutio, who also understands the code of honour, cannot understand or tolerate Romeo's refusal to take up the challenge. When Mercutio is killed, Romeo feels ashamed, and his sense of honour tells him that it is his duty to get revenge for his friend's death.

FATE

Romeo and Juliet are described in the Prologue as 'star-crossed lovers'. This means that their love is doomed not to succeed. Shakespeare's audience would have understood the idea that fate controlled people's lives and would have noticed all the references in the play to 'the stars'. For audiences today, Romeo and Juliet's tragedy seems more a case of simple bad luck. The young lovers certainly do seem to have their share of ill fortune, and a lot of it is to do with unlucky timing. It is particularly unfortunate, for example, that the Friar arrives at the tomb only seconds after Romeo has drunk the poison. It is as though, whatever Romeo and Juliet do, the course of their lives is already written in the stars. Their love is 'death-marked' and they cannot avoid their fate.

TRAGEDY

A tragedy is a play that shows how a happy and successful person suffers a great disaster that ends in their death. The audience knows from the Prologue that Romeo and Juliet will die at the end of this particular tragedy. In a tragedy the hero's or heroine's destruction might be caused by fate, or by a weakness in the person's character, or by a combination of the two. Romeo and Juliet's tragedy is mainly to do with fate. They are victims of the hatred between their two families and a series of unlucky events that lead to their deaths.

THEATRES AND STAGES

Romeo and Juliet was probably first performed in the mid-1590s, in the playhouse simply called The Theatre, in Shoreditch, on what was then the north-east edge of London. Later performances took place at the Curtain, another theatre nearby, before Shakespeare's acting company (known then as the Lord Chamberlain's Men) finally moved to its new home at the Globe playhouse in 1599.

The earlier playhouses were theatres of the same familiar type as the more famous Globe. The Theatre, in fact, was pulled down and its timbers re-used for building the Globe, so the size of the stage, and the yard and galleries round it, were probably much the same. A performance of *Romeo and Juliet* in a reconstruction of the Curtain playhouse was featured in the film *Shakespeare in Love* (1998).

What we know about the early staging of *Romeo and Juliet* comes mainly from the action of the play itself and the evidence of its stage directions. Three features are most important: the continuous and varying use of the large main-stage platform; the famous 'balcony' or 'window' scenes involving the lovers acting 'aloft', as the old directions say; and the need for some special stagings, such as Juliet's curtained bed (on which she collapses apparently dead in Act 4), and the tomb or 'monument' of the Capulets (for the climax of the tragedy in Act 5).

ACTION AND SETTINGS

The action of the play in an Elizabethan theatre would have been fast and continuous, with no intervals between Acts or Scenes. New scenes are often marked simply by the entrance of new characters. When the Capulet servants hurry in to clear up in Act 1 Scene 5, for example, they show that we are now 'indoors' for the dance at which Romeo and Juliet will meet – even though the visiting maskers who were 'outside' before had remained on the stage. No scenery or stage-lighting, as we think of them, were used. The play's language and activity were enough to suggest places and settings to the imagination of its audience. Burning torches, used several times in *Romeo and Juliet*, were not for lighting, but to tell the audience, in the open-air afternoon daylight of an Elizabethan theatre, that it was watching a 'night-time' scene.

Costumes (indoor or outdoor dress, expensive or 'poor') would also have signalled different settings and different kinds of character for spectators. Montague and Capulet servants, for example, might well have worn different coloured 'uniforms', or badges to represent their family. Balthasar, in Act 5 Scene 1, enters wearing riding-boots as a signal that he has just ridden hurriedly from Verona, and the Apothecary, in the same scene, wears 'tattered' clothes to show his poverty, in sharp contrast with the expensively fashionable dress that most main characters would have worn.

Some changes of setting in Romeo and Juliet can seem odd or complicated. Act 2 Scene 1 begins, for instance, with Romeo hiding himself from Mercutio and Benvolio as they leave the dance. He does this, we are told, by climbing a wall into the garden or 'orchard' of the Capulet house, though he still overhears Mercutio's rude attempts to 'conjure him up'. When he comes out of his hiding-place a new scene begins, continuing straight on from the last, and he is *inside* the garden, 'in darkness', and will see Juliet appear above at her 'window'. On the stage there would almost certainly have been no 'wall' to climb: Romeo may well simply have scrambled behind one of the oak pillars that held up the canopy over the stage. When he emerges, the stage-setting has changed, but *only* in the imagination of the audience, from 'street' to private 'garden', and the stage-pillar may now seem to represent a tree.

When Romeo leaves Juliet after their night together, in Act 3 Scene 5, he climbs down the rope-ladder from her window and departs, again, through the garden. Juliet then comes quickly down herself ('*She goeth down from the window*', the old direction says – but not of course by the rope-ladder). She enters below, to meet her mother and hear the bad news that she is to be married to Paris. The main stage, which was the 'garden', is now only another part of her bedroom: one modern director remarked that she 'brings her bedroom downstairs with her'. The change depends, again, on the imagination of the audience. Characters and their words and behaviour tell us where they are. Juliet's parents, we imagine, invade her bedroom: they are not, of course, likely to have furious family arguments in the garden.

Windows and discoveries

As in the Globe playhouse, there would have been two main entrances to the stage from the dressing-room area behind it. Between them, centrally positioned, would have been another opening, usually covered by curtains. This was known as the 'discovery space', because special items, such as a bed or a tomb in *Romeo and Juliet*, could be pushed out through it or revealed ('discovered') inside it. Above this, on the back-wall of the stage (probably about three metres up) would have been the railed upper gallery, which would have served as Juliet's window or balcony, reached by a stairway behind the stage-wall. Juliet would have come down this in Act 3 Scene 5 to re-enter on the stage below.

All we can be sure of, however Juliet's bed or the Capulet tomb was staged, is that they would have had to be visible to spectators on three sides of the stage. Juliet's bed may have been inside the discovery space, or a curtained four-poster bed may have been pushed out. The Capulet tomb, in Act 5, is more of a 'special effect'. Romeo must break open its doors or gates to reach Juliet inside it, and action around and inside it during the final scene of the tragedy must also have been easy enough for spectators to see. In this case, perhaps, the 'monument' may have been a specially built structure pushed forward from the discovery space. Around the monument, the main-stage 'graveyard' would have been in full use, with characters hiding, fighting, arriving too late, and then crowding to see 'this sight of death'.

Demands, fights and doubles

Romeo and Juliet would certainly have been a challenging play for Shakespeare's company to put on. We know, for example, that audiences were keen fans of good sword fighting and several fast and thrilling fights (like the one that leads to Mercutio's death in Act 3 Scene 1) would have had to be skilfully managed.

The play also has more than thirty speaking parts. Yet the acting company, including the specialist boy-actors who took female parts (though Juliet's Nurse would have been a man), would have had no more than twelve to fourteen players. Parts therefore had to be 'doubled', which was usual enough in the Elizabethan theatre. Benvolio, for instance, may be missing from the end of the play because the actor who played him has taken on another role. There would certainly have been other minor roles for the actors who played Mercutio and Tybalt to play after their 'deaths' in Act 3. Some players may well have had three or four of the smaller parts. This would have been managed effectively by using changes of costume, and sometimes also by changing appearance with wigs and beards.

Staging in Shakespeare's theatre may seem crude or simple by modern standards, but it was extremely flexible and effective in playing to the imaginations of its audiences. And *Romeo and Juliet* had all the ingredients, of language (from fine poetry to rapid wit and dirty jokes) and of action (the thrills of young love, danger and death), to make it a theatrical success.

A play in performance at the reconstruction of Shakespeare's Globe

Romeo and Juliet is one of Shakespeare's most popular plays. Audiences have always been moved and inspired by the tragedy of the two lovers, perhaps because they are so young, and because their deaths seem such a terrible waste. Modern audiences, however, take a different view of the lovers' story from audiences of Shakespeare's time. Most people today, for example, don't believe that our lives are ruled by fate or that the future is written in the stars.

It also seems likely that Shakespeare's audiences would have sympathised much more with Juliet's parents than many modern audiences do because they expected parents to have complete authority over their children. In the poem by Arthur Brooke on which Shakespeare based his play, the young lovers are condemned for their disobedience and their deaths are partly seen as a punishment for their sins. Modern audiences will also be divided over the issue of arranged marriages. Many people will take the view that Romeo and Juliet have every right to choose who they want to marry, sympathising with them rather than with the parents.

As a result of these issues there are some basic questions that any modern director of this play has to address. Three of the most important are:
- Who or what is to blame for Romeo and Juliet's deaths?
- Who should we sympathise with?
- What time and place should the play be set in to get the chosen interpretation across to the audience?

WHO IS TO BLAME?
Hardly any modern productions take the view that Romeo and Juliet are responsible for their own downfall because of some weakness in their characters. And, as most people no longer believe in astrology or fate, stage and screen interpretations tend not to place all the blame on 'the stars' either. Instead, responsibility for the deaths is usually laid upon other characters, or upon the society in which the young lovers have grown up.

Baz Luhrmann's 1996 film places the lovers in a world in which order has completely broken down. 'Captain Prince' seems powerless to stop the violent rioting in the city's streets and can do little more than observe the chaos from a police helicopter. In this modern version of the story all the men carry guns (decorated with the Capulet or Montague badge) and use them with deadly accuracy. The message seems to be that, in a society such as this, young men like Romeo have little chance of avoiding violence.

Michael Bogdanov took a similar view in his 1986 RSC production set in modern-day Italy. Capulet was a mafia boss who had little interest in his daughter except as a way of extending his business empire. Bogdanov chose to end the play with a sort of press conference for the two fathers. Newspaper photographers rushed on to take their photographs as they posed, shaking hands, in front of an enormous gold statue of their dead children. The two fathers were not really affected by their children's deaths, but were using them as an opportunity for a business merger between their two 'companies', Capulet and Montague.

WHO DO WE SYMPATHISE WITH?
Directors also have to decide who they want the audience to sympathise with. Should their sympathy be only for the younger characters? Or should they have some for the older generation as well?

Franco Zeffirelli's 1968 film shows Romeo and Juliet as two sincere and innocent young people suffering because of their parents' inflexible attitudes. The Capulets only seem concerned with carrying on the feud and have little time for their children. In this version the audience feels hardly any sympathy for the older generation. Only the Friar seems to be good-hearted in trying his best to bring the families together.

Baz Luhrmann is even harder on the adults. In his 1996 film Juliet's parents are selfish, heavy-drinking drug-takers, much more interested in throwing a glamorous party than in caring for their daughter. The Friar, while trying to be in touch with the young people under his care, seems to give up when he realises that Romeo has not received his letter and does not even go to the tomb to take care of the waking Juliet.

One version that did show some sympathy for the parents was the **BBC Television** production first shown in 1978 and available on video. This concentrated much more on the family relationships, using effective camera close-ups to show the characters' feelings, and was especially sympathetic to Capulet. The old man seemed bewildered by the events around him and uncertain about how to cope with a headstrong young daughter.

THE SETTING

Productions of Romeo and Juliet have set the play in every period from the fifteenth century to the twenty-first, and in places as different as medieval Verona in Italy and modern-day 'Verona Beach' in the USA.

Zeffirelli's 1968 film chose to set the story in the time and place in which it is supposed to have taken place: fifteenth century Verona. This gave an opportunity to show some dramatic sword fights set in authentic medieval city streets and characters dressed in brilliantly coloured costumes: the Montagues wore blue-green, the Capulets red and yellow. The historical setting helped the audience to understand, for example, how someone banished from the city would be difficult to contact and how the crucial letter from the Friar could so easily fail to reach Romeo.

Two key interpretations, however, have chosen a modern setting: the 1996 **Baz Luhrmann** film and **Michael Bogdanov**'s 1986 RSC production. A modern setting has the obvious attraction that it can speak directly to today's audience, and both of these productions were extremely popular with teenagers. In the 1986 RSC version Tybalt arrived on stage driving a red convertible and the fight started when the aerial was snapped off his car for use as a weapon.

Romeo was played as something of an outsider in a group of friends who were constantly trying to impress each other. The Luhrmann film opened with shots of street-rioting and an American city skyline dominated by a gigantic statue of Christ and two towering skyscrapers housing the headquarters of the Montague and Capulet empires. A modern setting like this can help us to understand how a Friar could have been such an important and influential figure in fifteenth century Verona. He was played as a tough city priest and it was easy to see why the teenagers would be influenced by him. His huge statue-topped church showed why he would also have such power and status with their parents.

ASSESSMENT OF SHAKESPEARE IN YOUR ENGLISH LITERATURE GCSE

All students studying GCSE English Literature have to study at least six texts, three of which are from the English, Welsh or Irish literary heritage. These texts must include prose, poetry and drama, and in England this must include a play by Shakespeare.

The four major exam boards: AQA, Edexcel, WJEC and OCR, include Shakespeare as part of their specifications for English Literature. All the exam boards offer controlled assessment to assess their students' understanding of Shakespeare, although some offer a traditional examination as an alternative option, or as one element of the assessment.

This section of the book offers guidance and support to help you prepare for your GCSE assessment on Shakespeare. The first part (pages 242–4) is relevant to all students, whichever exam board's course you are taking. The second part (pages 245–62) is board-specific, and you should turn to those pages that are relevant to your exam board. Your teacher will advise you if you are unsure which board you are working with.

WHAT YOU WILL BE ASSESSED ON

In your English Literature GCSE you will be marked on various Assessment Objectives (AOs). These assess your ability to:

- **AO1: respond to texts critically and imaginatively; select and evaluate relevant textual detail to illustrate and support interpretations**
  This means that you should show insight and imagination when writing about the text, showing understanding of what the author is saying and how he or she is saying it; and use quotations or direct references to the text to support your ideas and point of view.

- **AO2: explain how language, structure and form contribute to writers' presentation of ideas, themes and settings**
  This means that you need to explain how writers use language (vocabulary, imagery and other literary features), structure and form (the 'shape' of the text) to present ideas, themes and settings (where the action takes place).

- **AO3: make comparisons and explain links between texts, evaluating writers' different ways of expressing meaning and achieving effects**
  This means that you compare and link texts, identifying what they have in common and looking at how different writers express meaning and create specific effects for the reader/audience.

- **AO4: relate texts to their social, cultural and historical contexts; explain how texts have been influential and significant to self and other readers in different contexts and at different times**
  This means that, where it is relevant, you need to show awareness of the social, cultural and historical background of the texts; explain the influence of texts on yourself and other readers in different places and times.

You will also be assessed on the **Quality of your Written Communication**. This means you need to ensure that: your text is legible and your spelling, punctuation and grammar are accurate so that the meaning is clear; you choose a style of writing that is suitable for the task; you organise information clearly and logically, using specialist words where relevant.

Not all exam boards assess all the AOs as part of the English Literature Shakespeare task. Here is a summary:

Exam Board	Unit	AO1	AO2	AO3	AO4
AQA	Unit 3 CA	✓	✓	✓	✓
	Unit 4 Exam	✓	✓		
Edexcel	Unit 3 CA		✓	✓	
WJEC	Unit 3 CA	✓	✓	✓	
OCR	Unit 1 CA	✓			

WHAT IS CONTROLLED ASSESSMENT?

Controlled assessment is a way of testing students' knowledge and ability. It differs from an examination in that you will be given the task in advance so you can research and prepare for it, before sitting down to write a full response to it under supervised conditions.

Exam boards differ in the detail of their controlled assessment rules, so do check them out in the board-specific section. However, the general stages of controlled assessment are as follows:

1. The task
   Every year exam boards either set a specific task or offer a choice. Your teacher might adapt one of the tasks to suit you and the resources available. You will be given this task well in advance of having to respond to it, so you have plenty of time to prepare for it.

2. Planning and research

Your teacher will have helped you study your text and taught you how to approach the topics. He or she will now advise you on how to carry out further research and plan for your task.

- During this phase you can work with others, for example discussing ideas and sharing resources on the internet.

- Your teacher can give you general feedback during this phase, but not detailed advice.

- You must keep a record of all the source materials you use, including websites.

3. Writing up the response

This will take place under timed, supervised conditions.

- It may be split into more than one session, in which case your teacher will collect your work at the end of the session and put it away until the beginning of the next. You will not have access to it between sessions.

- You may be allowed to take an **un-annotated copy** of the text into the session.

- You may be allowed to take in some brief *notes*.

- You may be allowed access to a dictionary or a thesaurus.

- You may be allowed to produce your assessment electronically, but you will not be allowed access to the internet, email, disks or memory sticks.

- During this time, you may not communicate with other candidates. The work you produce must be entirely **your own**.

- Your teacher will advise you on how much you should aim to write.

4. Marking

Your Controlled Assessment Task will be marked by your teacher and moderated (supervised and checked) by your exam board.

General examiners' note

Remember:

- you will get marks for responding to the task, but not for writing other material that is not relevant

- you must produce an **individual** response to the task in the final assessment, even if you have discussed ideas with other students previously.

How to succeed in AQA English Literature

Your teachers will decide whether you should write about *Romeo and Juliet* in a Controlled Assessment Task (Unit 3) or an Examination (Unit 4). These two units are very different, so you need to be absolutely sure which one you are taking. If you are in any in doubt, ask your teacher.

Examiner's tip

Refer back to pages 242–3 for more about the assessment objectives you will be assessed on in Unit 3 Controlled Assessment or Unit 4 Exam.

Unit 3 Controlled Assessment Task

If you take this unit, you have to write about a Shakespeare play and one other text that your teacher will choose. It may be a novel, a selection of poetry, another play or even another Shakespeare play. The two texts will be linked in some way and you are expected to write about both.

The task

AQA will give your teacher a number of tasks to choose from. There are two main topics:

1. **Themes and ideas**

   These tasks might involve writing about love or hate, conflict or power, families or outsiders. For example: *Explore the ways writers present different kinds of love in the texts you have studied* or *Explore the ways writers present and use ideas of fate and free will in the texts you have studied.*

2. **Characterisation and voice**

   These tasks might involve writing about relationships or parents and children or comic characters or old people. For example: *Explore the ways the texts show differences between young and old people* or *Explore the ways the texts show people changing their ideas and attitudes.*

Your response

- You have to complete a written response to ONE task. This should be about 2,000 words, but remember it's quality not quantity that counts.

- You have FOUR hours to produce your work. Your teacher will probably ask you to complete the task over separate sessions rather than in a single sitting.

- Your teacher will give you time to prepare for the task. You can use any resources you like, but do keep a record of them (including websites). You must include a list of these at the end of your task.

- You can work in a small group to research and prepare your material but your final work must be all your own.
- Watch different versions of the play. You can refer to the different versions when you write your response and you will be given credit for this.
- You can refer to brief notes when you are writing your response, but these must be brief. You must hand in your notes at the end of each session and on completion of the task. You can also use a copy of the play without any annotations.
- You can hand write your response or use a word processor. You are allowed a dictionary and thesaurus or grammar and spell-check programs. You are NOT allowed to use the internet, email, disks or memory sticks when writing your response.
- You can do the Controlled Assessment Task in January or June. When you have finished, your teachers will mark your work and then send a sample from your school to AQA to be checked.

> **Examiner's tip**
> The Controlled Assessment Task is worth 25 per cent of your final English Literature mark – so it's worth doing it well.

HOW TO GET A GOOD GRADE

1. Select what you write about carefully. It is better to write a lot about a little. Concentrate on one scene in Shakespeare and one chapter in a novel or a single poem, or on two characters, one from a Shakespeare play and one from a novel.
2. Use short, relevant quotations. Every time you include a quotation, consider the language the writer has used and the probable effect on the audience.
3. Never retell the story. You and your teachers already know it. If you find yourself doing this, stop and refocus on the question.
4. Check your spellings, in particular writers' and characters' names.
5. Always remember that Romeo, Juliet and the other characters in the play are not real. Do not write about them as if they are. They have been created by Shakespeare: he's the important person to consider.

Sample Controlled Assessment Task

Explore the ways writers present family relationships.

Here are extracts from responses written by two students. Both are writing about the Capulet family in Act 3 Scene 5.

Extract 1 Grade C response

> Statement of opinion, but not fully justified

In this scene Lord Capulet behaves really badly towards his daughter. For example, when he has been told that Juliet refuses to marry Paris he uses a long list, 'Day, night, hour, tide, time, work, play, Alone, in company' to emphasise just how much time and effort he has put into finding Juliet a suitable husband. Some of the elements in this list are contrasts, which emphasise his efforts even more. He then imitates his own daughter, 'I'll not wed', which must be very hurtful to her. He also threatens her by saying that if she does not do what he wants he will turn her out of the house and he will not care whether she starves or even dies. At the end of the speech we see the real reason why he wants Juliet to marry Paris: he has given him his word and does not want to have to take back his promise, 'I'll not be forsworn'.

> Relevant textual detail

> How is this evidence of bad behaviour?

> Could be developed more

> Good analysis of language

> Good point with relevant quotation

Examiner's comments

- The student clearly understands some of Shakespeare's ideas and uses of language in the speech.
- Not all points are fully explained and backed up; for example, Capulet's efforts to find Juliet a husband aren't really evidence of bad treatment.
- There is a general understanding of how Lord Capulet treats his daughter, though the effect on Juliet and the audience is not considered in much detail.
- This is a grade C response. To improve, this student needs to develop ideas in more detail and to link these details to a more thoughtful consideration of the speech and the scene.

Extract 2 Grade A response

Clear, detailed statement

In this scene we see a family at war with itself and the role of the father is established as being one of complete power over his child. At first Lord Capulet claims that he has spent all his time, 'Day, night', on his necessary task of finding a husband for his daughter. The contrast creates the impression of universality and utmost importance. Then he provides a brief tour of Paris' most engaging parts, beginning with the fact that he has 'noble parentage': a fact that would undoubtedly impress Lord Capulet as a self-made man. He then denigrates his daughter as a 'whining mammet', a sulking doll or puppet, incapable of independent thought. This is further emphasised by Capulet's statement 'I'll give you to my friend'. His daughter is a commodity to be used in furtherance of his own career; an item with a value. The use of pronouns and the simplicity of the statement provide it with considerable power. The hurt he does her is given an added bite by his imitation of her. Any audience now feels for Juliet's misfortune. Then, as in many family arguments, come the threats ('die in the streets') and finally the truth: Capulet has given his word and claims 'I'll not be forsworn'. Capulet's exit underlines his power. There can be no further argument.

Analytic use of detail

Exploration of themes and ideas

Clear explanation

Awareness of effect on audience

Insight into the core reason

Examiner's comments

- The student shows a clear engagement with Shakespeare's ideas and the attitudes of Lord Capulet.
- There is evidence of a sophisticated interpretation and a perceptive exploration of Shakespeare's use of language.
- The student has written a lot about a little but has also explored some of the themes of the text as a whole.
- This is a grade A response.

UNIT 4 EXAMINATION

If you take Unit 4 in your AQA English Literature course then you will answer a question on a Shakespeare play in an examination. Your answer is worth 20 per cent of your total Literature mark and you will need to spend about 40 minutes on this question.

The Shakespeare question will always have **two** parts. Each is worth 10 per cent of your total mark so you must spend equal time on them.

- Part (a) of each question will ask you to write about a specific extract that is printed in the exam paper. This extract may be a monologue (spoken by one character) or a part of a scene where two or more characters are talking.

- Part (b) of each question will ask you to write about the same topic but relating to a different part of the play (there will not be a printed extract in the exam paper to refer to).

SAMPLE EXAMINATION QUESTIONS AND RESPONSES

Part (a)	How does Shakespeare show Romeo's thoughts and feelings in the extract below?
Part (b)	How does Shakespeare show Romeo's feelings in a different part of the play?

ROMEO:	O, she doth teach the torches to burn bright!
	It seems she hangs upon the cheek of night
	As a rich jewel in an Ethiop's ear –
	Beauty too rich for use, for earth too dear.
	So shows a snowy dove trooping with crows,
	As yonder lady o'er her fellows shows.
	The measure done, I'll watch her place of stand,
	And, touching hers, make blessèd my rude hand.
	Did my heart love till now? Forswear it, sight! –
	For I ne'er saw true beauty till this night.

Examiner's tip

The first part of each question asks 'How does Shakespeare . . .?' The 'how' is important. It means you must consider Shakespeare's _use_ of language, referring to specific words and phrases and the effect they create.

On the next page are extracts from essays by two students. Both are answering Part (a) of the question on _Romeo and Juliet_.

Extract 1 Grade C response

Appropriate comment on theme

In this extract Romeo sees Juliet for the first time and it is love at first sight. He is speaking to himself and uses images of light and dark. He compares her brightness to 'a rich jewel in an Ethiop's ear' because an Ethiopian's ear would be black and the jewel would stand out against it. This is how staggeringly beautiful he thinks Juliet is and the audience can see that he has fallen in love with her right away. The contrast between black and white is continued with the idea of 'a snowy dove trooping with crows'. Crows are black and so a dove would stand out because it is white. This particular dove is 'snowy' which might imply that it is innocent – just like Juliet.

Explanation of effects on audience

Sustained response to language

Examiner's comments

- The ideas here are expressed clearly and appropriately.
- The response explains the first of the images and considers the effect this would have on the audience. It is sustained as it considers a second contrast and begins to explore the word 'snowy'.

Extract 2 Grade A response

Analytic use of detail

In this extract Romeo sees Juliet for the first time. Such is the immediate impression she makes upon him that he sighs with wonder, using the highly romantic exclamation 'O' to indicate how he has been startled into adoration. This is an indication of how passionate he feels: for a second he is speechless and has to convey his feelings with an expression of sheer wonder at Juliet's beauty. Words, quite literally, fail him. When he does find words, Juliet is seen as a dominant figure: it is she who 'doth teach', the combination of soft and hard sounds being continued in the rest of the line 'to burn bright'. Here the alliterative 'b' sounds and the repeated 'r' and 't' sounds create an impression not just of light but also of heat. The torches may look beautiful burning brightly but they are nonetheless burning. There may be a suggestion that Juliet poses some kind of danger. His sense of wonder at Juliet's beauty contains an ironic foreshadowing of what is to come: 'for earth too dear'.

Exploration of ideas/ themes

Clear interpretation

Good analysis of language

Insight and interpretation

Examiner's comments

- The ideas are expressed cogently and persuasively, with apt text references.
- There is evidence of imagination in the development of the interpretation and a confident exploration of the use of language. The student has written a lot about a little but has also managed to explore some of the themes of the text as a whole.

How to succeed in Edexcel English Literature

The response to Shakespeare in Edexcel GCSE English Literature is a Controlled Assessment Task. You must produce your work at school or college under supervision and within two hours, although you may do some preparation for it in advance.

The task

The task will ask you to compare and make links between your own reading of the Shakespeare text and an adaptation. The adaptation can be a film, TV production, musical, graphic novel, audio version or a cartoon, but all must be based on the original play. The task will focus on **one** of the following aspects of the play:

- **Characterisation**
  For example: *Choose one central character in* Romeo and Juliet. *Compare your reading of the character with the presentation of the same character in an adaptation.*

- **Stagecraft**
  For example: *Choose one dramatic device used in* Romeo and Juliet. *Compare your understanding of the dramatic device with the way the same dramatic device is presented in an adaptation.*

- **Theme**
  For example: *Choose one key theme in* Romeo and Juliet. *Compare your reading of the theme with the presentation of the same theme in an adaptation.*

- **Relationships**
  For example: *Choose one important relationship in* Romeo and Juliet. *Compare your reading of the relationship with the presentation of the same relationship in an adaptation.*

Note that your answer should include some discussion of dramatic devices. These include a range of theatrical techniques and styles used by the playwright to create a particular effect on the audience, such as soliloquies, monologues; juxtaposition and contrast; use of dramatic irony; use of the stage and props; actions and reactions.

Preparing your response

When preparing, you will be able to use a range of resources available at your centre, which may include the internet, TV, DVDs and film, live performances and notes made in class.

You must complete your tasks individually, without intervention or assistance from others. However, you will be able to use: copies of the text without any annotations written in them; notes (bullet or numbered points), but not a prepared draft or continuous phrases/sentences or paragraphs); a dictionary or thesaurus; grammar or spell-check programs.

Examiner's tip

If possible, see several different adaptations of *Romeo and Juliet* and compare the ways they treat the story and characters.

HOW TO GET A GOOD GRADE

To get a good mark in this response, it is important that you:

- respond to the chosen drama text critically and imaginatively
- make comparisons and explain links with your own reading
- look at different ways that a production or adaptation expresses ideas
- consider what Shakespeare means and how he achieves his effects
- support your ideas by including evidence from the words of the play.

ACTIVITIES

The following approaches will help you to explore *Romeo and Juliet* in preparation for the controlled assessment.

Activity 1: Characterisation

Draw up a page with two columns, one for Romeo, one for Juliet, and list key headings under which to note down your ideas about each character. Include references from the text that support them. Do the same for the main characters in the adaptation, e.g. Tony and Maria in *West Side Story*.

Activity 2: Stagecraft

In a group, plan the production of a performance of *Romeo and Juliet*. Give each member of the group a non-acting role in the production, such as producer, stage manager, costume and make-up, and set designer. Decide on the three most important decisions or tasks that each member has to undertake, and make notes on each of these.

Activity 3: Theme

As you study *Romeo and Juliet*, decide on **two** important themes and use them as headings for two columns. Underneath, note moments in the play that deal with these themes, giving your ideas and any reference from the text that supports them.

Activity 4: Relationships

Note down your key ideas about Romeo and Juliet's relationship. Try to divide them into positive and negative aspects, to help you form an overview. Use references from the text to support your ideas.

Sᴀᴍᴘʟᴇ Cᴏɴᴛʀᴏʟʟᴇᴅ Assessᴍᴇɴᴛ Tᴀsᴋ

> Choose one central character in the Shakespeare drama text you have
> studied. Compare your reading of the character with the presentation of the
> same character in an adaptation.
>
> Use examples from the text in your response.

Here are extracts from essays by two candidates who had each watched
the film *West Side Story* and compared this with *Romeo and Juliet*.

Extract 1 Grade C response

*States
intentions
in clear but
rather simple
way*

I have read Shakespeare's play and seen the film West
Side Story. I am going to compare the two male leading
characters, Romeo and Tony. Both of these are in love with
a girl from a different background, and both die at the end,
which makes the girls very sad. Romeo is a Montague and
Juliet is from the Capulets. There is rivalry between these
families, and Shakespeare makes this clear right from the
start in the Prologue: 'Two households, both alike in dignity.
. . . From ancient grudge break to new mutiny'.

*Important
quotations*

The situation is different in West Side Story because Tony
and Maria come from different groups. Maria is a Puerto
Rican who has come to America and Tony is from New
York. She is advised to 'Stick to your own kind!' Both
Romeo and Tony are involved with a group of friends who
often fight. Romeo kills Tybalt in a quarrel and Tony kills
Bernardo when there is a battle between the Jets and Sharks.

*Appropriate
comparisons*

Romeo and Tony are both young men who try to calm the
situation. Romeo is wealthy and people look up to him. Tony
also takes responsibility and wants to stop the fighting.
Romeo and Tony are both presented as very attractive to
women. Tony is shown in the film as really good-looking so
you are not surprised Maria falls for him. In both Romeo
and Juliet and West Side Story, Romeo and Tony don't seem
to like violence, but because of bad luck and quick tempers,
they get pushed into things which end in death: 'I am
fortune's fool!'

*Needs
development to
consider events/
people that
cause them to
act as they do*

Examiner's comments

- This extract indicates a sound response. There is an appropriate
  emphasis on comparison of the two characters and situations.
- The writer responds personally and gives her/his own views.
- To raise the grade, the answer needs to refer to the text closely and
  discuss the plots in a less narrative way. Points need fuller development.

Extract 2 Grade A response

Clear opening shows awareness of context

The film of West Side Story, released in 1961, maintains much of the plot of Romeo and Juliet but is adapted and set in New York to reflect the mid-twentieth-century and its popular culture. The central characters (Tony and Maria) take the place of Shakespeare's pair of 'star-crossed lovers'. This study explores how the writers shaped their heroines.

Effective use of language

Strong comparison with very clear points

The most obvious difference is that of age. Shakespeare's text showed that Juliet was still only thirteen years old, an age which I, as a modern reader, certainly found very shocking. Maria's age is not stated, but she is probably about eighteen, even if portrayed as rather naïve, seen particularly when she sings, 'I feel pretty!' The age difference is reflected by the fact that Juliet is closely watched over by her nurse and her parents, while Maria is protected by her brother Bernardo, the leader of the Sharks, and by the other girls, especially the somewhat older Anita. Maria and Juliet are both more down-to-earth and practical than the highly idealistic and impulsive young men with whom they fall in love, both of whom are capable of violence and are responsible for deaths (Bernardo and Juliet's cousin, the 'fiery' Tybalt).

Helpful contrasts

Perceptive link

The relationship of the two lovers is central in both. At the Capulet ball in Romeo and Juliet, all of the characters speak in blank verse, but when Romeo and Juliet converse, they speak in sonnet form. Although this contrast in diction cannot be replicated in West Side Story, throughout the dance, both gangs dance a mambo; however, Tony and Maria dance a cha-cha and stand out by the language of their dance.

Examiner's comments

- It is clear that the writer has a very good understanding of both *Romeo and Juliet* and *West Side Story*.
- The comments show a very high ability to make close reference, whether to Shakespeare's text or to elements of the film script and staging.
- The candidate has clearly grasped, at an assured level, the similarities and parallels, and has also pointed out clear contrasts.
- The writer's language is marked by well-chosen vocabulary and confident, fluent sentence construction.
- This is a grade A response.

How to succeed in WJEC English Literature

If you are entered for English Literature GCSE (or English GCSE) you will be assessed on Shakespeare in a Controlled Assessment Task. This task will be a linked assignment, which means you need to write about the Shakespeare play you have studied, in this case, *Romeo and Juliet*, and some poetry you have studied in class. The play and poems will be linked by a theme. The possible themes are:

- love
- family and parent/child relationships
- youth/age
- power and ambition
- male/female relationships/role of women
- hypocrisy/prejudice
- conflict
- grief.

The exam board will specify which themes are set for the year you take the exam, and your teacher will decide which theme to focus on, according to the Shakespeare play and the poems you have studied.

The task

The examination board will provide teachers with 'generic tasks'. These are general tasks that your teacher will modify to suit the class and the texts you are studying. For example, the generic task could be:

> Many plays and poems are concerned with the relationship between men and women. Choose one relationship in a Shakespeare play and link it with the way a similar relationship is presented in poetry.

Your teacher will modify the task and may break it down into three sections, such as:

> Look at the way Shakespeare presents the relationship between Romeo and Juliet at key points throughout the play.
>
> Consider the way romantic relationships are presented in some of the poems in the collection. Choose one poem to write about in particular, but make references to others.
>
> What is your personal response to the literature you have studied? In your answer, explore links between the poetry and *Romeo and Juliet*.

Activity

Think about how you would approach the task above, and write a plan for your response to the first part of the task.

You might want to:

- choose three or four points from different parts of the play that you think clearly illustrate the relationship between Romeo and Juliet
- look closely at the way Romeo and Juliet speak and behave in these parts of the play, and at how this suggests the character of their relationship.

PREPARING YOUR RESPONSE

- You will have up to fifteen hours to prepare your response, then up to four hours to write it up.
- While you are doing your research and planning, you will have limited supervision; you may use research materials, you can work with others in your class, and your teachers will be able to give you general advice.
- Any worksheets your teacher provides to help you will be sent to the external moderator, and your teacher will have to tell the exam board about the support you have had.
- You are allowed to take an A4 sheet of notes into the final assessment with you. This will be checked to see that it is not a draft or detailed plan of any kind.

WRITING YOUR RESPONSE

- Once you start writing, you will be formally supervised (a bit like in an exam).
- You may complete the assignment over several sessions, in which case, your teacher will collect the work in at the end of each session.
- You are not allowed to discuss your work with others (students or teachers) during this part of the assessment.
- You will be allowed to use a dictionary or thesaurus if you need to, and you may be allowed to produce the work on a word processor.
- The approximate length for this assignment is 2,000 words but quality is more important than quantity.

HOW TO GET A GOOD GRADE

Be prepared to discuss characters and relationships sensitively in both the Shakespeare play and the poetry. You will be expected to show detailed knowledge of both, through well chosen, brief quotations and direct reference to the texts, in order to back up the points you make.

You should show your understanding of how the texts are written, by exploring, for example, the use of language and its effects. Do not try to simply identify literary features, for instance writing 'There are several metaphors used' or something similar. These features are only of interest if you explain why and how they are used and the effects they create.

Do explain the links and connections between the texts carefully.

SAMPLE CONTROLLED ASSESSMENT TASK

> Look at the way Shakespeare presents Juliet's relationship with her mother in *Romeo and Juliet*. Consider the way Lady Capulet speaks and behaves with Juliet at different points in the play, and the different ways in which Juliet responds.
>
> Consider the way some of the poets in the collection present relationships between parents and children. Write about the way the relationship between a parent and child is presented in one poem in particular, but make reference to others.
>
> What is your personal response to the literature you have studied here? In your answer, explore the links between the poetry and *Romeo and Juliet*.

Extract 1 Grade C response

Shows an awareness of characters and relationships

Direct reference in the form of a quotation is appropriate

Apt support for judgement of character

Relevant reference to support the point made

Comment needs to be more developed, perhaps by discussing Juliet's words in more detail

The relationship between Juliet and her mother starts out as Juliet being a very good and obedient daughter to her mother, Lady Capulet. It seems that the Nurse is closer to Juliet than her own mother. We see this when Lady Capulet is sent by her husband to tell Juliet about marrying the County Paris and she has to get the Nurse to help her out. When she is talking to Juliet she tells her she should marry Paris and Juliet just says:

'I'll look to like, if looking liking move.
But no more deep will I endart mine eye
Than your consent gives strength to make it fly.'

This means she will just do what she is told. This shows that Juliet is a very obedient daughter at this point in the play. As soon as Juliet meets Romeo at the party everything changes and she starts keeping secrets. She doesn't let on to the Nurse why she wants to know who Romeo is, and then when she is on the balcony talking to Romeo after the party she acts as if she's still a good obedient girl, when the Nurse calls her and she calls to her, 'I come', when all the time she is planning how she can meet Romeo again, and even asking him to marry her!

Examiner's comments

- This starts with a clear focus on the question and shows awareness of the relationship between Juliet and her mother at the beginning of the play.

- There is some use of apt reference to the events of the play to support the points made.

- To improve the grade, better use could have been made of the main quotation, by looking more closely at the impression it gives of the relationship between Juliet and her mother.

- More focused comments on Juliet's speech and behaviour would have improved this opening to the response. For example, thinking of other ways, as well as 'good' and 'obedient', of describing her.
- Additional close reference to actual text could be included.
- This is a grade C response.

Extract 2 Grade A response

'I'll look to like, if looking liking move.
But no more deep will I endart mine eye
Than your consent gives strength to make it fly.'

Clear focus, overview, evaluative

These words, spoken by the thirteen-year-old Juliet in response to her mother's suggestion (or order!) that she should marry 'the valiant Paris', would be typical of that of a daughter of that time, portraying Juliet as compliant and submissive to her parents' demands. The rhyming couplet and regular rhythm and rhyme used here almost give it a sing-song quality, as if Juliet had rehearsed what she says. As soon

Appreciation of style and effect

Tight summary of events/overview

as Juliet falls in love at first sight with the gatecrasher Romeo, before she is even aware that he is of the age-old enemy Montague family, all that changes. Within hours, when she secretly meets Romeo after the party, in the balcony scene, she is fully prepared to forgo her family, '. . . be but sworn my love / And I'll no longer be a Capulet', in order to be with Romeo. Her rapidly developing maturity is evident in her confidence in proposing to, and offering to arrange, her marriage to Romeo:

Well-integrated reference

'If that thy bent of love be honourable,
Thy purpose marriage, send me word tomorrow'
Her earlier obedience to her mother is a distant memory, it seems, as she can now contemplate life with no one but Romeo.

Point made and supported with evidence

Examiner's comments

- This answer really hits the ground running, with supported evaluation right from the start.
- The analysis of the stylistic features of the first quotation is detailed, astute, and appreciative.
- The response is confident and assured, and is concisely and clearly expressed, with not a word wasted.
- Quotations and details are blended into the text, showing high level of control of material.
- This is a grade A/A* response.

How to succeed in OCR English Literature

The Shakespeare task in OCR English Literature will be tested by controlled assessment. This means that you will be required to write your essay on Shakespeare, in school, under controlled conditions using notes you have made earlier.

The task and your response

- The task will ask you to show an understanding of Shakespeare's play by referring to a particular scene or scenes as they were acted and directed in either a film, staged or audio version of the play that you have watched or heard.
- Your teacher will know what the task is before you start to study the play and will give you advice on how much time you should spend preparing for it. (This time will include formal teaching, research, watching videos/live performance of the play, writing notes, etc.)
- In total, the final writing of the task is expected to take up to three hours and can be done over more than one session.
- Your final written response should be about 1,000 words.
- You will be allowed to have a clean copy, without annotations, of the play with you while writing your assessment. You can also refer to notes made in advance but these should be short bulleted points, not a full draft essay.

How to get a good grade

- Focus clearly on the terms of the question and ensure that any notes you have made also do this.
- Base your answer on the scene identified in the question but remember to show an understanding of its significance in the play as a whole.
- Show a thorough knowledge of the both the written text and the performed version by using quotations and close reference to details of the performance in your response, wherever relevant. Often short quotations are as effective as long ones, particularly if you embed them fluently into your writing.

Examiner's tip

This Shakespeare task is worth 10 per cent of your total GCSE English Literature exam, so it is worth working hard to get a good grade.

Activities

The following activities may help you prepare for writing your response. If possible, work in pairs or small groups so that you can discuss your ideas in full. Remember, you will know the task in advance so make bullet-point notes for reference for when you write your final essay.

Activity 1

Think about how the film/stage/audio version of *Romeo and Juliet* reflects or alters the view you formed from reading the text. For example, Baz Luhrmann's film is a very conscious attempt to put the play in a contemporary setting.

- List the main differences between the film and Shakespeare's text (e.g. the use of guns, video screens, etc.).
- Discuss how these modern additions alter the mood of the original play.
- How far do they fundamentally change the story and how far are they simply superficial changes?

Activity 2

Think of ways in which you could convert the scenes you are going to write about into your own immediate world.

- Think of characters you know who show the same characteristics as those in Shakespeare's play.
- Role-play or 'hot-seat' the scenes from the perspective of these contemporary characters.
- How does the film version help you to appreciate the complexities in the characters and their actions?

Examiner's tip

Remember, there is no 'right' or 'wrong' way for a Shakespeare play to be performed and produced. However, you must be prepared to justify your own opinions with close reference to the text and to the detail of the film/stage/audio version.

SAMPLE CONTROLLED ASSESSMENT TASK

Remind yourself of Act 1 Scene 5 and Act 2 Scene 2 in the text and in one or more performed version(s) of the play.

Explore the ways the characters of Romeo and Juliet are presented in these scenes and elsewhere in Shakespeare's play and in the performed version(s) you have studied.

Here are extracts from essays by two students who had each watched the Baz Luhrmann film *Romeo and Juliet*.

Extract 1 Grade C response

Clear understanding of events; appropriate quotations

In Shakespeare's text Romeo first sees Juliet at Capulet's party and immediately falls in love with her. 'Did my heart love till now?' Tension is built up when Tybalt wants to challenge Romeo but is stopped by Capulet as Romeo is 'a virtuous and well-governed youth . . .'

When Romeo and Juliet meet they speak to each other in the words of a sonnet, which makes their meeting seem rather formal. In the second scene, Romeo has jumped into Juliet's orchard and overhears her confessing her love for him ('What's in a name?'). This leads to them exchanging vows and deciding to get married straight away.

The film version is different. At the start of the ball scene, a voice says 'Thy drugs are quick' which comes from somewhere else in the play; just like some modern parties there's a lot of drugs being taken.

Could make more of this point

More comment needed, rather than description

The next scene takes place in and around Juliet's swimming pool. The action is light-hearted as they both fall in while they're declaring their love for each other. This made me think that they're really just ordinary teenagers and made the thought of their deaths later in the play much sadder.

Shows some awareness of the rest of the play

Examiner's comments

- This response shows the candidate has a secure knowledge of the text of the play and what happens in it.

- There is a sensible use of appropriate quotations to support the account of the action and a sound awareness of the difference between the film and the original text.

- In order to reach a higher grade, the candidate would need to make more detailed comparisons between the original and filmed versions. He/she would need to link the comments to explain more fully how the two versions complement each other in showing the complexities of the characters and how different interpretations of them can shed light on the key issues of the play.

- As it stands, this is a grade C response.

Extract 2 Grade A response

At the start of the scene in the film, a voice says, 'Thy drugs are quick'. This is a line taken from Romeo's last words at the end of the play, reminding the audience of the tragic outcome awaiting the two young lovers.

Juliet's angel costume suggests her purity and reinforces the imagery of light and brightness which is associated with her ('she doth teach the torches to burn bright . . . so shows a snowy dove . . .'). The film contrasts the innocence of the meeting between Romeo and Juliet with the coarser nature of the other characters – Tybalt's unpleasantness is emphasised by the devil's horns he is wearing.

The scene that follows allows the audience to take a different view of the characters from that which they may have gained from reading Shakespeare's text. It takes place mainly in Juliet's swimming pool (and not orchard). There is much comedy: Romeo appears rather accident prone and Juliet is portrayed as being very positive and independently minded – later in the play her strong will leads to her arguing with her father and agreeing to Friar Laurence's plan for her to feign death which ultimately leads to the tragedy of the two 'star-crossed lovers'.

Annotations:
- Good link to rest of play
- Perceptive understanding of imagery
- Good, perceptive understanding of the play as a whole
- Appreciates how costumes can emphasise key details of character

Examiner's comments

- This is a very good critical appreciation of well-selected details of the play and performed version.

- The candidate shows an excellent awareness of how the events of this scene relate to the wider issues of the play as a whole and of how the different versions emphasise and illuminate key points.

- There is a clear understanding of the text and perceptive explanation of how Shakespeare's language and imagery help to convey character.

- There is also clear explanation of how elements of the performed version (costumes, in particular) reinforce the effects of the language.

- This is a grade A response.